EDUCATION AND DEMOCRACY

EDUCATION AND DEMOCRACY

Principles and Practices

A .V. KELLY

P·C·P
Paul Chapman
Publishing Ltd

Copyright © 1995, A. V. Kelly.

Paul Chapman Publishing Ltd
144 Liverpool Road
London
N1 1LA

British Library Cataloguing in Publication Data

Kelly, A. V.
Education and Democracy: Principles and Practices
I. Title
370.115

ISBN 1-85396-205-8

Typeset by Palimpsest Book Production Limited,
Polmont, Stirlingshire
Printed and bound by Athenaeum Press, Gateshead.

A B C D E F G H 9 8 7 6 5

*For Benjamin, Matilda and Sophie,
my grandchildren, and for all young
people, in hope of a more genuinely
democratic future*

CONTENTS

ACKNOWLEDGEMENTS

My thanks are owed to Roy Birch and Gwyn Edwards who provided telling and insightful comments on the first draft of this book, which helped me significantly to strengthen my argument. They pulled no punches, as I hoped – and knew – they would not. Friendly criticism is of little value if it is too friendly and insufficiently critical.

I must express my further gratitude to Gwyn whose spoon-feeding reduced my leg-work considerably.

As always, however, any residual imperfections are my responsibility.

Vic Kelly
October 1994

PREFACE

There are several important ways in which this book seeks to pull together a number of threads which have formed the woof of my work.

That work has been directed, first, at attempting to establish, maintain and extend the many insights into the curriculum, and especially its development, which have been achieved over a number of years of inter-related research and practice. Second, my approach to that has been greatly influenced by considerations deriving from moral and political philosophy, which was the intellectual arena in which my academic career began. Third, within that broad context, my particular concern has been to challenge the certainties – the eternal verities – which have been a major feature of much theorizing about education and curriculum, both through the rationalist stance adopted by 'the philosophy of education' and the positivism of much educational psychology and sociology. My intellectual leanings have always been towards the questions of Socrates rather than the answers of Plato.

For this Platonic stance has had the effect of discouraging debate where debate is vital, of thus inhibiting development where development is vital, and of offering certainty of knowledge and of values where no such certainty exists or can exist. Its effect has thus been to retard the continuing development of democratic forms of education and thus of democracy itself. There can be no democracy and, indeed, no freedom in a context where the most important aspects of life, and of education, namely those values which underpin both, are treated as given, as non-problematic and as not themselves subjects of the continuing debate nor, as a consequence, open to modification and change.

Finally, I have also been concerned to argue that, at the level of practice, the same certainties, the same apparent acceptance of eternal verities, the same lack of awareness, even of tolerance, of the validity of alternative views have led to the imposition on the educational systems of many countries, and especially the UK, of highly *dirigiste*, and thus repressive, political controls. And the effect of these is to establish a system, and thus a society, in which debate on the fundamental issues is discouraged, even debarred, so that their consequences must be the creation of a society which, in several very important aspects, falls short of the standards any definition of democracy would seem to set and/or require.

The book has been written, however, not merely as an attempt to draw together some threads of my own intellectual concerns but also, and primarily, to draw attention to the fact that the basic principles of democratic existence are being put seriously at risk and eroded by current educational policies.

INTRODUCTION

Democracy is currently at the forefront of many people's minds. Events in eastern Europe seem to mark the advent of democratic forms of government in states which hitherto have been communist controlled. And the ending of apartheid as official policy along with the attempts to establish a democracy in South Africa appear to represent an end to yet another undemocratic political system. These events, however, are raising important and complex questions about what might constitute truly democratic forms of government.

Conversely, elsewhere, and especially in the so-called 'free world', events seem to be taking some societies further away from democratic ideals and from the democratic structures they have slowly, and often painfully, achieved. These events too are raising similar questions. And, at the same time, we are daily made aware of the repressive forms of totalitarianism which continue to exist, even to emerge anew, throughout the world, especially the 'third world', and even in member states of the British Commonwealth.

In this context, it is of interest to note that the year 1992/3 marked the 2500th anniversary of the birth of democracy in ancient Athens. For it was in the year 508/7BC that Kleisthenes introduced and carried through those changes to the political constitution of Athens which were to create the first (and, some might say, the last) form of government to merit the description 'democratic'. In ancient Athens this newly born democratic constitution was to survive for little more than a century and a half before it was overturned by the forces of reaction. Later, in ancient Rome, a burgeoning form of democracy was to give way to dictatorship, as the Roman Republic became the Roman Empire. And there have been few examples in history since that time, certainly prior to the present century, of constitutions one would confidently describe as 'democratic'.

Further, as we have already noted, the present century has seen, and continues to see, the regular emergence, establishment and maintenance of forms of government which are the very antithesis of democracy, however one might define it. And there are those who regard many recent developments, even in societies which would expect to be, and usually are, described as democratic, as undemocratic in a fundamental sense and as inhibiting, often deliberately so, rather than promoting the continued growth of democratic styles of government and democratic forms of social living.

'Democracy', along with all other concepts to be found in political theory, is like 'trousers' in that it is something we tend only to talk about when it is not there or looks likely to fall. This book has been written for precisely that reason – from a conviction that true democracy is seldom in evidence in present-day social institutions, especially that social institution we call education, that consequently it is very much at risk of falling, and moreover that this risk is, in many instances, a result of deliberate attempts to undermine it.

For the research which has led to this publication has not only confirmed the original thesis that most developed societies are becoming less democratic and that democratic principles are seldom realized in practice but has also led to a further conviction that this is not accidental. Democratic principles are often transgressed by default, because of the sheer compexity of operationalizing them. They are also frequently breached, however, by deliberate, although seldom overt, attempts to undermine them. And again the research has led to the view that this is particularly true in relation to policies for education.

The hold we may feel we have on democracy, therefore, is both recent and tenuous. And the continued survival of even that form of democracy which is seen as a significant feature of the present-day 'free world' cannot be taken for granted. Some may see hopeful signs in the current democratization (if that is genuinely what it is) of eastern Europe and of South Africa, and may even regard this as an indication that human societies are subject to some evolutionary process which leads inexorably and ultimately to democracy. Such historicism, however, has been shown to be unwarranted as well as dangerous – it is after all a major premise of Marxism itself – and a study of world history in any case does little to support such a thesis. On the contrary, a far more plausible conclusion to be drawn from such a study is that, if those democratic constitutions which exist are to survive, they need to be continuously cherished and protected, and to be defended rigorously against the forces of reaction which constantly threaten them.

And democratic forms of educational provision need to be particularly cherished and protected. For education is a powerful political tool, as advocates of totalitarian political systems have long appreciated. It can be used to support and promote democratic forms of society; and it can be used with equal, even greater, effectiveness to undermine and destroy them.

It is a trend towards the latter which is increasingly coming to characterize current educational policies in many countries. And if we are to protect present and future societies from its effects, we need not only to recognize that it is happening but also to be aware of its many nuances and manifestations, the many subtle devices by which it is forwarded. In short, we need to realize that democracy can only be cherished and protected by constant vigilance on the part of its members.

For, too often these days it seems to be assumed, especially by governments, that free elections are not only a necessary but also a sufficient condition of democracy. Yet it is more than two hundred years since Rousseau (*The Social Contract*, Book IV, Chap. XV) said of this form of democracy, as practised in the England of his day: 'The people of England regards itself as free; but it is grossly mistaken; it is free only during the election of members of parliament. As soon as they are elected slavery overtakes it and it is nothing.' It is perhaps also worthy of note that he adds, 'The use it makes of the short moments of liberty it enjoys shows indeed that it deserves to lose them' (*ibid.*). It would be extremely difficult to argue that the two centuries which have passed since Rousseau made these comments have witnessed any significant progress from this position.

It is a major purpose of this book to demonstrate that there is, indeed that there must be, far more to democracy than the right to elect a government, and far more to democratic government than the assumption of some kind of *carte blanche* once elected. There are basic democratic principles which must be adhered to, and reflected, in every context of life in a democratic society, and which must underpin the actions and policies of every elected government.

Democracy is an ideal construct. In its ideal form it has never existed and almost certainly never will exist. However, ideal constructs encapsulate moral principles, and this central feature of them must be recognized in all attempts to implement or act on them. And it is very important to reassert this at a time when, in all areas of public life, including educational and curriculum planning, policy issues are being increasingly viewed as technical rather than recognized as moral. For to conceal their moral dimension is in itself to create one of the most serious threats to the maintenance and development of democratic forms. Democracy as a political concept, then, is not confined simply to issues of control and decision-making. It is not merely a mechanism for the election of governments. Far beyond that, it is also a moral concept; it encapsulates a system of moral values which set the parameters within which control must be exercised and determine the kinds of decision that can and cannot be made. Democracy is more than a form of political organization or system of government; it is a way of life.

There are two important things to be done in relation to ideal constructs. First they must be analysed in order that we might be quite clear about the ideals they encapsulate. And, second, that analysis must be used to evaluate all practices, policies and institutions which lay claim to being founded on these ideals. This book will tackle both of these tasks, with particular reference to current policies for education. The central theme which the book sets out to develop, then, is that to have a concept of democracy, or to claim to be operating a democratic system, is to be committed to certain principles in the creation of social institutions and the framing of social policies.

Furthermore, those principles must go well beyond the need for ratification by a properly elected government. And they must also go beyond mere majority approval since, as we have seen on more than one occasion, the majority can vote for policies and systems which are undemocratic and even inimical to democracy. It must never be forgotten that it was a majority of Athenian jurors which voted for the execution of Socrates. All social institutions and all social policies in a democracy must be founded on democratic principles of a more sophisticated kind than mere approval by a duly elected government or by majority vote. They must represent the essence of democratic living, and they must support and promote its continuation.

In particular, it will be argued that the social institution we call education cannot be merely the product of government policy or even majority opinion but must, whatever the governmental or the majority views may be, reflect certain principles which are endemic to, and logically entailed by, the notion of democratic living. These principles this book will seek to identify, elucidate and explore, not least because we need such clarity of vision particularly as a defence against those who use the rhetoric of 'democracy', and many of its associated terms, such as 'equality', 'entitlement', 'freedom', 'rights' and so on, to conceal and impose a political reality which is far from democratic. The style will thus be conceptual rather than empirical; the aim to unpack the concept of democracy; the focus not on what democracy is in a variety of contexts but on what it might be, or even should be; the concern not to analyse actual democratic systems but to identify the essential principles to which all such systems must seek to conform.

The products of this approach, then, will be ideals rather than realities. It is important to be clear about this from the outset, and to be clear too about the purpose of such an exploration. This is expressed very well by Plato, in his defence of the 'idealism' of *The Republic*. For when it is suggested to Socrates in the dialogue that his city 'exists in words only', his response is to say that 'perhaps it is laid up in heaven as a paradigm for whoever wishes to see, and, seeing, to make of himself such a city . . . For his behaviour will reflect the principles of that city and of no other'. In short, the search is for moral principles and, in our case, those moral principles which constitute the moral system we call democracy.

These principles will supply the criteria by which we can assess the acceptability and the compatibility of all aspects of any society which claims to be democratic. They will offer us a template which can be applied to policies and practices so that we may see if they fit. They will provide a means of testing the veracity of claims made to democratic processes. And it is essential that we apply them to all institutions of major social and political importance.

The second task this book will undertake, therefore, is to apply these criteria to the idea, and the practice, of education in a democratic society, to seek to determine what practices are acceptable within and compatible with such a society and, conversely and perhaps more significantly, which are not. For this is one important aspect of the way in which educational practices must be evaluated and assessed in a democratic context.

Educational systems, however, have a further crucial role to play in society. For any society's educational system will exercise a high degree of influence, and indeed control, over the kinds of citizen which will make up that society. This is why totalitarian governments have always placed great emphasis on the control of education, and especially of the curriculum, and have used that control to seek to ensure the production, the training, even the indoctrination of a compliant and obedient citizenry. The role of education in a democratic society is no less crucial, even though it is diametrically different.

For the maintenance, protection and development of democratic forms of living require not merely that we achieve conceptual clarity over what are the essential features of such forms, nor even that we ensure that these are reflected in all social institutions; they require also, as an equally essential by-product of this, that the education system be designed, planned and implemented in such a way as to ensure that the products of that system are effective citizens. And this means, among other things, that they be both willing and able to contribute to, as well as recognizing the importance of the maintenance, the protection and the continued development of, the democratic style of social and political life. For the notion of democracy entails individual participation in government, however this is conceived and/or operationalized; and such participation requires in turn levels of awareness and understanding, along with an openness of mind, which only a truly democratic form of education can provide.

A third task this book will undertake, therefore, will be to consider what might be the major criteria by which we may evaluate the suitability and appropriateness of educational provision in a democratic society – not only in terms of its compatibility with the underlying principles of democracy but also, as a major aspect of that, in relation to the degree to which it succeeds in producing citizens adequately prepared to take their proper places in such a society.

One major theme will underpin our discussion. Views or stances taken on the nature and status of human knowledge, along with consequent views or stances on the issue of human values, are a central and inevitable feature – even if left implicit – of all political theories. From the time of Plato, totalitarian, or anti-democratic, theories have found it necessary to establish a base within a rationalist epistemology, while democratic political theories, when they have been fully thought through, have had to take a less certain or confident view of human knowledge and values. The former have sought certainty and permanence; the latter have accepted, even embraced, uncertainty and change. Mainstream rationalist epistemology has thus provided the intellectual basis for totalitarian rather than democratic political systems – both fascist and Marxist – and only by the most tortuous forms of sophistry and convoluted reasoning, such as that of Hegel, has it been rendered compatible with notions such as those of freedom, individual rights and equality, which some would regard as essential to any concept of democracy.

This epistemological difference, this book will argue, is crucial; and an understanding of its significance is equally central – not merely to conceptual clarity but also to effective practice. If we are to protect, let alone extend, those democratic features of our societies which have been extremely hard won by our ancestors, therefore, we need to address both current practices and the intellectual positions they reflect, assume and adopt, whether consciously or not.

In summary, then, the book will set out to do three main things. First, it will seek to identify those essential principles of truly democratic living about which we must be crystal clear if we are to create and maintain a supportive context for democratic life. Second, it will attempt to tease out the implications those principles have for the operationalizing of democratic social institutions and especially that social institution we call education. And, third, as the obverse of this coin, it will endeavour to identify features of educational practice which may be incompatible with notions of democratic living, and to evaluate current practices against the criteria its earlier explorations will have revealed.

The book is offered in three major parts. First, in order to provide a platform for the discussion of the forms of educational policies and practices appropriate to a democratic society, an attempt will be made to elucidate the basic elements of democratic theory and to identify the main sources of threat to these. This will be the concern of the first two chapters.

Part 2 will then explore the issue of theories of knowledge and the implications of these for democratic forms of social living. For it is a major theme of this book that it is from this source that the most serious, and least recognized, threats to democracy, and especially to democratic forms of educational provision, come.

Part 3 will then focus on questions concerning the essential features, form and role of educational provision in a truly democratic society and, in the light of that discussion, will seek to evaluate current practices and identify their theoretical and ideological underpinning, whether implicit or overt.

It may be that readers whose concern is to get to the heart of the educational issues will wish to concentrate their attention on this third part of the book. They would be well advised, however, to consult from time to time, and certainly not to ignore completely, the points of political theory which form the substance of Part 1 and what is said about the problem of knowledge in Part 2. For it is an understanding of those theoretical positions which provides the only sound base for the planning of genuinely democratic forms of education.

PART 1:

The Fundamental Principles of Democratic Living

1

DEMOCRACY AND POLITICAL THEORY I:
NON-DEMOCRATIC THEORIES

Democrats, at the end of the eighteenth and the beginning of the nineteenth centuries, were seen, commonly, as dangerous and subversive mob agitators . . . democracy and democrat, in their entry into ordinary speech, record the effects, in England, of the American and French Revolutions.

(Williams, 1958, p. 14)

It is not the intention of this book at any point to offer arguments in support of those forms of social organization we call 'democratic'. Democracy is accepted throughout as a 'given', and the intention is to attempt to elicit what that implies. In other words, a commitment to democratic values is presupposed, and the focus is on what such a commitment involves, what in detail are these democratic values.

The main task of the first two chapters is to attempt to identify the essential features of democratic forms of social organization. For these will then lead us to those values we call democratic, and will provide us with the criteria by which we can evaluate such organizations. In attempting to identify these essential features, however, we must first ensure that we recognize the appropriate level for, and the precise focus of, such an enquiry.

First, we need to note that the concern is not with the trappings of democracy but with its essence or first principles. The trappings may vary from one democracy to another, as indeed they do; the essence and the first principles, however, must be common to all.

Further, the trappings may exist in the absence of that essence and those first principles; they may even exist to conceal that absence. This is the case currently in a number of societies where universal suffrage through the ballot-box, for example, is clearly a mockery since, although the machinery of democracy may be in place, its essence is nowhere to be found.

It is that essence which is the object of our quest here. 'Universal suffrage, recurring elections, responsibility of those who are in political power to the voters, and the other factors of democratic government are means that have been found expedient for realizing democracy as the truly human way of living. They are not a fixed and final value' (Dewey, 1938). And even if they are a necessary condition, they can never be a sufficient condition of democratic living. It is the sufficient conditions, then, that we must attempt to identify. For what we are seeking is a conceptual template which we can apply to any political system, or any institution within such a political system, which claims to be democratic, in order to assess the strength and validity of its claims. In short, as was indicated in the Introduction, democracy is being viewed as a way of life and not merely as a mechanism for the election of governments or the making of policy.

Second, it follows from this that our concern is not to compare and contrast different types or models of democracy which can be identified as having been implemented at different times in history or in different countries. Held (1987), for example, delineates nine such models, ranging from the 'Classical Democracy' of ancient Athens to the currently observable model he calls 'Democratic Autonomy'. Our concern here, however, is to seek for their common denominator, those features in virtue of which all of these systems are given the common description of 'democratic'. Indeed, we may even wish to ask whether they are all appropriately so described.

Our concern then is not with actual types but with what we may call the 'ideal type', with democracy as an ideal construct. And our style must therefore be conceptual rather then empirical.

We must not, however, fall into some form of essentialism, in which we find ourselves illicitly deriving value positions from what purports to be some form of objective, value-free conceptual analysis. What we shall be doing may be described as essentialism only in the sense that it will be seeking to identify what is logically entailed by a commitment to that value position which is called 'democracy', what further values a person is committed to once he or she has declared an allegiance to democratic forms of social living. We will be endeavouring to find out what it would be difficult, or even impossible, for a person who claims to be a supporter of democracy to deny or oppose without being open to a charge of unreasonableness or even outright irrationality. In short, our concern will be to discover what might be the sufficient conditions for describing any form of social organization as 'democratic', the essential features whose absence might render such a description inaccurate and unjustifiable.

In attempting to discover these sufficient conditions, these essential features of democratic forms of social organization, it is natural to turn first to political philosophy. When one does so, however, one is immediately struck by how little attention has been directed by political philosophers over the centuries to promoting democratic forms of social organization or even to analysing the concept of democracy or seeking to identify its central features. From the time of the first major political theorist, Plato, the efforts of most of those engaged in this field seem to have been focused on justifying alternative forms of political organization. Democracy itself has had few advocates in this area of intellectual enquiry. It is worth considering, therefore, the kinds of theory which have been adumbrated, especially those which have been non-democratic, or even anti-democratic, in their thrust, before going on to consider the support that democratic systems have been offered and the features of such systems which have been regarded as important.

The intention is not of course to provide any kind of potted history of political theory. To attempt that would be silly. This chapter will merely seek to pick out those major forms of political theory and elements within them which seem to be inimical to notions of democratic living, whether deliberately so or not, and thus to identify negatively, through their absence, some of the features we would expect to see in democratic systems. Chapter 2 will then explore the main features of liberal and liberal-democratic theories which will point us in a more direct and positive way towards those basic democratic principles we are seeking.

AN EARLY STATEMENT OF DEMOCRATIC PRINCIPLES

One of the most interesting – and certainly one of the earliest – public statements of democratic political theory appeared about half a century before the publication of Plato's *Republic*, not in the form of a political or philosophical treatise but as a public address by a major advocate of democratic politics, the Athenian statesman, Pericles. This is the only published statement of support for democracy to be found in ancient Greek literature. And, interestingly, it is recorded not by Pericles himself but by Thucydides, who was no supporter of democracy but was an historian with a high respect for accuracy and truth.

At the end of the first year (431BC) of a war with Athens's main rival, Sparta, which was to last for almost 30 years, it was decided to hold a public funeral for those who had died in that first year of warfare, and Pericles was chosen to pronounce their eulogium.

In this funeral oration, he took the opportunity, among other things, to emphasize some of the major features, and advantages, of that form of democracy which, in his view, had made Athens the kind of state it had become and which had given it its pre-eminence.

> Our constitution . . . has been called a democracy because it is governed not for a few but for the many. In private disputes, there is equality for all according to the laws; public advancement is based on individual merit rather than on social class; and no-one who has something of value to offer the state is prevented from offering it by obscurity . . . We are tolerant in our private relationships and in public matters we adhere to the laws . . . In education, while our opponents from birth seek to attain manliness by arduous discipline, we live without such restrictions and yet are no less ready for equal dangers . . . We promote culture with moderation and pursue the intellectual without effeminacy . . . We

alone consider the person who takes no interest in public affairs not as
impractical but as useless, and we are able to make sound judgments
on public policies even if we cannot originate them; we also regard
as a hindrance to effective action not debate but the failure to discuss
matters fully before taking necessary action ... In summary, I say ...
that it seems to me that each of our citizens in all circumstances is able
to demonstrate complete self-sufficiency and to do so with grace and
versatility.

(Thucydides, *History*, Book II, paras 37–41)

This is a compelling statement, worthy of a place in any political treatise and
perhaps the stronger for having as its context a public address by a practising
politician.

It has of course often been pointed out that the democracy which Pericles
is eulogizing in this passage was a form of government which excluded
participation by large sectors of Athenian society – most notably, women,
slaves and immigrant workers; and that 'whereas classical Democracy was a
form of sectional government, to the modern mind Democracy is opposed to
all forms of sectional government' (Wollheim, 1962, p. 72).

This is of course true. But while this consideration may affect our judgement
of Athenian society, it is irrelevant to our purposes here. For it is our concern
to seek out the fundamental principles of democratic living, and they are
there to be identified even in what we might regard as a form of democracy
of limited scope. For the Athenian of the sixth century BC, democracy was
the rule of equals by equals. And, while we may quarrel with the Athenian
view of which members of a society shall count as equals, we must not let
that concern deflect us from recognizing the fundamental principle which is
there to be grasped.

Pericles' statement, therefore, is likely to offer us more help in our search
for the essential features of democracy than many more closely or cogently
argued discussions.

For, as we noted above, most of these more cogently argued discussions
focus their attention on justifying alternative forms of political organization,
Plato's *Republic* setting the tone and style with its concern to argue that
efficient and effective government comes not from the participation of all
members of a society in that government but from the placing of power,
control and responsibility in the hands of an élite. It will be as well for us to
begin, therefore, by identifying the main kinds of alternative political theory
which have been offered.

MAJOR STYLES OF POLITICAL THEORY

In broad terms, three main types of theory can be identified in political
philosophy, three major, but very different, approaches to the two basic
questions of political theory, that of the obligation of the citizen to the

state and that, for some but not all theories, of the reciprocal obligation of the state, through government, to the people.

First, there are those theories, usually based on some notion of a social contract, which advocate government by benevolent, or even merely self-interested, individuals or groups. The prime concern of such theories is to curb and control the competitive tendencies of individual members of society and/or to ensure effective and stable government. Such theories, at least in this form, are clearly incompatible with any notion of democracy.

Second, there are metaphysical theories, which see the state as having a life, an existence, a direction, an evolution of its own, as moving in some way inexorably towards a stage of perfection. Such theories are fundamentally totalitarian rather than democratic since, as we shall see, they must stress the primacy of the state over the individual or even collectively over all of the individuals who live in it.

And, third, there are various forms of liberal political theory, which stress such things as equality, individual freedom and human rights. These theories, therefore, are the only kinds of theory which offer support for democratic forms of social organization. And they are the only theories which seek to offer and, indeed, to demand, moral justifications for policy decisions. For the most part, however, they are, as we have seen, relatively recent arrivals on the stage of political theory.

We must consider each of these kinds of theory in a little detail, not least because of the light each can throw on the concept of democracy itself and the views taken of it.

The need for strong government: early social contract theories

Before we look at the major features of early social contract theories, there are two general points we should note. First, the notion that society is held together by a form of social contract should not be seen as some kind of historical assertion about the ways by which societies first came into existence; it must be recognized as an analogue, a device used to explain the bases of political obligation – whether that of the citizen to the ruler or of the latter to the former. It is not concerned to explain how states came into being but to explain what makes them legitimate. There is of course potential for confusion here, and such confusion can be discerned in a number of social contract theories.

Second, the theory of a social contract is a device which can be used to support very different, indeed diametrically opposed political theories. For it can be used to stress the obligation of government to the people or, as we shall shortly see, to argue for the absolute power of government over the citizenry.

It seems that it was first introduced to political theorizing in the western world to support the former kind of argument (Popper, 1945). For we learn from Aristotle that the sophist, Lycophron, saw the law of any state as a 'covenant by which men assure one another of justice' (Aristotle, *Politics*, III, 9, 8), and claimed that the state exists for the protection of its members and should be a 'cooperative association for the prevention of crime' (*ibid.*). This is not a historical version of the social contract; there is no suggestion that Lycophron thought that such a contract had actually been drawn up or happened. He is concerned with the purposes and the legitimacy of the state, and is attempting to introduce notions of equality, individuality and protectionism. Indeed, Popper (op.cit., p. 115) asserts that he was using the device of the social contract to outline 'the most fitting expression of the humanitarian and equalitarian movement of the Periclean age'.

He is thus adumbrating a more liberal political theory than was to take hold in the ancient world. And we shall see in Chapter 2 that it was in this form that the notion of a social contract was taken up by the liberal theorists, such as John Locke and Jean-Jacques Rousseau, in the seventeenth and eighteenth centuries.

Before then, however, our attention was firmly switched to a more negative version of the social contract, presented to us, although not advocated, by Plato, who, in Popper's view robbed us of this egalitarian version by handing the theory down in a distorted form, 'as the historicist theory of the origin of the state in a social contract; or as an essentialist theory claiming that the true nature of the state is that of a convention; and as a theory of selfishness, based on the assumption of the fundamentally immoral nature of man' (*ibid.*).

Whatever Plato's motives – and it must be remembered that in the *Republic* his concern is to set out this view in order to refute it – there is no doubt that on the two occasions when he presents this kind of theory in his dialogues, in the *Gorgias* and *The Republic*, it is expressed in a selfish and nihilistic form.

In *The Republic*, for example, the search for 'justice' and the basic principles of harmonious living begins as 'Socrates' seeks an answer to the problem put to him by a fellow participant in the dialogue, Glaucon. Glaucon's case is, put briefly, that people behave with moral responsibility towards each other only because they fear the chaos and anarchy that would otherwise ensue and that anyone who is able to transcend the normal human state of vulnerability (such as, in his account, the ancestor of Gyges who comes into possession of a ring which renders him invisible) would have no reason to adhere to any moral, social or political principles at all.

Clearly, this kind of theory begins from a pessimistic view of human nature as concerned totally with self-interest and as controllable only through fear. In what is perhaps the starkest version of the theory, that of Thomas Hobbes, we are offered a picture of what he calls 'the state of nature', the condition of people living 'without a common Power to keep them all in awe'. We are further told that this is 'that condition which is called Warre; and such a warre, as is of every man, against every man', and that in this context the life of man is 'solitary, poore, nasty, brutish and short' (*Leviathan*, Chap. 13). For, in such a condition, 'there can be no security to any man, (how strong or wise soever he be) of living out the time, which Nature ordinarily alloweth men to live' (op.cit.,

Chap. 14). And so reason suggests that 'every man ought to endeavour Peace, as farre as he has hope of obtaining it' (*ibid.*). This he calls a 'Fundamentall Law of Nature' and he claims it has two aspects – first, 'to seek Peace, and follow it', but, second, 'by all means we can, to defend ourselves' (*ibid.*).

Hence there comes a second law:

> that a man be willing, when others are so too, as farre-forth, as for Peace, and defence of himselfe he shall think it necessary, to lay down this right to all things: and be contented with so much liberty against other men, as he would allow other men against himselfe.
>
> (*ibid.*)

And so the basis of society is a social contract, an agreement between all members to abide by certain rules in the interests of self-preservation. There is no scope here for any more positive view of social living.

From this kind of concept of society it is but a little, although perhaps an inevitable, step to the notion that in such a society the government should be in the hands of an individual or group strong enough to maintain the contract. Within Hobbes's system, the individual person, having made a contract with his fellows (the sexist language is Hobbes's) to renounce certain rights and freedoms by mutual agreement, makes a further contract with a 'sovereign', thus creating a 'Commonwealth by Institution'; or perhaps he accepts the imposition of the sovereignty of another person or group of persons, thus acceding to a 'Commonwealth by Acquisition'. In either case, the motivation is fear – fear of one's fellows and fear of the power of the sovereign.

It is interesting to note that a flavour of democracy creeps into his scheme when he suggests that, when a commonwealth is *instituted*, it is created by the appointment of a sovereign by a majority decision. However, it is more important to note that, in Hobbes's view, that is the point at which democracy ends, since, from then on, 'everyone, as well he that *Voted for it*, as he that *Voted against it*, shall *Authorise* all the Actions and Judgements, of that Man, or assembly of men' (op.cit., Chap. 18).

A cynic may be inclined to say that this is close to being the form of government we currently have in the UK, since it increasingly appears to be the case that, once a government has been voted into power, it takes the view that every voter, however he or she actually voted, 'shall authorize' all its subsequent actions. This is of course the thrust of Rousseau's accusation, which we noted in our Introduction, concerning the slavery which overtakes the British people as soon as it has voted.

For Hobbes, however, this is the only basis for stable government, and the commonwealth or state is to be held together by an absolute sovereign who, once instituted – or, indeed, once having seized power – is to be obeyed implicitly, since only in that way can every individual member of the state be confident of retaining that security of existence for which he or she entered into the contract in the first instance.

A similar solution is offered by Machiavelli, although on pragmatic rather than philosophical grounds. For him, human nature (of both ruler and ruled) is such that strong government is all that one can reasonably hope for. The ruler, Machiavelli's 'Prince', will be as self-seeking as his subjects (again the sexist language is Machiavelli's), although better than them at getting what he wants, so that he will rule in a manner designed to promote his own advantage rather than that of the state, except of course where the two coincide.

Machiavelli's work is thus aimed at advising rulers on the techniques they might use for acquiring and maintaining power and for securing what they want. If the mass of the citizenry gain anything from this form of government it is, first, an element of security and, second, whatever incidental advantages may accrue from living in a state which is being successfully governed in the sense of being effectively policed and protected from external threat.

Plato's response to the notion of society as based on a social contract is more optimistic than the theories we have considered so far. Plato's 'ideal state' as presented in *The Republic*, far from being democratic, is overtly totalitarian; indeed, it is not unreasonable to see it as deliberately anti-democratic, as a response to what he saw as the excesses and follies of that Athenian democracy which Pericles had eulogized but which had ultimately, in Plato's view, led to political and economic downfall. In fact, when in *The Republic* he traces the process by which constitutions degenerate from his ideal, the last stage of that process (short of actual tyranny), the nadir of political organizations, the very worst form of human associated living he identifies as democracy. And he sets out at some length why he sees it in this way, as just one step removed from tyranny and, perhaps more interestingly in the light of current events, as ultimately leading to tyranny.

Plato's 'ideal state', therefore, is a totalitarian state. However, it is an élitist form of totalitarianism, not only placing power in the hands of those best qualified to wield it but also judging their fitness to hold power in terms of their moral qualities as well as their other strengths.

Plato's society is to be ruled by 'philosopher-kings', chosen not by birth nor by their propensity for seeking their own political advancement, but entirely in terms of the intellectual and moral qualities they display and which will have been fostered and developed through a lengthy and elaborate form of education. That form of education is designed to produce a small, élite group of people, both men and women, who will have 'perfect knowledge' of all things, including all things moral. Such people will be eminently fitted to take responsibility for the government of society and to conduct its government in a morally responsible manner, because they will *know* what is morally right. The rest of the citizenry of course must accept the judgements made by their 'philosopher-kings' and, indeed, must be prepared by their 'education' to do so.

The root of this theory is a rationalist epistemology which regards the ultimate attainment of 'perfect knowledge' as possible, and perhaps even, in evolutionary terms, inevitable. For the only justification Plato offers for the unquestioned authority of his 'philosopher-kings' is that they will have such perfect knowledge, so that their decisions will always be the correct decisions. Such an epistemology, we shall see when we explore it in greater detail in Part 2, is not only highly problematic but also politically dangerous.

What we must note here is that Plato's theory provides the bases for two different, and indeed incompatible, subsequent forms of political philosophy – those versions of the social contract theory, such as those of Locke and Rousseau, which, as we shall see in Chapter 2, represent the beginnings of a thought-out liberal political philosophy, offering a moral view of society and demonstrating a more optimistic view of human nature, and those metaphysical theories of the state which have provided an underpinning for various forms of totalitarianism.

The work of Hobbes and Machiavelli, however, lead only to the latter. For they offer us the notion of the state as conceptually distinct from society, especially by separating out the government and the citizenry and viewing their inter-relationship as contractual. They thus pave the way directly for the emergence of those metaphysical theories of the state which were developed to combat the rise of liberalism, and which have been a feature of both the theory and the practice of politics in the western world for more than two centuries.

Metaphysical theories of the state

We shall see in Chapter 3 why the rationalist view of human knowledge which Plato adopted is ill-conceived and, indeed, mistaken. We shall also see how dangerous it is politically and, in Chapter 4, it will be argued that this view of knowledge constitutes the most serious barrier to the achievement both of a clear concept of democracy and, consequently, of effective strategies for its realization.

We must note briefly here, however, that, in the late eighteenth and early nineteenth centuries in parallel with, in response to and in deliberate opposition to developing notions of liberalism, there emerged, in direct line of descent from Plato's *Republic*, and relying on the self-same rationalist epistemology, that metaphysical theory of the state, most closely associated with the work of Friedrich Hegel, which was to be seen as offering an intellectual justification for fascism and which was the direct forebear of Marxism.

The rationalist's conviction that there can ultimately be perfect knowledge, which was a key element in Plato's philosophy, requires of us that we accept that nothing can, again ultimately, be a matter of individual opinion, everything being either right or wrong. And within rationalist epistemology, indeed central to it, is the claim that this applies equally in the moral sphere. It follows from this that questions of right and wrong are never matters of opinion but always of *truth*, and that, like all truths, these moral 'truths' are attained through reason or rationality (hence the term 'rationalism'). For Plato, this meant that those people whose rational faculties were most fully developed had access to these moral 'truths' and thus were entitled to govern and direct the lives of the other members of their state who were not so fortunate or gifted.

A more sophisticated version of this epistemology emerged in the second half of the eighteenth century through the work of Immanuel Kant, and was later given a political dimension in the work of Friedrich Hegel. In Hegel's political philosophy, the state is the embodiment of reason; it represents the current stage that the development of reason, of 'perfect knowledge' has reached. Knowledge develops by a triadic dialectic of thesis, antithesis and synthesis. A thesis is accepted as true until it is opposed by an antithesis, a piece of contrary and conflicting evidence; that piece of contrary evidence must be reconciled with and accommodated to the original thesis in the form of a synthesis; the synthesis so formed becomes a new thesis; and so the dialectic proceeds until finally 'perfect knowledge' is attained.

In human affairs, Hegel argues, the dialectic takes the form of conflict between states or nations. It is through this conflict that progress towards perfection proceeds. The state thus comes to have an existence of its own, independent of its members; it becomes a metaphysical entity and is seen as also having a status which transcends that of its individual members. And those individual members must be forced to accede to the claims of this entity, the state, and to accept the rightness of those claims, a rightness which derives from the fact that the state is the embodiment of reason, so that it cannot be wrong. They must be 'forced to be free', their freedom consisting in acceptance of the will of the state, since to express their freedom by holding or asserting alternative opinions would be to fly in the face of reason.

For, 'the only idea which philosophy brings with it', he tells us, 'is the simple idea of reason, that reason dominates the world and that world history is thus a rational process' (*Philosophy of Right*, para. 352). To argue against it, therefore, or to seek to hold one's own, contrary opinions, is to fly in the face of reason. And it is similarly irrational to criticize it as immoral. It is neither good nor bad, it just *is*. 'The insight to which . . . philosophy is to lead us is that the real world is as it ought to be' (op.cit.). 'What is, is right, because it is' (op.cit.).

Fundamental to this kind of theory is a view of history as some kind of rational process, as the unfolding of some predetermined pattern of development or evolution, a view which has been called 'historicism' (Popper, 1957). The acceptance of this view of history must of course lead on to an acceptance either of the possibility of predicting the future direction of the historical process (in the way, for example, that the study of science may permit some prediction of the future behaviour of inanimate objects) or, at the very least, to an acceptance of the fact that there is nothing human beings, either collectively or individually, can do to change the inevitable course of things.

It is a theory, therefore, which considerably reduces the scope of human morality, since to be moral now becomes a matter merely of aligning one's behaviour to this inexorable and predetermined process. And since, for Hegel, the state is the embodiment of reason, or 'the Divine Idea as it exists on Earth' (*Philosophy of Right*, p. 39), and the process of the development of reason towards the 'Absolute', i.e. perfect rationality, is forwarded through the activities of the state, it must follow that to align one's behaviour with rationality one must be an obedient citizen. This is the road to freedom. 'For Law is the objectivity of Spirit; volition in its true form. Only that will which obeys law is free; for it obeys itself' (*ibid.*).

One can see, therefore, why it is important for those who wish to establish a more open view of morality and of social living to refute this historicist position. And this has been done most effectively in Karl Popper's *The Poverty of Historicism* (1957), in which he argues, among other things, that 'if there is such a thing as growing human knowledge, then we cannot anticipate today what we shall only know tomorrow' (p. vi). This is an issue we will need to return to.

For the moment, however, we must merely note how such a philosophy offers a theoretical justification for totalitarianism, whose essence is an acceptance of the interests of the state as being more important than those of its citizens, individually or even collectively. One can see too how such a philosophy came to underpin that nationalism which was a feature of much of the nineteenth century and, indeed, is still to be seen. One is not surprised to hear that Mussolini's doctoral thesis was a study of the work of Hegel, nor to note Dewey's claim that most of German cultural and philosophical thought reached its natural fruition in Hitler.

We must note too that the philosophy of Karl Marx was a natural development of that of Hegel. For Marx, the dialectic is economic and material rather than political, the conflict is between classes rather than between nations or states, but the rationalist epistemology remains, the historicism remains and the essence of his theory continues to be the notion of a continuing progression towards perfection – a perfection of knowledge and a perfection of society. Again, therefore, it is a process which can brook no opposition, no contrary opinion. Marxism is thus essentially anti-democratic, in spite of its championing of the interests of the proletariate and in spite of its constant claims to be supporting the democratic process.

There is no doubt that when the inexorable historical process has reached its apparent conclusion, when it has reached the stage of the classless and stateless society, something akin to democracy will have emerged. However, it seems that this will be a democracy of citizens who all think alike and hold the same values since, by that stage, perfection of human knowledge will also have been attained, as Hegel predicted. And the notion of a democracy in which everyone agrees with everyone else does not help us in our search for the basic principles of a democratic form of social living for people who have many differences of opinion, taste, morals and culture.

Furthermore, it is quite clear that, before this level of perfection is reached, before the stage when the state itself withers away, there is to be an interim or transitional stage, the dictatorship of the proletariate, which, on some interpretations, will consist of what Marx himself described as the raising of the proletariate to the position of the ruling class, the victory of democracy, in short a stage where majority rule is all, where the state continues to exist but government is now in the hands of the proletariate.

On other definitions, however, including most significantly those of people, such as Lenin, who had the actual responsibilities for setting up communist systems of government, during this transitional stage the majority would not have reached an appropriate level of competence to become the ruling class, so that equality would remain merely an ideal. 'In short, during the "first phase" we are to have government *for* the people by the party elite' (Lancaster, 1959, p. 187).

This view of course illuminates the actual systems of government which emerged in the USSR and explains why they were far from being of a kind one could genuinely describe as democratic. It also reveals, however, why Marxism, however interpreted, could never offer a base for a democratic form of social organization. For its fundamental rationalism, and especially its historicism, can leave no scope for differences of opinion. Those who might have different views from the 'party line' are regarded as having these either because they are members of the minority 'bourgeois right' or because, even as members of the proletariate, they lack 'true' knowledge and understanding and thus need to be 'educated' before they can be given power.

All will be well of course when the classless, stateless society arrives. For then everyone will have 'true' knowledge and will conform to the 'true' values. Some form of democracy will thus have been reached. But it is a poor form of democracy and, as we have just seen, not one that will help us in our search for a form of social living which will create a context for those genuine differences of opinion which many people regard as constituting the enrichment that social living can offer and, indeed, much of what it means to be human.

We can now see perhaps why Karl Popper (1945) identified as the three great enemies of 'the open society' Plato, Hegel and Marx. For what they all have in common is a commitment to a rationalist view of knowledge as developing inexorably towards perfection, a consequent view of moral and political issues as matters of knowledge rather than of mere opinion and a conviction that the organization of society cannot be left to people who do not possess this knowledge or demonstrate a belief in its validity.

Religion and political theory

A final point should perhaps be made before we conclude this brief discussion of metaphysical theories of the state. What we have just been exploring in the work of Plato, Hegel and Marx is a philosophical version of a view of knowledge, society and the place of individuals in society which is also that of organized religion. Many organized religions have a view of knowledge as developing towards some form of perfect knowledge, not by the mystical and metaphysical processes of Hegel's 'Absolute' or Marx's dialectical materialism, but by divine revelation, the progressive revelation to humankind of that perfect knowledge which at present only an omniscient God possesses.

As a consequence, most religions regard moral issues as being matters not of personal opinion but of 'God's law':

> Laws which never shall be broken
> For their guidance hath He made.

Thus they encounter serious difficulties if they seek to permit personal opinion, since this can only operate within the broad moral parameters of the particular doctrine. And this serves to illustrate the epistemological inconsistency. As a further consequence, most religions have their own fixed views on how society should be organized and governed – on the scope of individual freedom of thought, for example, as the recent Salman Rushdie case illustrates, and on many other matters which affect the lives of individual members of society, whether they happen to be adherents of the dominant religion or not.

Finally, most religions have some concept of a perfect world towards which we, or at least some of us, are moving, when God creates 'a new heaven and a new earth'. Religion thus shares many of the basic tenets of rationalism, of historicism and of metaphysical theories of the state.

It is not surprising, therefore, to discover that there has been little genuine support for democracy in the works of religious philosophers. We may note, for example, the 'nationalism' of the Judaeic tradition and its concept of sin as disobedience to the holy law. We may note too the Christian concept of 'original sin' and the influence that had on the development of philosophy in the western world. We see St Augustine presaging Hegel in his view that to exercise our freedom to choose what is 'wrong' is not to be free at all. We see him also implying, in the manner of those social contract theorists whose views we considered earlier in this chapter, that the state's prime function is to restrain the evil tendencies of human beings. And we see his historicism in his 'insistence that the history of the Church was "the march of God in the world" and that the true Christian ought not to focus on the problems of "this temporal life"' (Held, 1987, p. 37).

We find St Thomas Aquinas, not surprisingly as one wedded to the work of Aristotle, taking a more positive view of the state as a natural form of human living and as concerned to promote the good of its citizens. As a consequence, he regarded government not as supreme and unchallengeable but as obliged to seek to translate, where necessary, 'natural law' into actual law or, to express it differently, not to enact laws which are 'unjust' in the sense of contravening 'natural law'. Nevertheless, his preferred form of government seems to have been what we would now call constitutional monarchy, the main requirement being that 'the ruler or rulers devote themselves to caring for and promoting the objective common good' (Copleston, 1955, p. 233).

Once one has a concept of 'the *objective* common good', as all religions must have, the idea of democratic debate over what that common good might be becomes unacceptable. Again, therefore, we see that the rationalist position over knowledge and especially morals is inimical to the notion of democratic forms of social living.

Christian theology dominated western thinking in all spheres for many centuries. And this is why we can detect little if any political theorizing throughout this time. John Dewey once said that thinking begins in a forked-road situation, that people only begin to speculate about matters when they see a problem or dilemma to be resolved or, more importantly, a choice or a decision to be made. For many centuries, however, the church was supreme in all fields and, so long as this was the case and was accepted as the case, political speculation was unnecessary.

Even when philosophy itself re-emerged in the seventeenth century, through the work of people such as Rene Descartes, who is regarded as the founder of 'modern' philosphy, the Christian influence continued to be strong, so that there is little evidence of political speculation at this time. The theory of the divine right of kings, for example, which was prevalent for most of this time, did little to encourage speculation that there might be other forms of government than monarchy. And this is a major explanation of the fact that, after those brief periods when democracy flourished in ancient Athens and in republican Rome, it disappeared even from the political debate until the eighteenth century.

It was only when the authority of the church in the temporal sphere began to be challenged that a fork in the road appeared. In the first place this created civil and political unrest and raised many problems in the sphere of practical politics. However, it also raised again the age-old problem of political philosophy, the problem of political obligation (Plamenatz, 1963). It thus created a forked-road situation and attracted forth political philosophers who sought to advise us on the fork we ought to choose. The issue of political obligation was not a serious problem when church and state were one. While the doctrine of the divine right of kings held sway, it provided a simple and ready-made answer to the problem of political obligation – we are obliged to obey the king because his authority comes from God and is absolute.

History of course reveals the emergence of challenges to this view of monarchy and political authority, most notably the English Civil War. The intellectual challenge, however, first came in the form of the Protestant Reformation which 'did more than just challenge papal jurisdiction and authority across Europe; it raised questions about political obligation and obedience in a stark manner' (Held, 1987, p. 40). For it left it no longer clear who had the 'divine right' or whose 'divine right' was to predominate. Such a simple answer to the question of political obligation ceased, therefore, to be tenable, and the question returned to the political agenda for alternative solutions.

There was a further dimension of the Reformation that was also crucial for this issue. For a major tenet of Protestantism is the notion that Christianity is a matter of the relation of each individual to God. 'The teachings of Luther and Calvin contained at their very heart a new conception of the person as "an individual"' (*ibid.*). And this notion of individualism is in direct conflict with the collectivism of previously held views of church and state. As we shall see in Chapter 3, it was precisely this kind of individualism that was the central feature of those philosophies of 'existentialism' which emerged as a reaction to German idealism as exemplified in the metaphysical theories of the state of people like Hegel. And so, 'this development, when joined with the momentum for political change initiated by the struggle among religions, and between religions and secular powers, constituted a major new impetus to re-examine the nature of society and state' (Held, 1987, p. 40).

Some other basis for political obligation had to be found and temporarily the social contract theory was seen as providing the answer. And with later versions of that theory came a new notion – that of the rights of a subject *vis-à-vis* the king, including the right, under certain circumstances, to resist the authority of the state.

Thus it was only when the influence of the church came to be weakened that space appeared for the development of more liberal views of social organization.

THE MAJOR ASSUMPTIONS OF ANTI-DEMOCRATIC THEORIES

We thus see that there has been much political theory over the centuries which has been fundamentally anti-democratic in its thrust, whether deliberately so or not. We can see too that this kind of theory has derived from at least two major assumptions.

The first of these is a pessimistic view of human nature, as being essentially self-seeking or burdened with original sin, and consequent doubts about the capability of people, or at least most people, to participate effectively in the government of the society in which they live. This has led, in some accounts, to the 'down-to-earth' or 'commonsense' view that it is a waste of time to moralize about society or to propound idealistic notions about forms of social organization. And, indeed, if this is the view one has of human nature, the debate about the essence of democratic living becomes an irrelevance.

The second major assumption to be seen in more closely argued forms of anti-democratic political theory has been a rationalist epistemology which has led, as it must lead, to a view of knowledge as transcending individual human opinion and thus to a conviction that the state (or the church) and its interests must take precedence over the views, interests or wishes of its individual members.

In both contexts, individuals are required to obey their 'sovereign' or government, either out of self-interest or because that 'sovereign' or government represents the will of the state and is *ipso facto* right and *knows* what is best for everyone. In neither case, therefore, is there room for any individual opinion.

What we must note here, then, is that these theories are predicated on quite distinctive views not only of knowledge but also of human nature, of social living and, indeed, of morality.

For social contract theories see human nature as essentially competitive, self-seeking and *a*moral. Within such a view of human nature, social living can be no more than a device for individual protection. And morality is a social construct – we create moral rules to protect ourselves and each other.

Metaphysical theories see 'man' as a rational animal whose reason, and thus whose behaviour, is constantly distorted by emotions, and who, as a consequence, needs to be forced into the path of rationality and rational morality. Society is a stage in the process of development towards something better, towards some form of ultimate perfection. For Hegel this is the 'Absolute'; for Marx the 'stateless society'; for religion 'the next world' or 'a new heaven on earth'. It is part of the unfolding of knowledge and rationality; it is consequently right and moral; it has, therefore, to be accepted. And morality is a rational morality; ultimate values cannot be questioned because they are firmly based in reason, or on God's law. Morality is not a matter of opinion but of *knowledge*.

Neither kind of theory, then, can provide a basis for a democratic theory of society. Such a theory, as we shall see, requires a more positive view of humankind as capable of self-directed moral behaviour. It requires a positive view of social living as a natural rather than an artificial environment for human beings. And it requires a moral theory which can allow for and accommodate individual preferences and choices.

THE MISSING DEMOCRATIC PRINCIPLES:
SOME NEGATIVE LESSONS

It was suggested at the beginning of this chapter that a brief survey of the kinds of non-democratic, or even anti-democratic, political theories which have dominated western thought since the time of Plato would perhaps reveal to us not only how recent and tenuous is our hold on democracy but also, in a negative sense, through their conspicuous absence, some of the principles of democratic living we are seeking to identify. Before we move on then, in Chapter 2, to consider those liberal political theories which, it might be hoped, will provide us with more direct pointers towards a definition of democracy, it may be worth while to pause here to pick out the negative points which may be seen to emerge from our discussion so far.

It may be claimed of course that our methodology is bogus, flawed or at least ingenuous, and that we have already adopted a definition of democracy, according to which we have been describing other theories as non- or anti-democratic, that we have, in other words, been pre-empting our own conclusions. There may be a certain truth in that.

Some of the theories we have considered, however, such as that of Plato, have defined themselves as anti-democratic, or at least have offered overt criticisms of democratic political systems. And, as was suggested earlier, what we have in fact been doing is working with a minimal definition of democracy, fundamentally that of Pericles, as implying – at least at this point in our argument – little more than the equal participation of all citizens in the decision-making process. What we are thus attempting to do, from that simple base, is to identify further principles that are implied by such a basic view and to discover any additional features which seem to be essential to those systems we would be prepared to accept and describe as democratic in this minimal sense.

Thus the two major kinds of theory we have so far considered fail to qualify as democratic because, in the case of the negative version of the social contract and the views related to it, they accept the legitimacy of government by a minority or even by a single sovereign; and, in the case of those metaphysical theories we also noted, they cannot accommodate differences of opinion on moral, social or political matters, and thus cannot provide even a majority of citizens with any voice in decision-making which is not in accord with the 'will' of 'the state'.

We must now briefly consider whether there are other features of these non- or anti-democratic theories which might highlight, even in a negative way, by their absence, other principles which might be fundamental to democratic living.

We should first develop a little further the point we touched on earlier, that those theories which claim either that democracy is not an acceptable political system, or that there are better systems, or both, do so because they take a pessimistic view of human nature and hence a negative view of human social organizations. They see human beings as fundamentally self-seeking, as congenitally evil, as constantly deflected from the paths of rational morality by their emotions, feelings and desires, as burdened with original sin, or even merely as ignorant. They thus see the mass of humankind as incapable of intelligent, sensible and wise self-government, and as requiring the external control of a strong government or sovereign.

Some, such as Plato, take the view that it is possible to find rulers who themselves transcend this basic human condition. Others, like Machiavelli, are not even that optimistic, regard everyone, including the ruler(s), as self-seeking, and advocate as the best political system one in which the ruler's self-interest coincides with that of the citizens.

And those who subscribe to a metaphysical theory of the state, and require that every individual should be, or should be brought, in line with the collective 'general will' of the state, rather blandly assume that it is possible to identify what that 'general will' is. And so, when, like Lenin, they find themselves seeking to operationalize such a theory, they are forced to accept that this cannot be done by the mass of the citizens, that they continue – perversely – to hold their own views, and they are thus driven to the conclusion that all citizens must be directed into the paths which the 'general will' dictates; they must be 'forced to be free'.

A major feature, then, of non- or anti-democratic theories is that they are characterized by a negative and pessimistic view of human nature and of human beings.

Such a negative view is reflected also in much current social policy, based, as it is, on the notion of the individual as a competitive, self-seeking and self-interested consumer:

> Conceiving the public alone as self-interested consumers or 'possessive individuals' (MacPherson 1973) presents, however, a degraded and distorted psychology of human nature. Not only does it mistake the diversity of qualities which inform individual motivation, . . . it also misconstrues the nature of individuality itself. It is to assume that my purposes, my development, must always be at the expense of someone else's . . . my success depends upon your defeat. The point is not that individuals are by nature possessively self-interested, but that the institutions of the market make them so. The institution of the market demands a singular currency of transaction.
>
> (Ranson, 1993, pp. 334–5)

Such policies are thus in themselves non- or even anti-democratic. Yet increasingly they dominate public discourse and permeate public policy. It has been claimed, for example (Carr, 1991a, p. 189), that

> more often than not, democracy is now defined as the political system which most effectively protects the freedom of individuals to make their own autonomous choices and implement their own private preferences. It is thus unsurprising that the public institutions now deemed necessary for the preservation of democracy are not those institutions identified with public discussions about the common good but those within which private choices and individual preferences can be freely displayed and satisfied (Levitas 1986).

And, again, the emphasis is on the institutions of the market, 'institutions sensitively attuned to the competing wants and interests of individuals' (*ibid.*).

The point being made here seeks to take us beyond this claim and to argue that this is not an acceptable definition of democracy, and that, further, it is a view of social living which is inimical to democracy. For democracy, as was stressed in our Introduction, is a moral concept. It is a concept which encapsulates certain ideal principles and moral values, to which anyone who proclaims adherence to democracy must be committed. And such a moral system must address itself, first, to the reconciliation of the interests of individuals and, second, as a major feature of that process, to the maintenance of a sense of commonality of interests, a sense of 'belonging and sharing common purposes and experiences' (Soltis, 1993, p. 152).

A significant principle of democratic living and of democratic government arises from this, therefore; and that is that democratic political theories are, and must be, predicated on a more positive and optimistic view of human nature. For even to accept Pericles' basic principle of the participation of all in government is to assume the capacity of all so to participate. And it is further to assume that humankind, if not perfectible, is at least capable of altruism, is able to recognize the needs of others and to consider what may be right for the community as a whole and not merely for him or herself within it. Another way of expressing this is to say that human behaviour can be motivated by an assessment of what is in the general interest and not merely by individual desires, that 'when the citizen chooses a certain policy or prefers one policy to another, he [or she] is expressing not a want but an *evaluation*' (Wollheim, 1962, p. 77).

A further principle follows from this. For, if we accept that all citizens can participate in government and can do so with more than their own narrow interests in mind, we are already a long way down the road towards taking a more positive view not just of human nature but also of human society and of its purposes. In particular, we are well on the way to recognizing that society exists not merely to protect individuals but, much more than that, to enhance and enrich the quality of their lives, to acknowledging that society is a natural rather than an artificial environment for human beings to live in. The notion of democracy as concerned with the enrichment of the life of all its citizens becomes, therefore, an important consideration and one to which we must return.

Finally, it may not be going too far to claim that democratic systems can offer a far more satisfactory form of morality as a basis for social living. For the non- or anti-democratic views we have considered have either no view of morality at all and are essentially *a*moral, regarding it as irrelevant in a context where expediency, self-interest and self-protection are the only concerns, or they take a fixed view of morality as rational, objective and non-problematic.

Democratic theories, conversely, must accept the possibility of devising a moral system which can accommodate differences, which can allow for individual preference and choice. Such a moral system does not take the view either that all is a matter of expediency or that all is a matter of obedience; it accepts the reality, indeed the desirability, of cultural and moral diversity, of difference, and seeks to offer a mode of social and moral living which will allow for, and indeed celebrate and benefit from, the richness which such difference and diversity can bring.

One of the weaknesses of classical Athenian democracy as a model is that, because it was relatively small and, as we noted earlier, sectional, it was in fact largely consensual, 'united in interest, and therefore uniform in desire or want' (Wollheim, 1962, p. 73), whereas 'in any modern state the people is bound to be both *numerous* and *diverse*' (Wollheim, op.cit., p. 72). It is precisely this diversity of modern societies which makes it essential to devise a moral and social system which can accommodate diversity, and to create mechanisms for reconciling differences where these may be in conflict.

All of these are points we must return to, since they will emerge more positively when we move on, in Chapter 2, to consider those liberal political theories which have offered more optimistic views of human nature and of human society, and have contributed in a direct way to the emergence of those basic principles of democratic living for which we are seeking.

2

DEMOCRACY AND POLITICAL THEORY II: LIBERAL POLITICAL THEORIES

A democracy is more than a form of government; it is primarily a mode of associated living.

(Dewey, 1916, Chap. 7, sec. 2)

The political theories which we looked at briefly in Chapter 1 revealed features which it was claimed entitled us to describe them as non- or even anti-democratic. We noted, however, that in a negative way they assisted us in our quest for the sufficient conditions, the basic principles of democracy by drawing our attention to those features of social living which were conspicuous in these theories by their absence – faith in human nature, a positive view of social living and a sophisticated moral system which seeks to accommodate, even celebrate, moral and cultural diversity.

We must latch on to these, then, as some of our first principles of democratic living, and proceed now to seek out in the literature of political philosophy those theories which have also taken this basic stance, in order that we might identify the kinds of positive feature of society they have been concerned to emphasize.

SOME POSITIVE EARLY THINKING ABOUT SOCIAL ORGANIZATION

The point we have stressed about the social nature of human beings is developed in a positive way in the political writings of Aristotle; and there are other positive elements there which we must also note briefly besides his conviction that 'man' is a social animal and that social living is thus 'his' natural state.

For example, he supports that further point we made earlier in claiming that 'a state exists for the sake of a good life, and not for the sake of life only' (*Politics*, III, Chap. 9). If it did not, he argues, then animals might form a state. For him, a state does not exist merely to protect individuals from each other or to prevent individuals from using their freedom only when such use might restrict the freedom of others. For Aristotle, these are necessary but not sufficient conditions of statehood since, in his view, the state has a further responsibility; it must help its citizens develop into good persons, it must help them to become virtuous. This, incidentally, it does through education which, for Aristotle as well as for Plato, has as its prime function the development of moral understanding and rectitude.

There are of course difficulties with such a view, especially in its rationalist assumption that virtue has some kind of objective status and that values are not problematic. For the present, however, let us note the positive support he offers for that principle of democracy we have already adumbrated, that society exists not merely to protect individuals but to offer them an enriched form of existence; so that a democratic society is one which seeks to provide positive rather than merely negative advantages to all its citizens and is to be judged by the degree to which it seeks, and is able, to do this. How far these positive advantages need to go is another matter to which we must return.

A second feature of Aristotle's political theory which is worthy of note is the emphasis he places on the notion of equality. Again, this is a concept which we will need to explore more fully since, although it is clearly central to most people's concept of democracy and has loomed large in most theoretical discussions of democracy as well as in many attempts, most notably perhaps that of the French Revolution, to achieve it, it is open to a wide range of meanings and interpretations.

This will be clear from a momentary glance at what Aristotle has to say about it, and we will want to express severe reservations about his concept of equality which, as we saw when discussing Athenian democracy in Chapter 1, is essentially a concept of equality within categories, equality of equals but not of 'unequals'. Thus, for Aristotle, as for the architects of Athenian democracy, while all men are considered equal, women are not, nor, clearly, are slaves. Each category has its own place in society; the husband is superior to the wife; the father to his children; the master to his slaves. For anyone to step beyond his or her place or category is unjust since, in his oft-quoted assertion, injustice arises as much from treating unequals equally as from treating equals unequally.

We are right of course to have serious reservations about this concept of equality – or at least Aristotle's application of it. We must not, however, let it deflect our attention from the fact that *some* notion of equality is essential to any concept of democracy. And we should note, again as we did when considering Athenian democracy, that we must not let one interpretation of this principle deflect us from recognizing the importance of the principle itself. Aristotle recognized the importance of equality between equals; the question of who is to count as an equal is a secondary issue – secondary not in the sense of being less important but in the sense of not affecting the equality principle itself.

The form of democracy which we know as the Roman Republic was even less egalitarian than that of Athens. For it was overtly based on a clear system of social class and differentiation by wealth. Every adult male citizen, whether patrician or plebeian, had a right to take part in the government of the state, but not the right to an equal part in that government, the level at which any individual could participate depending on birth and/or (later in its history) property.

Thus, although all adult male citizens participated, through membership of the three *comitia*, in the elections to all the major offices of state, only those of a certain level of wealth were permitted to stand for those offices. And, although the Plebeian Assembly (*concilium plebis*), which was restricted to members of the plebeian class, had the power to make laws – and did so to some effect from time to time – effectively legislation was in the hands of the Senate and, for the most part, laws made by the Plebeian Assembly were engineered by members of the Senate who had failed to win the support of their peers.

The Roman constitution, then, is an example of a very limited form of democracy. Nevertheless, again, as we saw in the case of Athenian democracy, limited as it was, it can still offer us pointers to the essence of democratic living.

One of those pointers comes from the emphasis that is placed within Roman culture on the concept of *virtus*. This is usually translated as 'virtue' or 'goodness' or even 'courage'. In fact, its connotations go far beyond those of these words. For *virtus* is public or social morality; it suggests the level of public responsibility which is expected of a public figure, a politician; and it stresses the undesirability of self-seeking on the part of those who would take charge of the affairs of the state. Its later interpretation as 'statesmanship' goes some way towards capturing this nuance of meaning, although today that term is not always used as one of total approval.

It is worth noting further that it is a concept which survived the destruction of the Republic and the establishment of the Roman Empire, ruled no longer by the people or even by the well-born and wealthy but by those who seized power as 'emperors'. For, even those whose actions led to the downfall of the Republic felt the need to justify the seizing of power by asserting that they were doing so in the best interests of the state. And once imperial rule had become the established norm, even in this context of complete autocracy, the merits of those holding the imperial power continued to be judged (although prudence usually dictated that this should not be done during their lifetimes) by reference to the concept of *virtus*, the degree to which they had used their power responsibly and in the general interests of all citizens.

A general point emerges from this that we should not lose sight of. That is the suggestion that the concept of a democracy requires that those elected to hold office in that democracy can reasonably be expected to perform the functions of that office in a manner designed to ensure the best interests of the nation as a whole and not merely to uphold the sectional interests of themselves or their party. This may appear to be an ideal, but it is ideals we are concerned with, since what we are seeking are the criteria by which we might be able to assess the merits of any system which has pretentions to being called democratic, and evaluate the performance of those who claim to be agents of democratic government.

A second pointer to be found in the history of the Roman Republic is one we will again return to often. The Roman Republic had emerged as a consequence of the revolt against, and expulsion of, the last king of Rome, Tarquinius, nicknamed 'The Proud', a notable tyrant. Liberty had been hard won, and was all the more prized for that fact. Political liberty thus became a further major feature of the Roman view of politics. Indeed, for many writers and thinkers of the time, it seems to have been viewed as an essential prerequisite of, and concern in, the exercise of *virtus*, so that the reconciliation of these two concepts became a serious problem for those living during the period of the Empire. Nevertheless, the notion of political liberty persisted far into that era – a clear indication of the important part it played in the Roman way of life.

It may seem self-evident to claim that political freedom is a prerequisite of democratic living. In one sense this is true. However, there are different levels of freedom and different interpretations of what it actually entails. To a discussion of these we must return later. At this point, however, it is worth noting the link the Romans identified between political liberty and the exercise of *virtus*. For this is likely to be an important consideration when we come to our discussion of the complexities of defining (not to mention operationalizing) political freedom.

The last point to be made about the Roman period is that there is little literature to be found emerging from it that we would call political theory. The Romans were notoriously people of action rather than of speculation. And most of what we know of their thinking is gleaned from our knowledge of their practical politics – most notably, through speeches, letters and historical treatises. Furthermore, the establishment of the Roman Empire eventually put a stop to such free philosophical speculation as there was on most issues, and especially those of a political kind. And the later advent of Christianity, for the reasons we discussed in Chapter 1, had the same effect.

The idea of democracy as a form of social living or even of government is thus difficult to detect in thinking at any level for several centuries. Indeed, associated concepts, such as freedom, equality and human rights, are also little in evidence. Christian theology reigns supreme. The divine right of kings is unchallenged. The central point at issue is whether the state or the church should rule, or which should have precedence over the other and in what circumstances. The idea that the people should govern themselves seems not to enter anyone's head.

It is for this reason that Raymond Williams, in his survey of *Culture and Society 1780–1950*, is able to say that '*democracy*, which had been known, from the Greek, as a term for "government by the people" . . . only came

into common English use at the time of the American and French revolutions'
(1958, p. 14). He also quotes Weekley as saying, in *Words Ancient and
Modern*, that 'it was not until the French revolution that *democracy* ceased
to be a mere literary word, and became part of the political vocabulary'.

Furthermore, as the quotation at the beginning of Chapter 1 indicates, the
term 'democracy' returns to common usage with a largely pejorative meaning.
Democracy was seen, for example by Edmund Burke, as a threat to the social
order. It was equated in the minds of many people with revolution, so that
whether one looked favourably on it or not depended on whether one wanted
the political status quo to be maintained or overturned.

However, the American and French Revolutions, along with the threat of
similar events in most other nations in the western world, prompted in part
by the 'Industrial Revolution', had the effect of accelerating the debate which
had begun in the later part of the seventeenth century as a response to the
cynicism of the political theories of men such as Thomas Hobbes. That debate,
to which men like John Locke in England, Jean-Jacques Rousseau in France
and Thomas Paine, who at various times lived and worked in England,
France and America, were major contributors, marks the re-emergence of
a liberal position in political theorizing, although it would be wrong to seek
to characterize it as in itself at that stage democratic. However, while not
specifically addressing the issue of democracy, it nevertheless began to raise
several associated questions.

And, in those questions, we can see reflected the major preoccupations and
features of the liberal theories of the classical world. Locke, for example, has
much to say about 'natural equality', about 'natural liberty' and about the
consequent need for there to be a moral justification for both the existence
and the practices of the state. Rousseau rejects the notion of original sin. 'God
makes all things good; man meddles with them and they become evil' (*Émile*,
Chap. 1). He also supports the notion of 'natural liberty'. 'Man is born free;
and everywhere he is in chains' (*The Social Contract*, Bk 1, Chap. 1). And
Tom Paine is best known for his assertion of 'The Rights of Man', his book
of that title having been written as a response to Edmund Burke's *Reflections
on the Revolution in France*.

Both Locke and Rousseau offer us a version of the social contract which is
a positive reaction and response to those negative versions of this theory we
considered in Chapter 1. We noted there that, as a device, as an analogue, this
theory could be used in support of diametrically opposed political positions –
to assert the rights of the citizenry against the government or to support the
absolute authority of government. And we saw that the version of the theory
which people like Thomas Hobbes inherited from Plato was of this latter kind,
and that Hobbes used it to argue the opposite of what it seems to have been
invented for.

What we now see in the work of both Locke and Rousseau is a shift to
the former, to what, as we also saw in Chapter 1, was the original thrust
of the theory as offered by the sophist, Lycophron. The concern is now with

liberty rather than security, with developing a case for resistance to the abuse of political power rather than for abject acceptance of it.

What we have here, then, is, first, at the practical level, a response to the historical events of the time, an attempt to press the claims of the citizenry to forms of government which take account in some way of their interests; and, second, at the theoretical level, a movement away from those anti-democratic theories, which would support strong government at any cost, towards a more liberal set of considerations.

This move was soon to render the social contract theory itself superfluous. As David Hume was to point out, it had become an unnecessary tool. Its use by the first of the liberal theorists can be explained simply in terms of its being there, of its being the material at hand on which they had to work. Those who followed were soon to realize that there were better ways of arguing the liberal case.

We thus see the re-emergence of a full, free and moral debate about social living, prompted in part by the slow emancipation of philosophy from theology, a process which was much accelerated by the Reformation, in part by those changing social conditions associated with the 'Industrial Revolution' and in part by the dramatic reaction to those conditions reflected in the events in France and in America, and threatened elsewhere.

We have thus entered an era when the essential elements of democracy will begin to emerge both from an ongoing philosophical debate and from major changes in political practices. It will now serve our purposes better, therefore, to explore these essential elements individually. For, while the brief historical survey which this and the previous chapter have so far attempted has taken us some way towards identifying them, now that we have reached a period when the issues themselves are being directly addressed, to continue to adopt a historical approach would be likely to obscure rather than to illuminate them.

KEY ISSUES, BASIC PRINCIPLES, SUFFICIENT CONDITIONS OF DEMOCRATIC LIVING

There are four major themes which can be identified in the work of those who have attempted to offer us a positive, liberal view of human society and its potential. The first of these – logically – is the notion, the claim, that all human beings have certain inalienable 'natural rights'. These 'natural rights', it is claimed, entitle everyone to certain minimal levels of treatment and, conversely, forbid, in some way, forms of treatment which fall below those levels.

Pre-eminent among these 'natural rights' is entitlement to equality of treatment, and this is the second major theme. It is a theme which is evident not only in the work of political theorists but also in the arena of practical politics. The American Declaration of Independence of 1776, for example, in what is a precis of John Locke, asserts that 'all men are created equal' and that 'men are born and live free and equal in their rights'. And the more recent 1948 declaration tells us that 'all human beings are born free and equal in dignity and rights'.

These quotations alert us also to the third of the major themes we must explore, that of 'natural liberty'. Not only must human beings, within these liberal, democratic views of society, be accorded equality of treatment, but they must also be allowed the maximum possible degree of freedom – of thought, of speech, of opinion and even of behaviour.

Finally, it follows from these three claims that, if the conditions they lay down for human society are to be met, the full participation of every member of society in government and decision-making is an essential prerequisite. The notion of popular sovereignty, therefore, becomes a fourth major issue we need to address.

We must now consider all of these essential concepts in some detail. Before we do so, however, there are two general points to be noted, both of which we have noted before. First, all of these themes reflect certain ideals of social and democratic living. In practice they are difficult to attain, and the machinery which is set up to attain them is often, indeed usually, imperfect. Our quest in this book, however, as has been pointed out on several occasions, is precisely to identify those ideals, to analyse that ideal construct, the moral system, we have claimed the concept of democracy is and identify its major component parts. The concern is not to produce a blueprint for a perfect democratic society. Rather the task we have undertaken is to discover the criteria by which we can evaluate the merits and the defects of those existing attempts to create social organizations which might approximate to democratic forms, to fashion a template by which we might measure how far they meet or fall short of the basic principles of democracy. Politics is a far from perfect form of human activity. Some approximation to the ideal is all that one can look for. In order to do so, however, one needs to be clear about what the ideal is, what the ultimate criteria of judgement are.

The second – and related – general point is also one we have drawn attention to on previous occasions. It is not at any stage the intention or concern of this book to seek to justify democracy and its related practices: the aim is merely to define it. We have not set out to justify democratic forms of social organization, to argue why anyone should be committed to these, but to show merely what such a commitment entails, what is implied by the acceptance of such a commitment or, perhaps more importantly, what anyone who claims or declares him or herself to be so committed can be held to.

We might express this by saying that it is not the intention to become embroiled in the controversies of the debate over values. A particular value stance, that entailed by an initial commitment to the ideals of democratic living, is assumed and adopted. Our discussion then proceeds within the parameters of that value system, and the task undertaken is that of identifying what precisely such a system entails.

It has already been argued that to be committed to democratic forms of social living implies a commitment to upholding human rights, to maintaining equality, to promoting individual liberty and to supporting the idea of the participation of all in decision-making. The concern in what follows is to dig a little deeper than this, to try to tease out some of the complexities of these notions and to ascertain what further implications these subsequent commitments may have.

In that frame of mind, then, let us turn to a more detailed consideration of the four major themes we have identified.

'Natural rights'

The concept of 'natural rights', along with the associated concept of 'natural law', is another feature of political philosophy which has been around since the time of the Greeks. For them, as for others who have appealed to the concept since then, it has been seen as offering a basis for defining social justice, for suggesting that the actual laws of any given society may not always be 'right'.

And, in spite of its manifest conceptual problems, it is a continuing concern. Today we are more likely to hear '*human* rights' being advanced and demanded, but the concept is the same. People continue to believe and to claim that they have rights which are in some way independent of, and different from, those rights which are granted them by the laws of their society.

Again too, it is a concept which re-emerged both in political theory and in assertions of political doctrine at that point we have identified when a challenge began to be mounted to autocracy or authoritarianism in politics. Its prime purpose was to offer a basis for questioning political authority, and even for justifying disobedience and resistance to such authority in certain circumstances. It was adduced in order to provide a check on, and a court of appeal against, the absolute nature of political power, the arbitrary rule of Hobbes's 'sovereign' and Machiavelli's 'prince'. Its concern was to furnish criteria by which we might judge whether an actual law or decree was 'right' or 'wrong', whether we should obey it or not. And it did this by attempting to assert that it is not only kings who have their rights – divine or otherwise; subjects, citizens, the common people have rights too. Thus the French Declaration of the Rights of Man and of Citizens informs us that 'men are born free and equal in respect of their natural and imprescriptible rights of liberty, property, security and resistance of oppression'.

A major difficulty with such a claim, however, is the question of where these rights derive from. 'Right' is a legal term; it connotes an entitlement conferred by a system of law; it indicates what that system of law permits us to do and will support us in doing. It is thus an odd term to use when the intention is to provide us with a court of appeal against what any particular legal system might or might not permit. It is even odder to suggest that we enter this world somehow bearing with us rights which may be at odds with the legal system of the society into which we are born. Hence Hobbes tells us that the subject has rights only to whatever the sovereign allows.

To say this, however, is to deny the very thing which the concept of 'natural rights' was devised to assert. And it is for this reason that in Locke's version of the social contract 'natural rights' are seen as the rights which people enjoy in the hypothetical state of nature, i.e. before they enter the compact which is society, and of which they cannot, or should not, as a result be deprived by society.

It is difficult to deny, however, that the term 'right' is only meaningful in a legal context, and that the notion of a 'natural right' may be a contradiction in terms. Hence, those who wished to set up a court of appeal in which certain legal decisions might be challenged also set up their own legal context for their natural rights. They invoked the notions of 'natural law', and later of 'natural justice'. The claim now is that human beings have certain rights which transcend the laws of whatever political or social organization they happen to live in because these rights are conferred by a system of law which also transcends any particular social or political organization. And this system of 'natural law' provides the court of appeal against particular systems; it offers a model against which all individual systems can be evaluated; it tells us whether a particular law or political decision is 'just' or 'unjust'.

It is not difficult to see the difficulties political theorists have found in this notion. For it confuses several meanings of the term 'law'. We can understand 'natural law' as a concept in science; we have no problems with law as a regulatory device within society; we can even understand the idea of a moral law. The term 'natural law', however, as it has been and continues to be used in this kind of political context, fits into none of these categories and yet seems to seek somehow to partake of all of them. 'Natural law' is so called because it is seen as in some way deriving from human nature; but this does not help us in determining what kind of law it is; it merely compounds the confusion.

It is perhaps more easy to accept if offered in a religious framework, as the law of God – the form in which it is offered by Aquinas when, as we saw in Chapter 1, he expresses the view that rulers should seek to translate 'natural law' into actual law, or at least not to enact laws which contravene 'natural law'. And there is an element of this appeal to religion, to revelation, in a number of the views of 'natural law' and 'natural rights' developed later by such people as John Locke.

However, without this theological basis, both terms become confused and confusing. And we can appreciate why Edmund Burke opposed the notion of 'natural rights' as metaphysical and suggested that the term 'right' can only be used meaningfully in the context of a particular society, and why Jeremy Bentham tells us that 'the rights of man are plain nonsense; the imprescriptible rights of man nonsense on stilts'.

The notion of 'natural rights', however, is clearly an important one, as is the idea that we need some court of appeal against laws or political decisions which appear to contravene what we might regard as basic principles of natural justice. And that is why the notion has come to be important within liberal and democratic political theory and why we must make some attempt to show that it is not nonsense, whether on stilts or not.

In doing so, the first point we must note is that it is indeed nonsense to see 'natural rights' or 'natural law' in any *descriptive* sense, to regard both or either as having some kind of existence. We can only do this if we are prepared to accept some form of religious argument which declares 'natural rights' to derive from the 'law of God'.

If the term 'natural rights' is to have any kind of meaning outside this form of religious doctrine, that meaning cannot be a *descriptive* meaning; it must be recognized as *prescriptive*. The term 'natural rights' must be seen not as describing some readily identifiable feature of humanity, but as constituting a claim that human beings *ought* to be treated in certain ways. It thus becomes a part of that sophisticated moral system we suggested in Chapter 1 is a *sine qua non* of democratic living.

The term came to be used, as we have seen, in contexts where many human beings had few, if any, legal rights, and was thus coined to offer the basis of a demand that they should have such rights. For, clearly, if such rights existed in a society, there would be no reason for inventing a concept of 'natural rights'. The purpose of that concept, then, is to claim or demand rights. Its force is fundamentally moral. And only conceptual confusion can result from regarding it in any other way. Indeed, it might be argued that the use of the term 'right' in this context in itself invites such confusion; although there is no denying its rhetorical force.

The term thus seeks to make a claim for certain kinds of entitlement for all citizens. It sets out to define what have been called 'the conditions of a good society' (Macdonald, 1956, p. 48) and to provide a moral basis for demanding that these be met. But it is important to recognize that 'what these conditions are is not given by nature or mystically bound up with the essence of man and his inevitable goal, but is determined by human decisions' (*ibid.*). It is a fundamental error, and the source of much conceptual confusion, to treat the concept of natural rights as in any sense a priori or metaphysical.

The notion of natural rights, then, seeks to do no more than offer us a set of criteria by which we can evaluate particular laws or decisions within particular social settings. The notion of 'natural law', provided again that we do not interpret it in descriptive or metaphysical or even legal terms, but recognize it as moral and, indeed, political in its force, provides a model, a humanitarian model, against which actual laws can be assessed. There is no logical reason why we should be committed to its claims, but it is difficult not to be so when those claims in essence amount to little more than the need for some kind of moral regulation of the interactions of all members of any human society.

It is for this reason then that, properly understood, the concept of 'natural rights' is crucial to our understanding of democratic forms of social living. For although, as we have just seen, individual rights must be determined 'by human decisions', and those decisions may well vary from one democratic society to another, what cannot vary is the requirement that any society wishing to claim to be democratic must undertake all of its planning and decision-making in full awareness that the interests, the 'rights', of all citizens must be taken into account at every stage. Indeed, this is a major part of what is entailed by the recognition that democracy is a moral concept. A democratic society is by definition committed to recognizing, respecting and attempting to meet the needs of all its citizens.

There is a further point worthy of note which follows from this. For the concept of 'natural rights' must also be seen as part of that general movement of challenge to those metaphysical theories of the state we considered in Chapter 1. We saw there that such theories elevate the state to a status where its interests are supreme and are to be accepted as transcending those of individual citizens. And it was suggested there that such a view of the state is the essence of totalitarianism and thus quite opposed to any concept of democracy.

In its assertion of rights which it is claimed the individual has against certain kinds of action on the part of government, the doctrine of 'natural rights' is opposing this view with one which places the interests of the individual citizen at least on a par with that of the collective. It is asserting that the state, in the shape of its government, cannot ride roughshod over any of its citizens. Again, therefore, we can see how important this notion, whatever we are to call it, is for our definition of democracy.

This aspect of democratic living takes us naturally on to the second major issue we identified earlier, that of equality of entitlement. For this may be claimed to be one of those 'conditions of a good society' it has been suggested some people have described as 'natural rights'.

Equality

From the earliest known time in the history of western thought egalitarianism has been a recognizable phenomenon at both the popular and the philosophical levels. Like that positive version of the social contract theory which we considered earlier, it can be seen in the work of some of the earliest of the sophists. Popper (1945, Vol. I, pp. 69–70), for example, draws our attention to the words of the sophist, Antiphon, who tells us,

> The nobly born we revere and adore; but not the lowly born. These are barbarous habits. For as to our natural gifts, we are all on an equal footing, on all points, whether we now happen to be Greeks or Barbarians . . . We all breathe the air through our mouths and nostrils.

However, as Popper goes on to point out, again like that positive version of the social contract, this view was opposed and suppressed by the work of Plato and, albeit to a lesser extent, that of Aristotle. For at no stage does Plato acknowledge the existence of an egalitarian viewpoint, and he offers us, as we have seen, an élitist or meritocratic view of society. And we have seen Aristotle advocating equality as an essential element of the just society, but at the same time offering us a concept of equality within categories but not between them – equality for men, but not for women, for free men but not for slaves, and so on – and thus asserting that injustice comes not only from treating equals unequally but also from treating unequals equally. 'The only stable principle of government is equality according to proportion' (*Politics*, para. 1307a).

This view of equality as dependent on merit has a long history in both theory and practice. And it is still prevalent in much current thinking and practice. There continues to exist alongside it, however, the broader egalitarian principle of equality according to common humanity rather than individual merit. For it is the latter view that has been supported by Christianity, which has long taken the view that all are equal in the sight of God. It has thus enjoyed the support of most philosophers, even during the times when philosphy was barely distinguishable from theology, so that some attempt has been made to give the doctrine a basis in reason rather than in religion. We see, for example, Spinoza asserting that 'those men who are governed by reason . . . desire nothing for themselves which they do not also desire for the rest of mankind' (*Ethics*, Prop. xiv) and thus seeking to argue that it is irrational to think or behave otherwise.

We might also note here a link with the concept of 'natural law' For, according to 'natural law', all men are equal; and this 'law' was promoted largely to offset, or even to replace, the Aristotelian view of natural inequalities:

> The pivotal point of the Aristotelian argument . . . was the assumption that men are by nature unequal in rank, and that there is therefore a natural rank order among men. This presupposition collapsed in the face of the assumption of natural law that the natural rank of all men is equal.
>
> (Dahrendorf, 1962, p. 92)

It is not surprising, therefore, to find those liberal theories of social living which emerge with the work of Locke and others in the seventeenth and eighteenth centuries adopting and asserting this kind of equality principle as if it were almost self-evident. For Locke, for example, the state of nature is

> a State also of Equality, wherein all the Power and Jurisdiction is reciprocal, no one having more than another, there being nothing more evident than that Creatures of the same Species and Rank, promiscuously born to all the same Advantages of Nature and the use of the same Facilities, should also be equal one amongst another, without Subordination or Subjection . . . The *State of Nature* has a Law of Nature to govern it, which obliges everyone; And Reason, which is that Law, teaches all Mankind, who will but consult it, that being all *equal and independent*, no one ought to harm another in his Life, Health, Liberty or Possessions.
>
> (*Second Treatise*, 2.6)

And we have noted before similar assertions in the American Declaration of Independence, the French Revolution's statement of 'Les Droits de l'Homme', UNESCO's Universal Declaration of Human Rights and in other similar public documents.

The contrary view, however, as we noted just now, continues to appear from time to time. Indeed, it would not be difficult to argue that in practice it continues to flourish, that the reality of most present-day societies is that it is the meritocratic version of the equality principle that one can most often discern while the democratic view remains largely at the level of supporting rhetoric, and that, as in George Orwell's political satire, *Animal Farm*, 'All animals are equal' rapidly degenerates in reality into 'All animals are equal,' but some are more equal than others'.

Indeed, Dahrendorf (1962), in the chapter referred to above, goes on to argue that there are inevitable and unavoidable inequalities between people in any society, inequalities which derive from the accepted norms of the society. Whatever capabilities, for example, a society values – hunting or fishing skills, economic 'know-how', sporting prowess or whatever – some people will display these to a greater degree than others. Further, in a complex modern society, this inequality will be reflected in occupational patterns and, indeed, rewards.

It is not necessary, however, even if we accept the empirical force of this claim, to regard it as inimical to the recognition of equality as an essential principle of democratic living. Much talk and intellectual energy has been wasted over the years on debates concerning respects in which human beings may be said to be equal. The answer to this question is that people are not equal – in the sense of 'same' – in any respects; and that is one of the things that makes life interesting. And much of the confusion over the concept of equality stems again, as we saw when discussing 'natural rights' and 'natural law', from a failure to recognize that the concept's main force is moral and *prescriptive* rather than descriptive, that its use represents not an assertion of some 'fact' about human beings or human nature or some 'natural law', but a demand for certain kinds of treatment. To assert that all 'men' are equal, or that all are born equal is not in any sense to describe the human condition. Indeed, as we saw just now, taken as a description, it is totally and inevitably inaccurate. It is rather to make a demand about the ways in which everyone should be treated.

The problem is further complicated, however, by the fact that it is equally unclear what kinds of treatment are being demanded. For, although at first glance this would seem to be a demand that everyone should be treated in the same way, it has often been pointed out that that is far too simple an interpretation, and that in practice to treat everyone the same would be to create rather than to eliminate inequalities.

Fundamentally, the demand is for social justice, for fairness and impartiality of treatment. And in all aspects of social living – in education, in health, in the administration of the law – social justice requires that individuals be treated appropriately rather than identically. For it is self-evident that social justice must be tailored to individual circumstances, and that injustice and inequality must result from failing to take such individual circumstances in to account. The term 'equal', then, says little or nothing unless it is qualified in some way.

If this is so, however, if the principle of equality is in fact demanding that we treat people differently, according to their individual differences, then that principle in itself is offering us nothing more useful than a general demand that differential treatment must be justified. It is thus a negative plea against unjustifiable differences of treatment. What we need to know is the criteria of relevance we are to appeal to in justifying such differences, and the concept of equality in itself does not help us in this quest.

> If we accept the infinite variety of human personality, that no two people, not even identical twins, are qualitatively identical, then there will always be differences between any two people, which might be held to justify a difference of treatment. Many of these differences we may wish to rule out as not being relevant, but since the principle of Formal Equality does not provide, of itself, any criteria of relevance, it does not, by itself, establish much. It gives a line of argument, but not any definite conclusion.
>
> (Lucas, 1965, p. 297)

In other words, while talk about human equality may be another way of demanding social justice, it does little or nothing to help us to discover what social justice is or what kinds of behaviour it requires of us.

This is one major reason for the persistence of those two versions of the equality principle we identified earlier – the 'strong' or meritocratic and the 'weak' or democratic versions (Crosland, 1961). For the 'strong' or meritocratic principle justifies us in only differentiating between people in respect of their merit. To quote Orwell again, it then does become a matter of 'Four legs good; two legs better'. It does become a matter of equality within categories, as Plato and Aristotle both advised, although, as for Plato, those categories are determined by merit. In education, for example, it does become a matter of equal opportunity to succeed or fail according to one's natural abilities, to pass or fail regular tests on the basis of which the nature and availability of further provision will be based.

The 'weak' or democratic version of the equality principle, on the other hand, seeks to commit us to more than this. It is recommending that we accept the need for different kinds of treatment to match the differences which exist between individuals, but not differences in the quality of such treatment. It is seeking to extend the range of criteria which might count as relevant to differential treatment. In education again, for example, it advocates not a single form of provision within which pupils succeed or fail according to individual merit, but a range of quality provision which seeks to meet the requirements of children of different abilities, backgrounds, cultures, talents, interests, preferences and so on.

This version of the equality principle then offers us a different notion of social justice. What it is unable to do, however, is to provide any justification for adopting this interpretation. Nor again can it help us very much with the realities of implementation. It offers a different set of arguments for differential provision; it makes a claim for a wider interpretation of those inequalities which, as we saw above, the notion of equality is attempting to oppose; but, as we also saw above, it offers us no solid criteria in the light of which we can practise what it preaches. It gives us no help in identifying those criteria of relevance, by which we are to justify differences of treatment, and the identification of them is the key issue. It merely offers us a broader interpretation of what might more helpfully be called the principle of 'universal humanity'.

> We may call it, if we like, the argument from Equality of Respect, but in this phrase it is the word 'Respect' – respect for each man's [or woman's] humanity, respect for him [or her] as a human being – which is doing the logical work, while the word 'Equality' adds nothing to the argument and is altogether otiose.
>
> (Lucas, op.cit., p. 298)

What we seem to have learnt then, from this brief exploration of the concept of equality is that, while it is confused, capable of a range of interpretations and, perhaps, as Lucas claims, otiose and unhelpful, it does encapsulate at the very minimum the notion that in a democratic society an attempt to achieve social justice must be a central feature, and that a basic principle of that attempt must be the requirement that justification must be offered wherever differences of treatment are planned or practised. It may well not be helpful to call this 'equality before the law', since justice is seldom a matter of treating people equally, although always a matter of treating them humanely. Again we must note, however, that, whatever we call it, there is a principle here of some importance to us in our search for the fundamentals of democratic living.

There is one final point we should note before we leave this discussion of the equality principle. We will find shortly when we discuss individual liberty that in that case too, as with equality, it is much easier to define, and indeed to practise what we are preaching when we are operating at the largely negative level of identifying situations which transgress basic principles – examples of inequalities or of unwarranted intrusions on individual liberty.

When we move to the more positive versions of these principles, however, as we have just seen with the 'weak' or democratic interpretation of the equality principle, the plot thickens considerably and justification becomes more complex. It is also the case that at that point potential for conflict between these principles begins to appear. To attempt to make people 'equal', for example, by seeking to remove or overcome what might be seen as unacceptable inequalities – inequalities of birth, of wealth or of social background, for example – will almost certainly necessitate intrusions on their freedom and, indeed, on that of other members of society. Adequate educational provision, for example, for every child regardless of social background can only be achieved by limiting their freedom, that of their parents and that of the taxpayers who must ultimately foot the bill.

This then becomes another major factor to be borne in mind when planning all forms of social provision. It is another dimension to the complexities of operationalizing democracy we have noted before. Fortunately, operationalization is not the task we face here. What we must note, however, is that we have now discovered that, under some circumstances, and especially if we feel driven to a positive view of democracy, the fundamental principles we are identifying may be in conflict with one another.

This is a point we should keep well in mind as we turn to the third major principle of democracy we are to explore, that of individual freedom.

Freedom

Political freedom has come to be regarded as in some way the essence of what it means to be human. Rousseau, for example, in *The Social Contract*, claims that 'to renounce liberty is to renounce being a man'. And Philip Phenix (1958, pp. 259–60) tells us that liberty

> has come to be widely regarded as the birthright of every man [and woman] so that a person is somehow less than human without it. The struggle for freedom is probably the major objective in revolutionary movements of all ages, and particularly of the twentieth century. Freedom is not always completely realized in the life of man [or woman], but can be suppressed and denied in unfavorable social circumstances. Thus, freedom is a goal to be attained rather than a possession guaranteed by nature. If freedom is part of the essence of being a man [or woman], then there are individuals who are less than fully human, and the struggle to become free is at the same time a striving for complete humanity.

Few would wish to disagree with that assertion. For most people would see freedom as 'a necessary condition for individual and social progress, for the expression and development of personality or a society' (Wilson, 1964, p. 33). Indeed, it is our claim here that no one who embraces the ideals of democracy as a social system can disagree with such a claim. For, as Dewey pointed out, the major argument for a democratic way of life is the conviction that all other forms of political organization are hostile and restrictive towards individual and social development, precisely because they deny the kind of individual freedom which is an essential prerequisite of such development.

On the other hand, there are many circumstances in which we feel it appropriate to restrict this individual freedom, and there is much debate about what it might mean for everyone to be free. And so we need to be a little clearer about this concept if we are to hold it up as one of our essential principles of democratic living.

For Hobbes, concerned, as we have seen he was, with security above all else, freedom is whatever the laws allow. He thus offers us an essentially negative view of freedom, as concerned primarily with what people should be free *from*. Men have liberty in all those areas where 'the sovereign has prescribed no rule'. In Hobbes's society, the most important freedom people have is freedom *from* the excesses of others, from the dangers of the 'war of all against all'. To ask for more than this is to ask for anarchy and a return to that 'state of nature'. For, as he tells us,

> If we take liberty, for an exemption from Lawes, it is no lesse absurd, for men to demand as they doe, that Liberty, by which all other men may be masters of their lives. And yet as absurd as it is, this is it they demand; not knowing that the Lawes are of no power to protect them, without a Sword in the hands of a man, or men, to cause those laws to be put into execution. The Liberty of a Subject, lyeth therefore only in those things, which in regulating their actions, the Sovereign hath praetermitted: such as is the Liberty to buy, and sell, and otherwise contract with one another; to choose their own aboad, their own diet, their own trade of life, and institute their children as they themselves think fit; and the like.
>
> (*Leviathan*, Chap. 21)

As we have seen, however, those liberal political theories which we are here exploring, as having contributed to the re-emergence of theories of democratic living, were prompted as much as anything by what was seen as the abuse of this kind of power by governments and sovereigns. Such a view of freedom, therefore, does not go anything like as far as democratic theory requires (although it does reveal to us some of the difficulties surrounding the use of the term 'freedom' in political contexts, and in particular its potential ambiguities).

Later theories, then, took a more liberal view. John Locke, for example, as we have seen before, is primarily concerned with supporting the possibility of challenge to the authority of government when this is abused, and sees dangers in the undue interference by the sovereign in the personal liberty of the individual (a concept which for Hobbes is meaningless). For him the concept of freedom is designed to place checks and balances on the power of the sovereign or government, to delineate the boundaries beyond which it is impermissible for a ruler to go. If liberty is what the laws allow, then, in Locke's view, the law must allow the maximum possible.

And he goes further than this and sees liberty – and, indeed, society – in a much more positive light. Whereas Hobbes had taken the view that we surrender our liberty in return for the security of a strongly governed society, Locke believes that society actually increases, or should increase, our freedom by preventing others from interfering with it:

> That ill deserves the Name of Confinement which hedges us in only from Bogs and Precipices ... The *End of Law* is not to abolish or restrain, but to *preserve and enlarge Freedom*. For in all the States of created Beings capable of Laws, *where there is no Law*

> *there is no Freedom*. For *Liberty* is to be free from Restraint and
> Violence from others, which cannot be, where there is no Law: But
> Freedom is not, as we are told, *A Liberty for every Man to do what*
> *he lists.*
>
> (*Second Treatise*, Sec. 57)

If, then, the law is to promote liberty in the manner envisaged, we must be
sure that the sovereign or government only interferes with the behaviour of
the individual in order to secure this kind of liberty for all, and that it does not
interfere where interference is not justified. Liberty as the right to do anything
which the laws allow is no liberty at all unless we can be sure that the law
will only interfere when it is in the interests of the community as a whole for
it to do so.

The sovereign or government itself, then, must be restrained by law. And
it is for this reason that Locke built into his concept of sovereignty the
notion of 'checks and balances' on the powers of the sovereign, in particular
that separation of the legislature and the executive which is a continuing
and important feature of the British constitution, although currently under
serious threat.

It is the same kind of argument which is developed by John Stuart Mill in
what is often regarded as the classic statement of social freedom, his essay
'On Liberty'. For there he tells us that 'All restraint, *qua* restraint is an
evil . . . leaving people to themselves is always better, *caeteris paribus*, than
controlling them' (op.cit., Chap. 5). He suggests, however, 'one very simple
principle' (op.cit., Chap. 1), one fundamental justification for the existence
of restraints. 'That principle is, that the sole end for which mankind are
warranted, individually or collectively, in interfering with the liberty of action
of any of their number, is self-protection' (*ibid.*). People may be restrained
when their behaviour interferes with, or causes harm to, others. Authority
exercised to apply restraint in such cases is justified. It is not justified if it is
used to restrain people from doing things which affect them only, what might
be called 'self-regarding' actions.

Viewed in this way, then, the main force of the notion of freedom or liberty
is moral or prescriptive. To speak of freedom or liberty, as we saw earlier in
relation to both 'natural rights' and 'equality', is not to *describe* anything; it
is to *prescribe*, to make a demand for, certain kinds of treatment of human
beings, or to assert the unacceptability of other forms of treatment. When
Rousseau, for example, begins his *The Social Contract* by asserting, 'Man is
born free; but everywhere he is in chains' (op.cit., Bk 1, Chap. 1), he is not
making a *descriptive* statement as he would have been had he asserted, 'Man
is born naked; but everywhere he is in clothes'. He is making a demand for,
prescribing, certain conditions for social living.

Further, in essence the demand is that any interference in personal liberty
on the part of government must be justified. In other words, when a person's
freedom is being curtailed, the onus is not on him or her to show why it
should not be, but on the restrainer to show why it should. When we speak

of freedom, whether for ourselves or others, we are not demanding licence, a complete absence of restraints; we are simply requiring that good reasons be adduced for any restraints imposed.

It is worth pausing here to note one of the main concerns which prompted Mill's interest in this issue. Mill expressed a major concern about the possible domination of minorities by the majority view in a society. In any democracy this is a very real danger. And we sometimes see, in small communities as often as in society as a whole, circumstances arising in which minority views or preferences are ignored, opposed or even suppressed. There are situations of course in which only one preference can prevail. Preferences, however, which may be different from, but not incompatible with, the majority opinion must, on Mill's principle, be protected. For interference in them, and certainly suppression of them, can only be justified if they can be shown to be contrary to the interests of the community as a whole.

So far all of this would seem to be relatively straightforward, and to be an indisputable dimension of any democratic society and thus one of the essential principles of democracy for which we are seeking. However, it is one thing to say that all restraints need to be justified; it is quite another to define what might count as appropriate justification.

It is, for example, naive to claim that the only acceptable form of justification is the protection of other people's freedom. For, in the first place, it is far from easy to identify kinds of behaviour we might claim with confidence do not affect the freedom of others, forms of behaviour which might merit the description of 'self-regarding' actions. There is very little, if any, human behaviour which has no impact on others.

Second, and more important, a view of social freedom which attempts to adhere to this rather negative stance can readily be seen to conflict with another principle of democracy which we identified earlier, the obligation of the state to improve the quality of life of its members. For it may be claimed that a democratic society is justified in imposing restraints on its members not only to protect and maximize every citizen's freedom but also to enhance the quality of everyone's life or, as we have seen Aristotle asserting, to make the good life possible. To impose taxation, for example, and thus to limit the uses to which individuals can put their wealth, in order to provide social services of many kinds or to support the arts, in order to enhance life for all, is a practice that it would be difficult to argue against in a democratic society. Yet to do so is to go far beyond the principle of applying restraints only to protect individual freedom. It is to move beyond the notion of freedom *from* to the idea that what must also be of concern is freedom *to*.

This consideration created a serious dilemma for Mill in relation to his advocacy of the values of education (West, 1965). For, because he wished to argue for that improved quality of life which is, or can be, a result of appropriate educational experiences, he had to advocate restraints on the behaviour of parents to ensure that children were given these advantages. (The proper education of children, he argued, was an 'assignable duty' of their parents. The state, therefore, was to institute a system of public examinations to check that parents were fulfilling this duty, and to tax them appropriately if they were not, so that, as a result, the state had to do the job for them.)

This is of course a dilemma for Mill only when he takes a purely protectionist view of liberty and advocates that model of democracy Held (1987) calls 'protective democracy'. There are in Mill's work, however, as we can see in this concern for education, the seeds of what might be called 'developmental democracy' (MacPherson, 1974), 'a moral vision of a form of associative living that took the main purpose of democracy to be the provision of opportunities for each person to develop their talents and capacities to the fullest' (Soltis, 1993, p. 150). And, if one takes the view that, in a democratic society, laws need to be made in order to promote social reform, to enhance the quality of life for all citizens, to ensure, in Pericles' words, government 'not for the few but for the many', then no such dilemma exists. The task of justification, however, becomes considerably more complex.

This is also a problem for Mill when he appears to regard liberty as the only value and thus as the sole central principle and determinant of liberal government. If, however, we acknowledge those other values, which it is being argued here are equally central to democratic forms of social living, then we can see that the crucial issue becomes not merely that of safeguarding individual liberty but, more importantly, that of reconciling the demands of individual liberty with those of these other, equally significant, democratic principles.

We must note, then, that in a democratic context a further form of justification for interference with individual liberty, beyond that of protection, is that such interference may be required in order to protect or promote other essential democratic principles. Thus there might well be circumstances in which individual liberty may be justifiably curtailed in the interests of the protection of human rights, the promotion of equality, the maintenance of popular sovereignty or the safeguarding of some other essential ingredient of democratic life. On the other hand, its curtailment can never be justified in order to promote the sectional or individual interests of others – even of a majority.

However, perhaps we should pause to ask whether this further dimension of justification beyond the purely protectionist is logically entailed by the notion of democracy itself, whether it is a *sine qua non* of democratic living or merely a further preference, an additional value stance. At the beginning of this chapter we pressed this view strongly, and suggested that democratic societies must take a more positive view of their *raison d'être* and recognize their responsibility to do more than merely protect their members. This is again a major implication of recognizing democracy as a moral concept and not merely as political.

And it would seem very difficult to advocate, as both Bentham and Mill do, as the basic principle of legislation, 'the greatest good of the greatest number' at a purely protectionist level. A commitment to maximizing the benefits of society for a majority of its members would seem to imply more than merely protecting them from harm and leaving them otherwise to their own devices. We can at least assert, therefore, that to acknowledge the moral force of the concept of democracy is to accept a commitment to a view of legislation as justified if it can be shown to be in the best interests of the community as a whole, even though it may involve interference with individual liberty beyond the minimal level of protectionism.

This is a matter to which we will need to return, since it is highly pertinent to current social policies in the UK and elsewhere, and nowhere more evident than in current policies for educational provision. It is an issue which is central, for example, to the analysis of current educational ideologies which Denis Lawton offers us (Lawton, 1992), in which he identifies four current ideologies – those of the privatizers, the minimalists, the pluralists and the comprehensive planners. And we will need to address the issue of whether all of these positions are compatible with a declared commitment to social reform, or even to democracy.

The question of when and how one justifies the imposition of restraints in a free society, then, is a complex one; and what is to count as a good reason is difficult to define, except in so far as we have claimed that any such reason must be based on some appeal to democratic principles. We have also discovered again, as we did when we discussed the equality principle, that issues of this kind become much more complex when we adopt a more positive position and accept a commitment to social reform and development rather than to mere protectionism. Yet it has also been argued that this is precisely what democratic forms of social organization demand.

Furthermore, we must again note that it is at this point that conflict is likely to emerge between our fundamental principles, and that any proffered justification must be compatible with the other principles we have identified as central to democratic living.

This further alerts us to a general point we have noted before and will need to note again – the difficulties of operationalizing the principles we are in process of identifying. It is this difficulty too that leads to the many different interpretations, and models, of democracy which can be identified in practice.

This should not be allowed, however, to obscure the principle itself. For it should be clear that, whatever the complexities of justification, it remains a fundamental requirement in a democratic society that an attempt at justification be made for every act of legislation, for every action which limits the freedom of its citizens. At certain levels of refinement, this will prove to be far from easy; as a general principle, however, it will enable us quickly to identify and expose unacceptable extremes of practice.

One area in which it might be claimed that the curtailment of individual liberty can never be justified is that of freedom of opinion. It might be argued that some opinions should be curtailed since they represent a threat to democratic principles of one kind or another. A distinction must be made, however, between the holding of an opinion, on the one hand, and the expression of it or acting on it on the other. It is only the latter which might threaten democracy and thus only the latter which might justifiably be curtailed. Individuals or groups of people are entitled, for example, to hold views which are anti-democratic and which support the destruction of democratic forms of life and of government, such as the political convictions of the National Front and some of those current educational ideologies which we have just seen Denis Lawton (1992) identifies. In a democratic society, however, they are not entitled to offer these as a basis for the framing of social policies. For while it might be argued that a greater threat to democracy is likely to come from the suppression of opinions than from allowing people to hold opinions which may in themselves constitute a threat, the crucial distinction between thought and action must be maintained.

The corollary of this is equally important and raises a more general theme which we must explore more fully when we discuss democracy and the problem of knowledge in Part 2. For freedom of opinion requires the free availability of knowledge and information to all citizens as a basis for their reaching their own conclusions and decisions on all issues of public concern. And this free availability of knowledge must be a *sine qua non* of democracy, since it is a *sine qua non* of the proper exercise by individuals of their right to participate in the decision-making processes, if only by offering views on, and evaluations of, decisions made on their behalf by elected governments.

The involvement of every citizen in the decision-making process is also one kind of device for avoiding those extremes of practice in relation to the curtailment of individual liberty we referred to earlier. And although the practicalities of this are again complex and have resulted in the emergence of many different systems, again the fundamental principle, that of popular sovereignty, can provide us with a yardstick by which to evaluate particular forms. It is to an elaboration of this fourth major principle of democracy that we now turn.

Popular sovereignty

Taken simply as a question about who should rule, the issue of sovereignty in a democratic society is straightforward. For by definition the people should rule. And we might go further and argue that it is only in this way that those other principles of democracy which we have identified can be safeguarded. At one level, then, this may be all that is implied by the notion of popular sovereignty.

There is again, however, the question of how we are to operationalize this principle. And this time we cannot pass over this issue and leave it to the stage of implementation. For in this case the manner in which it is interpreted has implications for the principle itself.

In a small society such as that of ancient Athens, the notion of self-rule by the people offered few management problems. Popular assemblies could be held. The ordinary person could keep reasonably closely in touch with the political action. Those who held office, whether appointed by election or chosen by lot, could be made constantly accountable for their decisions and kept under some kind of control. Popular sovereignty was not, therefore, an issue; it was a virtual reality.

The advent of larger, more complex societies, however, rendered this simple model outdated and unworkable. And the means which have emerged for retaining popular sovereignty within such societies have opened the doors to much abuse, and have often threatened and even destroyed democracy itself. We have already noted, for example, Rousseau's comment about the British form of representative government, that 'the people of England . . . is free only during the election of members of Parliament'. And it would be difficult to argue, certainly in the context of the 1990s, that this is merely a caricature and has no semblance of accuracy as a picture of current political reality in the UK.

The point which it becomes important to stress, therefore, as a fundamental democratic principle, is that, within a democracy, the people cannot hand over their sovereignty or, to express it differently, there can be no separation between the sovereign and the people nor, indeed, between the state and society. In that same passage, Rousseau makes the point that 'sovereignty, for the same reason as makes it inalienable, cannot be represented'. Within a democratic society, the government, however elected, is not the sovereign; the people is sovereign. It is the government's task to make laws on behalf of the people and not on its own behalf. And it should be properly accountable to the people for so doing, and, especially, for not so doing.

Again we must note that other views might be expressed on this issue. In particular, we need to note that the complexities of operationalizing this principle in large, complex, modern societies has led some to argue against it, and to seek to separate out again the government from the people, and the state from society. Again, however, we must respond by asking whether, if the case is different, if governments can act in their own rather than the people's interests, there is any sense in which this process can be described as democractic, or any way in which this can be done without infringing, in an unwarranted and unjustified manner, the rights, the equality and the freedom of the democratic citizen, and thus conflicting directly with the other principles of democratic living we have identified. If we are right to claim that neither of these conditions can be met, then we must be right to assert that inalienable and unrepresentable sovereignty must reside and remain in the hands of the people. To place it elsewhere is to nullify democratic procedure.

To say that is not of course to say that representative government is unacceptable or unworkable. It is to say, however, that representative governments are obliged always to act in the best interests of society as a whole, to seek to display the Roman quality of *virtus*, to represent the will of the people in so far as they can determine what that will might be, or at the very least to be seen to be attempting to do this.

We must note too, however, that the concept of a 'general will' which seemed to Rousseau to go a long way towards resolving this problem is, first, a chimera, a fanciful and unrealistic conception, and, second, a dangerous throwback to those metaphysical theories of the state which we looked at in Chapter 1, and whose danger lies in the fact that they give the state a life, an existence, and thus a will, of its own.

We have noted on several occasions already that the central problem of democratic forms of social organization is the need to reconcile differences of view, opinion and values. Positive dangers exist, as we shall see in Chapter 4, in any attempt to ignore the existence and the legitimacy of such differences and to posit some kind of consensus.

There are also dangers, however, in resolving this problem by a simple reliance on the majority will. We noted earlier Mill's fear of the impact of majority opinion on individual liberty. And we must note here the warning of Berlin (1969) that the sovereignty of the people might in some circumstances destroy the sovereignty of individuals (Held, 1987).

We should also remind ourselves of a point we noted in Chapter 1 that, whereas classical Athenian democracy was, to a very large extent, consensual, complex modern democracies are characterized by a plurality of values and opinions. And so, in such societies, there is seldom to be found a clear majority, if by that we mean more than half the population, in support of any particular measure, even the election of government. Wherever several options exist, there must be correspondingly several points of view, and it is always possible, indeed likely, that none of these will command majority support. Again, therefore, there is potential for conflict between the basic principles we have identified.

The solution, then, yet again lies in a recognition that, since in any practical situation, as we have seen several times before this, the fundamental principles of democratic living may be in conflict with one another, the real problem lies in reconciling the demands of each with those of the rest. Practical politics, as we have also noted before, is an imperfect science. It entails the constant juggling of a variety of considerations – practical as well as ideal. The most important point to stress is that the ideals must be kept in mind, and no action taken which clearly transgresses any one of them without justification. Furthermore, such justification can only be found by reference to the ideals themselves.

There is a final point to be made here, and it brings us back to one of the claims made by Pericles in that assertion of the principles which underpinned Athenian democracy, which we quoted at the beginning of Chapter 1. If the people is sovereign and must remain so, there is an obligation on every individual in a democratic society to take this responsibility seriously and to seek to fulfil it conscientiously. For it is only in this way that the maximization and, indeed, the preservation, of democratic ideals can be reasonably assured.

That is the force of Pericles' assertion that 'we alone consider the person who takes no interest in public affairs not as impractical but as useless'. If democracy is to survive, then sovereignty must remain with the people, and that can only happen if the people, severally and collectively, maintain, guard and protect their possession of it. Apathy on the part of the populace, which can be deliberately induced and promoted in many ways, is one of the major threats to the maintenance of democratic forms of living.

SUMMARY AND CONCLUSIONS TO PART 1

The first two chapters of this book have undertaken a search for the basic principles of democratic living by undertaking a brief survey of the major features of political theorizing in the western world since the time of Pericles. That survey has revealed that democracy has not loomed very large in theory or in practice during that period of 2000 plus years, that for much of the time it has not been on the agenda of anyone, politician or theorist, and that, when it returned to the agenda, it did so not as a development deemed to be desirable but, for many people, as a threat to good social order. We have thus seen ample evidence of the point made in our Introduction that our hold on democracy continues to be a tenuous one.

Chapter 1 identified several powerful political theories which we described as anti-democratic. These, it was suggested, are important to our quest, because they indicate the basic assumptions or arguments which are inimical to democracy, which destroy its very foundations and which provide the platform from which opposing theories can be mounted. They thus alert us to the issues we need to address if we are to establish a case for democracy which cannot be demolished as superficial, a case which genuinely gets at the underlying principles both of democracy and of other theories of social organization.

We noted there too that they help us in our search for the essential principles of democracy by drawing our attention to certain features of democratic living which are conspicuous by their absence from such theories.

In Chapter 2 we turned to a consideration of some more positive and liberal views of society, and noted the beginnings of those debates about such concepts as human rights, equality, freedom, popular sovereignty and other such elements of democratic living which have formed the basis for the emergence of a theory of democracy. For they seek to offer a moral justification of certain forms of social living, a justification which can hardly support any form of political organization other than the democratic.

We have throughout stressed that this is a conceptual rather than an empirical inquiry, that we are seeking for the characteristics of an 'ideal' form of democracy. And we have reiterated the fact that actual forms must fall far short of these ideals. What we have been seeking for, however, is some delineation of what those ideals are, both so that we can be clear about what all societies, and all social institutions within societies, which call themselves democratic should be aiming for, and so that we have a template to apply by which to judge how near they are to or, especially, how far they are from what they should be seeking to become.

It will be helpful, therefore, if we conclude our search by attempting to summarize, to list, those fundamental principles we might claim to have identified.

We have first established that democracy is a moral as well as a political concept. Indeed, it might be claimed that the most important single characteristic which distinguishes democratic forms of political organization from other forms is that, unlike those other forms, they have firm moral roots, and are based on, and justified by, clear moral principles.

And the most central of those moral principles, the major features of truly democratic societies, are those we have listed and elaborated in this chapter – a concern for the protection of human rights, for the equality of all citizens, for the maximization of individual liberty and for the maintenance of popular sovereignty.

Further, we had noted in Chapter 1 that these values are predicated on a view of human beings as capable of altruistic and self-directed behaviour, and on an acceptance of the practicability of developing a moral system which can accommodate moral and cultural diversity. For it was the lack of a belief in these possibilities, and even in their desirability, which we suggested characterized those non-democratic or anti-democratic theories we considered there.

It was this feature of democratic theory which led us also to argue that a strong case can be made out for taking a positive rather than a negative view of democratic societies, for accepting the view that democratic societies exist not only for the protection of all citizens but also for the enhancement of their life standards and expectations.

If democratic theory starts from the conviction that social living is natural for human beings, that 'man' is a social animal, and that what makes it natural is the opportunities it offers for collaboration in the interests of all, then it must follow that its prime purpose is to promote such collaboration and not merely protect the individual in the pursuit of his or her private ambitions. For it is the availability of others for collaborative enterprise, economic, artistic, cultural or social, which is the essence of that enrichment which a properly organized society can provide. As we have seen Aristotle asserting, 'a state exists for the sake of a good life, and not for the sake of life only' (*Politics*, III, Chap. 9). Conversely, this must raise questions about the legitimacy of seeking deliberately to foster competitiveness as a fundamental social principle, or to promote sectional interests.

However, we saw that to take this positive view is to complicate the democratic equation enormously. It is clear that even those basic principles we identified can often be in conflict with one another, that considerations of individual liberty, for example, will frequently be at odds with a concern for human equality. And it was acknowledged that careful reconciliation of such conflicting demands will often be necessary.

What is even clearer, however, is that such conflict will be significantly increased and exacerbated by the adoption of that more positive view we have just discussed. For more extensive interference in individual liberty, for example, will inevitably become necessary, if the concern is not merely to make space for individual enterprise but to do so within the parameters created by a full consideration for the best interests of every member of the community and a concern to support and promote those interests, as we saw with Mill's problem over educational provision.

There is no straightforward, 'scientific' way of effecting the necessary reconciliations this will require. We will never find a formula for it that can be simply applied, any more than we will find a formula for any other moral decision. It must always be a matter of judgement.

It is important, however, to recognize it as a moral issue rather than to treat such matters as economic or technical problems, and to realize that the intention must be to satisfy as many of the basic principles of democracy as we can in any one instance. In other words, those elected or appointed to make these judgements on our behalf must make them with the best interests of the community as a whole at the forefront of their minds. As we saw earlier in this chapter, this was the essence of the Roman concept of *virtus*.

That governments too frequently do not have the best interests of all citizens in mind is easy to see from even the briefest review of the actions of any 'democratic' government. And the recognition of this reinforces what was said earlier about the tenuous hold we have on true democracy. Hence there is a need to explore and outline the major threats to democracy, the constant dangers to it for which we all need to be constantly on the lookout.

It is a central theme of this book that one of the most serious sources of threat to democracy is the adoption, or the blind assumption, of rationalist, universalistic, positivist views of knowledge, since this, it will be claimed, is essentially inimical to every one of the fundamental principles of democracy we have identified in these first two chapters.

It is thus to a consideration of the problem of knowledge that we must turn in Part 2.

PART 2:

Democracy and the Problem of Knowledge

3

THE PROBLEM OF KNOWLEDGE

The problem is not to kill reason, but to render bad reasons harmless, and to dissociate the notion of reason from that of truth.

(Umberto Eco, Travels in Hyperreality)

The first two chapters of this book have sought to identify the essential principles of democratic living, in order to provide us with a range of criteria by which we might evaluate any social organization which lays claim to the description of 'democratic'.

It has been stressed throughout, however, how slender is the hold we have on democracy and how rare it is that we are able to find these principles being effectively upheld in practice. It will be the concern of this and subsequent chapters to attempt to reveal what are the main threats to any continuing attempt to implement democratic principles, what are the sources of the kinds of danger which put their maintenance at risk. In setting about this task, we should perhaps first note that it is from within democracies that we must expect threats to come rather than from outside. For, as Benjamin Barber tells us (1984, p. xvii),

> It is easily overthrown – not from without, for democracies have rarely perished at the hands of armed aggressors or foreign enemies or alien ideologies. They have eroded gradually from within, consumed unprotestingly by complacency in the guise of privatism, by arrogance in the guise of empire, by irresponsibility in the guise of individualism, by selfishness in the guise of obsessive rights, by passivity in the guise of deference to experts, by greed in the guise of productivity. Democracy is undone by a hundred kinds of activity more profitable than citizenship; by a thousand seductive acquisitions cheaper than liberty.

It is these insidious internal threats, therefore, that we need to identify in order to guard against. In part, they arise from those imperfections of operationalization we noted in earlier chapters, the unavoidable difficulties in implementing, in large complex modern democracies, the principles we identified there. We saw that those principles are problematic, that they are often unclear in their precise import and that, in almost every context, they will need to be interpreted and reconciled one with another.

These features of democratic principles make it very easy to get things wrong, to take inappropriate action even with the best of intentions. More seriously, however, they make it very easy for those who wish to subvert the principles to get them wrong deliberately. Intention is all here. And mistakes made in genuine error will not constitute anything like as serious a threat to democracy as those made with malice aforethought.

The major threats arise, then, not so much from inadequate or misguided efforts to implement those principles we have identified, but from the deliberate refusal to acknowledge or recognize them and to adhere to them in the making of social policy and, further, from the implementation of policies which fly in the face of such principles or which, after due reflection, can be seen as unlikely to be compatible with them.

One category of threat, then, is that of those dangers which derive from deliberate attempts to manipulate social institutions to achieve ends which are clearly not aimed at the best advantage of society as a whole, but are directed at improving the lot of sectional interests within it. And since the social institution we are primarily concerned with in this book is the education system, it is the kinds of educational policy which militate in this way against the growth and maintenance of democratic forms of social living that will be our main concern. Much the most serious threat, however, because more insidious, is that posed by certain views of knowledge and, in particular, by the ways in which these can become enshrined in forms of discourse.

We saw in Chapter 1 how the adoption of a rationalist epistemology leads inexorably to the reification, even the deification of the 'state', to a separation of the concept of the 'state' from that of 'society', and to the anti-democratic view that the state is somehow bigger than the sum of its citizen parts, and that, as a consequence, its interests must always be allowed to transcend theirs.

Such a metaphysical theory of the state we have already seen to be inimical to democracy, and to be at the very root of totalitarianism. What we must now recognize is that it is predicated on and, indeed, is a necessary consequence of, the adoption of a particular view of human knowledge, a view which sees knowledge as in some way transcending human experience.

Such a view, although, as we shall see, now largely outmoded in the intellectual sphere, continues to be prevalent in popular thinking, since it continues to be enshrined in popular discourse. More significantly, it can be seen to underpin much current social policy. And certainly in the UK at the present time, it is within policies for education that this kind of rationalist epistemology, and the discourse it generates, can most readily be identified, so that it constitutes a serious threat, through this impact on educational provision, to the maintenance and development of democratic structures. Theories of knowledge are inexorably linked to political movements, so that any theory of knowledge which is incompatible with democratic forms must constitute a major threat to the maintenance and development of those forms.

The question of the nature of human knowledge, then, is central to issues related to the planning of education in a democratic society, not only because knowledge is the very stuff of education but also because how knowledge is viewed, and especially how it is conceived, are crucial to how an education system is to be planned. And since the education system is the means by which control of the distribution of knowledge is managed, then that too in turn has implications for the democratic health of that society.

It is for this reason, as we shall see in the third part of this book, that education has such an important role to play in the maintenance of democratic systems. For it is vital that the education system produces citizens who are both motivated towards and capable of effective participation in the affairs of the nation.

And so, since it will be claimed that one of the most effective devices available to us for the maintenance and development of democracy is a properly democratic system of education, this exploration of the problem of knowledge will lead us naturally into the third major part of this book, in which we will consider what a properly democratic system of education might look like.

I have argued elsewhere (Kelly, 1986) that an awareness of the problem of knowledge is crucial to educational and curriculum planning. What will be demonstrated here is its particular significance for the planning of a democratic system of education.

THE PROBLEM OF KNOWLEDGE

The problem of knowledge is arguably the oldest issue in western philosophy, and epistemology, the study of knowledge, its oldest branch. For the first clearly philosophical question which perplexed and caught the attention of those who came to be known as the Ionian philosophers was 'How can we have knowledge, or claim to have knowledge, of the shifting and changing world in which we live?'

These early thinkers saw the world around them in all its aspects – social, moral, and political as well as physical – as in a constant state of flux. In the words of Heracleitus, 'You cannot step into the same river twice'. Everything we experience is impermanent, uncertain, unstable, unreliable, even deceptive. How then, they asked, can there be knowledge of such a world? And that is the central question of epistemology.

This consciousness of the shifting nature of the world led some of the early philosophers to the view that it is not possible to generate meaningful knowledge in any sphere. And it led Socrates, for example, to embrace the notion of universal ignorance and to adopt the stance of eternal questioning, a view that asking questions was a more readily justifiable intellectual practice than proffering answers.

It seems, however, to be a feature of human nature that human beings evince a preference for certainty rather than uncertainty; that they cling to some notion of perfection rather than acknowledge that the concept of perfection may be merely an idealist construct; that they hanker after the security which a view of knowledge as fixed and permanent can give them rather than accept the insecurities of recognizing it as provisional and tentative. And this seems to be especially the case when they live at times of particular political instability.

It is not surprising, therefore, that the solution offered by many of the Greeks to this question which they posed themselves was a theory which sought to offer this kind of permanence and security of knowledge and, further, to do so in all fields – the aesthetic, the moral and the political, as well as the physical. Nor should we be surprised that many people continue to cling to such a view.

It is important, however, to recognize from the outset that this view, popular and comfortable as it is, is not the only view one can take of human knowledge, and that there are, as we shall see, some very serious dangers in making that assumption. It is also worth noting here that the alternative is, if anything, more intellectually compelling, especially when viewed in the context of the twentieth century.

The solution which took hold in the ancient world, however, and was given its first and most important statement by Plato, who was undoubtedly attracted to it because of the political instabilities of his own day, was the view that it is possible to discern behind the shifting uncertainty of human experience an unchanging and permanent reality and thus to gain 'true' knowledge, again in all fields, through an understanding of this reality. All that we learn from the observations of our senses falls far short of this status of being 'true' knowledge, since it lacks all permanence and certainty. It is possible, however, according to this view, to transcend these observations or experiences of the senses and to reach the 'truth', the reality, which lies beyond.

This epistemological theory has been called 'rationalism' because its fundamental claim is that it is through the exercise of reason, rationality, the rational mind, that this 'true' knowledge is attained. In some way the rational mind itself rather than the experience of the senses is the source of such knowledge. The theory thus opens up a metaphysical world, a world which literally goes beyond the physical, since it accepts the validity of knowledge which is a priori independent of the experience of the senses. Furthermore, it regards such knowledge as infinitely superior – in status and in certainty – to what we learn from our sense impressions since, it argues, while our senses are notoriously deceptive, our reason is not.

In Plato's view, human beings are characterized essentially as being rational creatures, the possession of rationality being that which differentiates them from other creatures. In short, as Aristotle was later to assert, 'man' is a rational animal, and rationality is seen as the essence or 'function' of the human being. From that premise Plato deduces that it is the purpose of human existence to act rationally and to extend and develop rationality and the knowledge which it generates.

Three things follow from this. First, we can readily see the source of that hierarchy of knowledge familiar to every educationist, the rationalist justification for claiming that abstract, intellectual pursuits are qualitatively superior to those which are practical or even artistic.

Second, we must note that this view of knowledge regards the development of knowledge as a progressive movement towards some kind of ultimate perfection. The 'forms' are perfect forms; the 'ideas' are idealist. And even if our present levels of understanding are imperfect, if we fulfil our duty, our function as human beings, and pursue rationality, human knowledge will eventually attain that state of perfection.

And, third, in order to promote this process, we have a corresponding duty to play down, to control, to eliminate as far as possible the passionate side of our nature, those desires and emotions that will, if we are not careful and vigilant, deflect us from the single-minded pursuit of reason. Plato offers us the analogy of the tripartite soul of 'man', the three elements of which are reason (which, as we have seen, is the essential characteristic of humanity), 'spirit' or self-assertiveness (which he likens in his imagery to a lion) and the appetites or passions (which he calls 'the beast with many heads'). These appetites, this beast must be tamed and brought firmly under the control of reason; and 'spirit', the lion, must be trained to support reason in this process. This, incidentally, encapsulates what Plato saw as the major functions of education.

Finally we must note that, since Plato's central concern is with creating a stable system of morality, all that we have noted so far applies equally to the development of our moral nature and of our moral knowledge. Rationalist epistemology is intended not only to provide a sound base for the development of our mathematical and scientific knowledge about the physical world but it is intended also – indeed, as we have seen, more so – to provide such a base for our 'knowledge' of matters of value.

All of these features can be seen to interlock closely with religious, and especially Christian, views of knowledge. For again knowledge is seen as universal, as ultimately perfectible, as rational rather than empirical, as extending to the moral sphere as well as the physical, and the superiority of the intellect is asserted over the domain of the emotions. And here there is the added advantage of a definitive source of this knowledge – a divine, omniscient being who progessively 'reveals' such knowledge to humankind.

It is thus not surprising to find this view persisting throughout the centuries and even up to the present. Nor is it difficult to understand why the challenge to rationalism which was offered by British empiricism in the seventeenth and eighteenth centuries brought an immediate response in the form of an attempt to give it a more sophisticated foundation.

This was the task Immanuel Kant took on. And in doing so he established that philosophical movement which came to be known as German idealism, as it was developed by such people as Fichte, Schelling, Hegel and, albeit in a somewhat different form, Marx, and which dominated western philosophy throughout the late eighteenth and the whole of the nineteenth centuries.

Kant's solution was to attempt to show again that there can be a priori knowledge and that the source of this kind of knowledge is reason or rationality itself, the rational mind. Sense experience can never be a source of certain knowledge, so that 'knowledge' which is dependent on experience, which is a posteriori, must always be of doubtful validity. Kant argues that the rational mind can go beyond this uncertain knowledge and make a priori assertions with full confidence and validity. For, in his view, the rational mind can transcend the experience of the senses by bringing to bear on that experience certain rational concepts by which that experience is understood.

These concepts are the concepts of rationality itself. They constitute what it means to be rational. The rational mind cannot view the world as a series of unrelated snapshots; the rational mind cannot but view this experience in rational terms, as a coherent whole. To use an analogy offered by Bertrand Russell, the rational mind views the world, as it were, through rational spectacles. It imposes on its perceptions certain standards of universality, necessity and causality. And this enables it to make assertions which, although they go beyond the simple experience of the senses and are thus a priori, nevertheless are valid and objective because they satisfy the criteria of rationality, they represent the only rational explanation of the phenomena under observation, and they thus have the acceptance of all rational minds. We cannot deny them without denying rationality itself, without ourselves being irrational.

Without pursuing Kant's theories of morals or aesthetics further than we have to for our purposes here, there are three aspects of them on which comment must be offered, since these are especially germane to our concern with the implications of this debate for education, and especially for a democratic form of education.

First, for Kant, the essential element in rationality, and thus the ultimate test for the validity of any knowledge assertion is the universal. It is the ability to universalize which characterizes rationality; and it is only by formulating universal laws that knowledge can be developed; so that his critique of knowledge is designed to demonstrate the validity of universal assertions.

Second, this notion of universalizability is extended to the realm of values – social, moral and aesthetic – again as we saw with Plato's view. It thus leads to claims for comparable levels of certainty of knowledge in these spheres.

Third, again we must note that this view also evinces that traditional concern of rationalism to reject the passionate, emotive dimension of human existence. Reason is seen as opposed to human feeling or passions, so that a rational morality must be one which transcends such feelings or passions. Moral behaviour, then, must not be prompted by desire or inclination or custom, since all of these are subjective and beyond the scope of rationalism. Moral actions are not those we perform because we want to perform them; they are those actions we do out of duty, out of that obligation which, as rational beings, we have towards rationality and rational behaviour. For Kant, the will is the crucial element in moral behaviour. What makes an action right or wrong is not the act itself but the intention or the motivation of the person performing it. And a truly moral act must be performed simply because it is the right act and not from any subjective desire or inclination or from mere usage or custom. It must also be performed because of an acceptance of the moral law and not merely out of obedience to it.

There is no denying the attractions of this theory. It offers us a basis for the development of scientific knowledge (even though it regards this development as a process of continuous accumulation rather than as transformatory). And at the moral level, indeed at the level of values of all kinds, it has appeal for those who want the reassurance of being informed that values are not matters of subjective opinion but are susceptible to objective judgement. Further, the value positions it leads to, especially in the moral sphere, are such as few would wish to quarrel with.

There are, however, serious difficulties, indeed dangers, in accepting this kind of certainty in both the moral and the aesthetic/cultural spheres. These difficulties and dangers will be explored more fully in Chapter 4. And an attempt will then be made to elucidate the threats such an epistemological position poses for the maintenance and the development of democracy.

We will need also to explore the implications of this kind of epistemological theory for education, and especially for a democratic view of education. One point should perhaps be noted here, however. For the significance of rationalism for education goes beyond the fact that it reinforces that hierarchical view of the curriculum with which we are all familiar, the view that places a superior value on those subjects which are abstract, cognitive, intellectual, those subjects whose 'cognitive concerns and far-ranging cognitive content give them a value denied to other more circumscribed activities which leads us to call them serious pursuits' (Peters, 1966, p. 160). Far more importantly, it is a view of knowledge which limits the curriculum debate, as the work of Richard Peters and most other 'philosophers of education' shows, to discussions merely of what the curriculum should consist of, and denies us the opportunity to address questions of how the curriculum should be conceived. Yet, as we shall see later, these are precisely the questions we must address if we are to develop a curriculum suited to a democratic society. It is for this reason that we must give careful attention to perspectives on knowledge which seek to offer an alternative to the certainties of rationalism and the threats to democracy which these certainties bring with them.

In the western philosophical tradition, the alternative major form of epistemological theory has been that known as 'empiricism'. This perspective is best seen as a challenge to the fundamental claims of rationalism. (It is not, of course, to be seen as a rejection of rationality itself, merely of the claim that this can be a source of knowledge or of truth, and certainly of eternal and timeless knowledge and truths.) In particular, it challenges the claim that there can be any knowledge which is independent of the experience of the senses and which comes a priori from the rational mind. It thus represents a complete rejection of all metaphysical speculation.

The fundamental tenet of empiricism, in complete contradiction to that of rationalism, is that there can be no knowledge which does not derive from empirical observation or logical necessity. In short, an assertion can only be claimed as true if it can be shown to reflect observable experience or to be logically entailed by some prior assertion.

As one of the earliest exponents of empiricism, David Hume, showed, this basic position denies us access to those universals – in the realm of physical science as well as in that of values – which were the central concern of rationalism. For universals cannot be empirically observed; they can only be deductions from reflection on what can be observed.

And it follows from this that there can be no knowledge for which we can claim the kind of permanent, timeless, unchallengeable status the rationalist is seeking for and claims to have found. It is not necessary, as Hume thought, to deny all possibility of generalization. But the certainties of rationalism must go and, in all spheres, on this view, knowledge must be seen as uncertain, tentative, provisional and hypothetical. This is of particular significance in the realm of values – aesthetic, social, moral, political – where it must be recognized that all such values are problematic and that, even where they may appear to have some kind of universal status, we must acknowledge that they are 'socially constructed'.

Again we must pick up later the implications for education of adopting this kind of epistemological view. Again, however, it is worth noting briefly that its main general thrust is towards a more tentative, less dogmatic view of the curriculum than we saw the rationalist perspective encourages. And, further, it raises questions about curriculum which require us to go far deeper in our thinking about it than the simple issue of what subjects or knowledge content it should consist of, which we saw earlier to be the limit of the rationalist's perspective on curriculum.

In particular, it suggests that, if all values are socially constructed, then educational values, those aesthetic, social, moral and, indeed, political values which underpin curriculum planning in all its facets, must be seen not as reflecting some kind of timeless, eternal set of 'truths' but as merely evincing the value stances of those doing the planning. In short, all such value stances must be recognized as ideological. And the implications of that for education in a democratic society are far-ranging, as we shall see in later chapters.

Before we move to an exploration of the ways in which knowledge has come to be regarded in the twentieth century, we should note one further aspect of earlier views. For that general rationalist predilection for universal and certain knowledge led also to the adoption of positivist approaches in the social sciences, and this too has had the same effect of discouraging debate and discussion and thus obscuring the problematic nature of human knowledge, especially in the area of human values. For positivism is an approach to the social sciences that begins from a conviction that human, social and moral issues can be studied by the same methods with which we undertake studies in the natural sciences, and that this kind of exploration can produce results which are similarly reliable. It reflects the view, criticized by Wittgenstein (1975, p. 18), that it is legitimate to ask social and moral questions 'in the way that science does'.

Thus, for example, early figures in the field of sociology, such as Auguste Comte (1798–1857), known as 'the father of sociology', adopted this kind of positivist approach to sociological inquiry, studying society as a botanist examines flora, seeking for the same kinds of universal knowledge and asserting the right to make similar kinds of predictive utterances on the strength of that 'knowledge'. In short, they laid claim to an expertise in social planning and engineering of a kind which others, lacking such expertise, could never aspire to. And these positivist approaches have persisted into the present century in all areas of the human and social sciences – most notably sociology and psychology.

Positivism in the social sciences, then, like rationalism in epistemology, has the same objective of producing unchallengeable universal certainties and thus of discouraging debate and a proper recognition of the problematic nature of knowledge. It has thus become a major target of those who in more recent times have wished to question this epistemological position.

It must be noted, however, that to oppose positivism is not to oppose empiricism. Many of the proponents of postmodernism tend to use the terms as though they were synonymous, and it is important to be clear, before we consider twentieth-century views of knowledge, that they are not. Positivism is the application of methods of inquiry devised for the natural sciences to the study of human affairs – to aesthetic, social, cultural, moral and political questions. Empiricism, from the time of David Hume himself, has not only challenged rationalist epistemology but it has also stressed the logical difference of value questions and assertions. It was David Hume, for example, who alerted us to the 'naturalistic fallacy', the fallacy of arguing from 'is' to 'ought'. And one of the best known exponents of empiricism in the twentieth century, A.J. Ayer, went so far as to argue (1936) that value assertions are not assertions at all, that they are 'literally meaningless', that they are mere expressions of feeling. Such views, therefore, far from being the targets of postmodernism must be recognized as having made their own contributions to its emergence.

Reflections on the problem of knowledge in the twentieth century, as we shall see, have gone well beyond this basic form of empiricism. Their general tenor, however, has been to accept the empiricist's rejection of the a priori certainties of rationalism and to view all knowledge as tentative, uncertain and thus problematic. On the one hand, this has contributed to those major technological advances which this century has witnessed, since most of these have resulted from an unwillingness to accept without question what has been offered as 'timeless' knowledge and, conversely, to challenge and reconstruct that knowledge. On the other hand, it has led, especially in the sphere of human values, to the chaos theory of postmodernism, a movement which can be seen as the current culmination of the rejection of certainty.

We must, therefore, continue our exploration of the problem of knowledge with a detailed analysis of those developments during the present century which have now brought us to this point.

KNOWLEDGE IN THE TWENTIETH CENTURY

The twentieth century has seen a revolution in the way in which knowledge is viewed. There has been a major intellectual movement, in almost every sphere of human activity, away from the certainties of rationalism. The shift has been away from positivism, from universalism, from absolutism, from idealism; away from assumptions of the objectivity of knowledge in all fields; away from the notion of the development of knowledge as the unfolding of some, ultimately perfect, tapestry, away from the Newtonian knowledge paradigm, and towards a recognition, an acceptance, even a welcoming of the uncertainties which must follow from the rejection of this kind of rationalism. As William Doll (1989, p. 243) expresses it, 'we see our vision of the universe turning from the simple, stable one of Newtonian modernism to the complex, chaotic, finite one of post-modernism'.

And this has been true even in the hitherto apparently secure fields of science and mathematics, where dramatic advances have occurred which are entirely due to the rejection of previously assumed certainties. As Wellington (1981, p. 21) says in mounting his case against the use of transcendental arguments in education,

> Kant and his contemporaries strongly believed that the mathematics and physics of that time, and even the moral code, were true beyond all doubt. Kant thus assumed that the schemata employed in mathematical, physical and moral thinking were unique and could not be otherwise. In 1981 we have non-Euclidean geometry, Einstein's relativistic view of the space-time continuum, Heisenberg's 'uncertainty principle' and the knowledge that Newtonian physics only applies to slow-moving objects. Kant's category of cause and effect has been replaced by the statistical probability that one event will follow another, while modern physicists assure us that 'matter' (Kant's category of substance) is mostly empty space, and particles often behave like waves.

These developments not only reveal the case for rejecting the certainties of rationalism but they also demonstrate the kinds of advance in human understanding (a better, because perhaps more accurate, term to use now than 'knowledge') which have resulted from that rejection and the acceptance of a more tentative, less dogmatic view of knowledge – a transformatory rather than a cumulative view (Doll, 1989).

Nor is it only in the fields of science and mathematics that such changes can be observed. There has been an important shift in the focus of philosophical inquiry from the search for 'truth' to the more humble and mundane attempt to analyse the concepts we use in all areas of exploration in the attempt to achieve greater clarity of thinking. In all forms of art, too, we have witnessed dramatic changes, attributable fundamentally to the offering of challenges to traditional forms and styles – in particular, perhaps, a shift from what Nietzsche called the Apollonian culture to the Dionysian. In most areas of the social sciences, positivism has given way to approaches which reflect more limited, but more intellectually honest and defensible, forms of endeavour, through the adoption, for example, of phenomenological and ethnomethodological perspectives.

In the intellectual sphere, then, the absolutes have been consigned to history. 'The Western/industrial world view based on certainty, predictability, control and instrumental rationality has become fractured and incoherent' (Slaughter, 1989, p. 255). The great intellectual message of the twentieth century is that which was put rather crudely by Nietzsche in the assertion that 'God is dead'. In other words, rationalism has had its day, metaphysical philosophy has had its day, certainty of knowledge in all spheres has had its day, and we must learn to live with the realities of change, and cope with the uncertainties these create. For the intellectual world we now live in is characterized by this shift to a new knowledge paradigm.

Nor is it only in the world of the intellect that these changes can be seen. In the real world of events, there have not only been those major technological advances which have resulted from these intellectual developments but there have also been many consequent shifts in values, moral and aesthetic, and, in general, a move towards the recognition that values are, after all, a personal matter. And, on the macroscale, we have seen the collapse of several forms of totalitarian political system, based on an assumed and spurious concept of moral and political certainty and universality, on an historicist view of development as evolution towards some form of perfection, and thus incapable of coping with the inevitabilities of social and political change.

There has thus been a questioning of the bases of every form of political organization. And this has led further to a linking of knowledge with power, since if knowledge is a social, even a personal, construct, then the theoretical bases of any political organization must be recognized as ideological and thus as a device for the maintenance and exercise of political power rather than as the pursuit of some ultimate ideal.

It is here, then, that links between theories of knowledge and views of social organization become apparent, so that this becomes perhaps the most important issue which anyone who wishes to analyse, and especially to promote, democratic political structures needs to address. And it will be argued in later chapters that it is precisely this shift that now makes possible the emergence of something more nearly approaching a democratic system of social living, and a democratic form of education, than we have yet seen.

We must now turn to an examination of the major features of this epistemological revolution. For we need to identify what have been, and are, its main strands, both the chief influences on its development and its major manifestations. There are several inter-related strands which have notably contributed to this intellectual development, and which we should identify here, since they will offer us a deeper understanding of its main thrusts.

Existentialism

Historically, the first of these strands is that movement usually called 'existentialism', which emerged in the nineteenth century in quite explicit opposition to German idealism, and especially to that version of it which was propounded by Hegel.

For, different as the views and positions of most of those philosophers who have been dubbed 'existentialist' have been, what they have had in common is the desire to re-establish the claims of the particular against the universal, the individual against the varied kinds of collective, whether class, state or even humanity as a whole, into which rationalism and essentialism would dissolve him or her. Each person, on this view, must be defined as an individual and not as a representative of some larger group; and each individual must be encouraged to define him or herself in this way. This is the significance of Jean-Paul Sartre's assertion that existence precedes essence; the individual first exists as an individual; what he or she becomes is his or her own responsibility and choice.

Rationalist philosophy has defined 'man' as essentially rational, rationality being in some way 'his' *raison d'être*. It has then proceeded, quite illicitly, to deduce from this definition that it is somehow the duty of every person to develop this 'essential' quality, to aim towards the perfect human being and the perfect state, as defined by Plato, towards the perfect 'man' of Christian theology, towards Kant's rational moral imperative, towards the unfolding of Hegel's 'Absolute' through identification with the will of the reified 'state'.

Existentialism can best be understood as the assertion of a position diametrically opposed to this, a polar view of existence and thus of morality. On this view, it is the duty of the individual not to merge into any collective but to assert his or her own existence as an individual. And this means that, since existence is an individual matter, the only moral obligation we face is to reach our own conclusions and work out our own solutions to the moral and other value issues which we face. It constitutes a denial of our existence and of our individuality, what Jean-Paul Sartre, for example, calls *'mauvais fois'*, 'bad faith', to seek to resolve these problems by identification with the general laws of some kind of rational imperative and to allow our choices to be made for us by the state or any other form of collective.

The implications of this assertion of individualism for the idea of democracy will be plain and we will need to return to it when we examine the relevance of this whole debate for political theory, and especially for educational provision, in Chapter 4. What we must note here, however, is the major impact it has had on the development of what we are claiming has been the prevalent intellectual climate of the twentieth century.

The 'revolution in philosophy'

The second major influence on, and indeed aspect of, this development has been those changes which we suggested earlier have occurred in the very conception of philosophical activity. It is often said that the present century has witnessed a 'revolution in philosophy'. The main feature of that revolution has been a shift away from the search for 'eternal truths' towards the lesser, but more readily defensible, activity of conceptual analysis. We must now consider the significance of this shift more closely.

Conceptual analysis is concerned to reveal the meanings people actually give to words, terms, concepts and, perhaps more importantly, the subtle differences and nuances given to related families of words. For these nuances and differences suggest in turn that there are subtle conceptual differences which need to be appreciated and understood. Thus, for example, within explorations of education, we can note that terms such as 'education', 'instruction', 'training', 'indoctrination' and so on are used to denote simple acts of conveying knowledge or information from teacher to taught, but that they tell us very different things about the purpose of those acts, or at least about how they and their purposes are viewed by the person selecting the appropriate term. In other words, an analysis of these concepts reveals significant conceptual differences of which it is important to be aware.

The importance of this kind of activity can be readily appreciated when one considers how often, even in official documentation, the term 'education' is used to denote teaching activities of widely differing kinds, some of which are clearly instrumental and thus more appropriately termed 'training', so that, even if one leaves aside the rhetorical aspects of this misuse of terms, one must note its effect in denying us important conceptual distinctions.

Conceptual analysis, then, can assist in the process of clarifying our thinking in all intellectual spheres by pointing up important, and often quite subtle, conceptual distinctions, and thus refining our use of language and raising the quality of our thinking. What it cannot do is to reveal meanings or essences in any absolute sense, in any metaphysical or essentialist sense, in any sense in which earlier philosophers can be seen seeking for meanings and essences, in short, in any sense which, it may be claimed, offers a basis for prescriptions.

It is here that most of the major exponents of the 'philosophy of education' have gone seriously wrong in that, while they have claimed to be engaged in conceptual analysis, they have also, illicitly, sought to derive prescriptions from such analyses. They have thus failed to understand the significance of this shift of focus for philosophical activity, have fallen into serious contradiction and have, as a result, introduced confusion rather than clarification into the educational debate.

For the move to regard the study of philosophy as conceptual analysis represents an attempt to establish a radical alternative to traditional, essentialist, rationalist and positivist approaches. It reflects a rejection of universals, and of all forms of metaphysical philosophy, all attempts to go beyond the physical, beyond the evidence of the senses, and a denial of the claim that there can be a priori knowledge. It must, therefore, be seen as a major feature, and component, of that intellectual movement we are seeking to analyse.

In particular, it has led to a recognition that assertions of value are logically distinct from scientific assertions, even to the view we noted earlier that they are not real assertions but are 'literally meaningless' (Ayer, 1936), that, at the very least, they are not to be seen as having any kind of universal status or force. And the task of moral philosophy has come to be regarded not as a quest for universal moral 'truths', for irrefutable moral prescriptions, but rather as the analysis of the language of morals and of the concepts which moral language encapsulates. Again, therefore, we can see its place in the intellectual scenario of the twentieth century.

Pragmatism

The third major influence on the intellectual climate of the twentieth century we need to identify is an influence which has especial relevance both for education and for democracy, since these were its specific concerns. This is the particular version of empiricism which was developed by John Dewey and which he termed 'pragmatism'.

We will need to return to Dewey's theory in Chapter 4, when we address the issue of the implications of particular epistemological positions for democracy, for education and, especially, for education in a democratic society, since it is Dewey who links these three most closely and explicitly. We need to note here, however, his general contribution to the development of the intellectual climate of the twentieth century which we are seeking here to unfold.

Dewey inherited from his predecessors in the philosophical system of pragmatism, notably Charles Sanders Peirce and William James, a view of truth, not as correspondence with some empirical 'fact', nor as some a priori rationalist construct, but as an essentially human construct, a property not of objects but of our assertions about objects. For the pragmatist, truth is that which 'works', and any assertion which 'works' is *ipso facto* 'true'.

This is a theory of truth which has come in for a good deal of criticism, much of it based on a misunderstanding of its full significance, since it has often been interpreted in the rather cynical form of implying that we can call anything true if it works for us (most notably, in the popular examples, successful burglary!). And, to some extent, Dewey has invited such criticism by his attempt to include values, and especially moral values, in this theory of knowledge.

However, properly understood, what we have here is another example of the rejection of rationalism, positivism, universalism. For Dewey is saying no more than that, in order to claim that any assertion is 'true', i.e. that it constitutes a piece of 'knowledge', we must not appeal to any a priori principle but merely seek to demonstrate that to accept it, and especially to act on it, brings about satisfactory results. And by 'satisfactory' he does not mean 'pleasurable' or 'rewarding' (as perhaps in the case of the burglar) but 'warranted' by the consequences. Peirce had likened this to the basic process of scientific verification; 'by their fruits shall ye know them'. Truth is a matter of experimentation, but not of subjective opinion. It is not personal, but public – agreed by all who consider the evidence. As Dewey tells us, 'the best definition of *truth* from the logical standpoint which is known to me is that of Peirce: "The opinion which is fated to be ultimately agreed to by all who investigate is what we mean by the truth, and the object represented by this opinion is the real"' (1938, p. 345).

The second important feature of Dewey's theory of knowledge which we must note is the emphasis it places on the evolutionary nature of knowledge. Darwin's *Origin of Species* was published in the year in which Dewey was born, 1859, and that theory of evolution has had its own influence on the subsequent intellectual climate. For Dewey, if all of the physical world is in a state of continuous evolution, then that which we call the knowledge we have of that world must also evolve. If truth is a matter of what works in a continually evolving situation, then truth itself must evolve and cannot be the fixed and final answer which rationalism seeks. Knowledge is not a body of 'facts' which grows bigger as we discover more and more about the world around us, or have more and more revealed to us by God; knowledge itself evolves as we find different solutions, different approaches which 'work', in response to the ever-changing, ever-new problems we must face in an evolving world. We must view the development of human knowledge, then, as transformatory rather than as cumulative, as we have seen Doll (1989) has suggested.

Again, therefore, we see emerging a view of knowledge as problematic, as hypothetical, provisional, evolutionary and thus as subject to constant challenge, modification and change. Again we see too the untenable nature of that rationalist epistemology which offers us a view of knowledge as largely static and unchanging, and as independent in some way of our experience of the world in which we live.

Finally, for Dewey, this view of knowledge implies a particular form of social organization, i.e. a democratic form; and, in turn, it also implies a particular approach to education, a democratic theory of education for a democratic society. These issues we will consider in some detail in Chapter 4, since they reinforce what is the main theme of this book.

The main thrust of this theory, then, is towards the same kind of epistemology we have seen emerging from other sources. And in this way it has made its own important contribution to the development of the intellectual climate of the twentieth century.

While the emphasis on the evolutionary nature of knowledge and on the importance of a democratic social context for that evolution are important steps forward, however, a major weakness of this theory is its attempt to view all human knowledge and understanding in the same way. The Hegelian influence on Dewey's thinking is nowhere more apparent than in this attempt to extend this theory of scientific experimentalism to the realm of values and to seek for comparable levels of public agreement there. For the attempt to adopt this knowledge paradigm in all areas of human understanding reflects an adherence to the view that all areas are susceptible to the same form of inquiry and exploration, that we must approach all questions 'in the way that science does' (Wittgenstein, 1975, p. 18). And there is no doubt this has had the effect of weakening the force of his case.

It also leads to a weakness in his theory of democracy. For there, while the intention is to create an environment for the smooth evolution of knowledge, the assumption is made that it will be some form of 'public knowledge' which will develop in all areas in such a context. His democratic theory, therefore, offers us little help with that problem of reconciling differences of values – cultural, social, moral or political – which we have identified as the major task of democratic government.

It is a rejection of this kind of totalizing theory – in all areas of human understanding – that constitutes the essence of that view of knowledge currently known as postmodernism, and thus renders it – on some, but by no means all, interpretations – a firmer epistemological base for the development of democratic theory.

Postmodernism

There are many senses in which postmodernism can be seen as the current culmination of the intellectual movement we are seeking to identify here. Like all such developments, however, it is difficult to pin down and delineate. For it is a concept which takes many forms, has many meanings and is thus susceptible to many interpretations. It is 'irritatingly elusive to define' (Featherstone, 1988, p. 195) and 'not a fully fledged positivity which can be defined comprehensively in its own right' (op.cit., p. 197).

There is thus much current debate over the meaning of the term 'postmodernism'. To a large extent, that debate derives from attempts to define it too precisely. It is also a result of the fact that the term is not merely used in the context of epistemological debate but is applied to literary and artistic movements too, as well as to cultural and political developments. Hence definitions vary according to the context of particular intellectual disciplines. Thus it may be given one nuance of meaning by those who are considering the phenomenon from a sociological perspective, another by those whose interests are literary or artistic, another by those whose intellectual focus is philosophical and so on. In some cases too, the differences are matters of degree rather than of substance.

At one level, however, it might be interpreted as a generic term which denotes the extremes of that shift in the view taken of knowledge which it is being claimed has been a feature of the intellectual scene of the twentieth century. It 'rejects the whole of "modern" philosophy from Descartes to Husserl' (Winter, 1991, p. 471, citing Madison, 1988). It questions that view of knowledge we have been designating as rationalist, 'the emphasis on the linearity of thought, the aesthetic of rationality and order, the rationality of science in the process of progress, the pre-eminence of Western European thought, and history as the process of the progress of Western culture' (Sholle, 1992, p. 274 citing Giroux, 1988a). It mounts 'an interrogation of Western discourse's desire for certainty and absolutes' (op.cit., p. 275). It is thus a concept which might be seen as embracing and extending all of the intellectual developments of the twentieth century we have been exploring. It does, however, add its important own dimension to those developments. And we must seek now to identify what that dimension is.

First, as we have just seen, it questions and rejects all theories which seek to universalize, to offer 'metanarratives'. Jean-Francois Lyotard (1984, p. xxiv), for example, defines postmodernism as 'incredulity toward metanarratives'. It is thus opposed to rationalism, to positivism, to any form of structuralism. As such, it is better established in aesthetic theory than elsewhere, where it reflects and extends that shift from traditional forms, that rejection of established structures we noted earlier.

It is important to add here, however, that that shift is seen as going a good way beyond what we have so far identified. For what might be seen as major developments in the literary and artistic fields, as instanced, for example, in the work of many major figures of the late nineteenth and early twentieth century, such as Joyce, Kafka and T.S. Eliot in literature, Picasso in painting, Strindberg in theatre and so on, are described by some as 'modernism', as that which *post*modernism seeks to transcend, and even opposes (Boyne and Rattansi, 1990). For, while these developments certainly represent major changes in artistic forms, they still 'cling to the belief that in principle the deep structure of reality is knowable, that it is intellectually and culturally penetrable, as it were, but requires aesthetic, philosophical and psychic strategies more complex, inventive and self-reflexive than the ones typically deployed in realist and naturalist forms' (*ibid.* p. 7).

To go beyond this, as postmodernism seeks to do, therefore, implies a rejection not merely of traditional forms and effectively the whole of post-Enlightenment western philosophy, but of all kinds of totalizing theory. It reflects a conviction that neither art nor philosophy nor the social 'sciences' can 'deliver totalising theories and doctrines, or enduring "answers" to the fundamental dilemmas and puzzles posed by objects of enquiry' (op.cit., p. 12).

On this kind of interpretation, then, postmodernism offers us a view of human 'knowledge' which takes us some way beyond those earlier strands of twentieth-century speculation we have just explored, which, although seeking to offer a critique of positivism and to transcend the traditional

search for certainties, have themselves sought after alternative narratives, or
'metanarratives'. In some senses, then, it 'may be said to extend and deepen
the critique already begun by modernism' (op.cit., p. 8). And, in doing so, it
offers us, as a 'vision of the universe', that 'complex, chaotic, finite one of
postmodernism' (Doll, 1989, p. 243), as we noted earlier.

In social, cultural and political theory, however, although those postmodern
artistic developments themselves have been seen as reflections of social, cultural
and political events, 'the present wave of political reaction sweeping the
Western world' (Gott, 1986, p. 10, quoted Featherstone, 1988, p. 195), it
is a comparatively new development. And, although an understanding of
its central thrust in aesthetic theory is helpful to an understanding of its
social, cultural and political significance, there are inevitable extensions and
differences of meaning which can have the effect of blurring the picture.

It is its significance within social theory, however, which is of prime concern
to us here. For our interest in postmodernism must focus on its implications for
democratic theory and for democratic education. Within social and political
theory, an important target for postmodernism has been Marxism, a major
totalizing theory which had permeated sociological enquiry for many years.
It is precisely this kind of theory which we have identified as offering serious
threats to democratic social forms, so that we might see here potential support
for the development of democratic theory. For postmodern thinking, as a
rejection of universals and an acceptance of difference, would appear to be
on the side of democracy and opposed to its enemies.

Nothing, however, is ever as straightforward as that – especially in a
postmodern world. For the theory of democracy might itself be viewed as a
totalizing theory of the kind which postmodernism finds unacceptable. Some
exponents of postmodernism, for example, 'want to regard postmodernism as
necessarily opposed to the political framework of modernity, namely liberty,
equality and freedom' (Turner, 1990, p. 10). On this kind of interpretation,
then, postmodernism would pose its own threat to those democratic principles
we identified in Part 1. This issue we must return to in Chapter 4 when we
explore theories of knowledge expressly in relation to democratic theory.

What we must note here is that the prime significance of postmodernism, in
the context of this book, is that it explicitly links theories of knowledge with
political movements. For that is precisely what is being sought after here in
relation to democracy, since the concern is to demonstrate that certain views
of knowledge are inimical to democracy as a system of social organization,
while others are supportive of it. Further, the linkage which postmodernism
makes is that of knowledge with power or empowerment, a linkage which is
effected through the concept of discourse.

Totalizing theories are expressed in language and thus become forms of
discourse. Those forms of discourse, as we shall see when we explore the
politics of knowledge in Chapter 4, have the effect of controlling our thinking.
Once one challenges the 'truth' of such theories, however, as we have seen
that postmodernism does, they cease to have universal validity and become

ideologies, so that our thinking is being controlled by the values implicit in particular ideologies. We might thus be said to be constituted by the 'knowledge' we are exposed to; we are in many ways the creations of, the products of, that 'knowledge'. In the view of Foucault, for example, 'it would be appropriate . . . to reverse the familiar notion that persons make statements, and say that statements make persons' (Shapiro, 1981, p. 141).

Thus discourse represents power and the legitimation of discourse the exercise of power. We are, or can be, manipulated by those who wield power through the control of discourse, through the propagation of particular ideologies, through totalizing theories of whatever kind, through 'the bureaucratic imposition of official values' (Turner, 1990, p. 11). And for some theorists there is an inevitability about this process. We live in a world in which there is no 'knowledge', no ultimate 'truths', in which all perception is subjective, so that we are the products of the discourse, the ideologies, we are exposed to.

Such a view of course provides no kind of base for a theory of democracy, since it would appear to admit of no freedom of action for the individual. It is, however, one kind of conclusion one can be led to once the notion of universal truths has been abandoned and the subjectivity of perception recognized. And it is in this form that postmodernism has been embraced by those seeking support for the political policies and practices of the far right. We must return to this when we explore the significance of postmodernism for democratic theory in Chapter 4.

It is not, on the other hand, the only conclusion one can draw. For, while it is true that 'postmodern theory makes us aware of how our subjectivity and experiences are constructed, how the meaning we attempt to grasp slips away in our failure to affectively commit to it' (Sholle, 1992, p. 274), nevertheless, 'Such a deconstruction of our present condition can lead us to question that condition and resist it (op.cit., pp. 274–5). There are two points here to note. First, it is not necessary to assume that, because knowledge can never be absolute, it must always be subjective. 'The question mark that post-modernism puts on the "truth" of all discourse means only that all knowledge is contextual, not that all knowledge is false, nor that one cannot support the validity of one claim over another in a specific circumstance' (op.cit., p. 276). Knowledge when viewed from a postmodern perspective can be seen as public, if not absolute and objective; there can be 'agreement between rational minds'.

And, second, it is not necessary to assume that because political power is exercised through the distribution of 'knowledge', the legitimation of discourse, 'the bureaucratic imposition of official values' (Turner, 1990, p. 11), we must remain powerless against it. On the contrary, to understand these processes can be interpreted as being armed against them, empowered to resist them, forewarned against attempts to manipulate our thinking. It is to be empowered to view the world 'reflexively', 'as constructed through experience, linguistic codes, cultural signs, etc.' rather than 'naturalistically', 'as it is' (Slaughter, 1989, p. 264). To do this is to gain 'greater freedom from ideological and linguistic traps, breadth of vision, the ability to "speak one's own words", direct access to fundamental negotiations of meaning' (op.cit., pp. 264–5). We need no longer be restricted to 'passively encoding finished structures of meaning' (op.cit., p. 265). And this enables us also to 'feel deeply involved in the process of cultural reconstruction and renewal' (*ibid.*).

The notion of discourse needs to be interpreted in a more subtle manner, and not simply regarded as a device for the exercise of power. As Foucault puts it in one of his later works (1979, pp. 100–101),

> Discourses are not once and for all subservient to power or raised up against it . . . We must make allowances for the complex and unstable process whereby discourse can be both an instrument and an effect of power, but also a hindrance, a stumbling-block, a point of resistance and a starting point for an opposing strategy. Discourse transmits and produces power; it reinforces it, but also undermines and exposes it, renders it fragile and makes it possible to thwart it.

It is this latter interpretation of the postmodern perspective, then, which offers support for democratic theory. For it provides a view of knowledge which, while rejecting all forms of universal, acknowledging individual differences of perception and plurality of values, and recognizing the dangers of manipulation through the control of discourse, is able at the same time to proclaim the potential empowerment of every individual and to provide a sound theoretical base for co-operative action.

In a sense, therefore, the chapter ends where it began. For the conclusion has to be that there are essential links between theories of knowledge and political movements; that theories of knowledge thus have enormous significance for questions of political organization; that different theories of knowledge lead to quite different positions in relation to political organization; and that those theories of knowledge which are incompatible with democratic social forms constitute a major threat to those forms.

Furthermore, these theories in turn have a crucial relevance for the ways in which we organize systems of education. It is, then, to a consideration of the implications of these distinctive views of knowledge for both social organization and educational planning that we turn in Chapter 4.

4

KNOWLEDGE AND DEMOCRACY

To know is to kill . . . Thinking is still alive.

(Daignault, 1992, p. 199)

The previous chapter explored a number of views of human knowledge, views displaying a spectrum from a conviction of the ultimate certainty and perfectibility of knowledge, through an acceptance of its tentative and provisional nature, to a complete scepticism. And it also sought to establish the importance of recognizing the significance of the links between knowledge and politics or, more specifically, between theories of knowledge and political policies and practices. In doing so it suggested that their very incompatibility rendered it impossible for all of them to be consonant with a democratic form of social organization. And, indeed, it had been briefly noted in Chapter 1 that the natural bedfellow of rationalism is totalitarianism rather than democracy.

This chapter sets out to elaborate and justify these claims. And it will seek to do so by identifying the implications these views of knowledge have for political theory and some of the consequences for social institutions of the adoption, whether conscious and thoughtful or uncritical and unquestioning, of any of them. It will also explore the specific implications of these views for the social institution we call education. For it is the purpose of this book to discover and define the essential ingredients of an appropriate form of education for a democratic society; and it has been claimed throughout that the way in which knowledge is conceived is a crucial determinant of this.

RATIONALISM, POSITIVISM AND DEMOCRACY

It is not necessary here to repeat what was said in Chapter 1 about the political implications of rationalism. For there it was shown how and why this view of knowledge must lead to a metaphysical theory of the state, to a reification of the state and to the view that the state is bigger than the sum of its individual parts. The reasons for this may now be more apparent in the light of those more detailed discussions of rationalism which were offered in Chapter 3. And it should now be clear that this kind of view of the state and of society is the quite unavoidable consequence, the inevitable corollary, of the adoption of a rationalist perspective on human knowledge. It should also now be clear why it was claimed there that the kind of view of social living which a rationalist epistemology must lead to is not merely undemocratic but is positively anti-democratic.

To that, in the light of our discussion of positivism in Chapter 3, we can now add the dangers of any attempt to regard human issues, social, moral or political, as subject to any kind of scientific study or productive of any form of reliable universals. Questions of value are logically distinct from scientific questions, and must be approached in an appropriately different manner. Claims for certainty of knowledge in any sphere, as we saw in Chapter 3, are impossible to substantiate and are politically dangerous and life threatening to democracy; such claims in the realm of human values offer dangers that are immeasurably greater.

For, as we saw in Chapter 2, democratic theory has emphasized freedom, equality, the protection of human rights and the maintenance of popular sovereignty. Indeed, it was stressed there that these principles are fundamental to any intelligible concept of democracy; they constitute what democracy *is*. And underlying these fundamental principles is a concept of the individual human being as possessing a worth in his or her own right, as being an end in him or herself not, as rationalism would have it, as a participator in rationality, as the proud owner of a rational mind, but as an individual, as someone with a distinctive personality and character.

A major part of that personality and that character is the possession of views and opinions which may not always conform with those approved by society as a whole, which may not always even coincide with those of the majority, which in fact, especially in a modern pluralist society, may reflect a quite distinctive aesthetic, moral and cultural position. And it was argued in Chapter 2 that it is the function of a truly democratic form of social organization to accommodate these distinctive value stances, to facilitate their coexistence, not least because they offer society the kind of variety – aesthetic, moral and cultural – which, when properly managed, can add richness to the lives and to the experience of all its members.

Such a form of social living, however, cannot be based on a view of knowledge as not in any sphere, and especially not in the aesthetic, moral or cultural spheres, open to this kind of variety of view or opinion. Yet, as we have seen in our earlier chapters, that is the essence of rationalism and, indeed, of positivism. For a view of knowledge, especially in the social sphere, as a slowly unfolding pattern of eternal and unchallengeable 'truths', or as derived from some kind of objective, scientific inquiry, cannot be compatible with any notion that there might be different shades of opinion on any matter; and it can only lead one to the conclusion that the individual must seek to understand that pattern in order to align his or her views and opinions with it.

And the corollary of that, as we have also seen, is that it can only support totalitarian forms of political organization, whether based on a metaphysical concept of the state, on some kind of reified view of the state, on claims to 'scientific expertise' or merely on a passive acceptance of the 'fact' that 'the government knows best'. It has thus been the underpinning philosophy of both fascism and Marxism. And, at a more general level, it has provided a justification for that development of the concept of the nation-state, of nationalism in all its forms, which has been a feature of the history of Europe during the last two centuries, and which has even in some contexts been adduced as a valid reason for 'ethnic cleansing'.

This concept of the nation-state has also given rise to the idea of national sovereignty, which has led, in many contexts, to the perpetration of all kinds of barbarous and inhuman acts and the apparent inability of other nations, and even of the United Nations Organization itself, to interfere to protect the individuals whose liberties, and in many cases whose lives, have been threatened, and even taken from them.

There are of course many situations in which one cannot find nationalism reprehensible. In sporting contexts, for example, it would seem unexceptionable. However, there is a significant difference between supporting one's national soccer, rugby or athletics team in international competition, in applauding the activities and achievements of one's fellow countrypersons abroad in any sphere, on the one hand, and adopting the 'my country right or wrong' philosophy which is what rationalism must lead us to. Indeed, taken to its logical conclusion, as in the philosophy of Hegel, it is not a matter of 'my country right or wrong' but 'my country unquestionably right all the time'.

For such a view must lead to an unjustifiable loss of individual freedom (even in some cases of life itself), to inequalities, to the infringement of human rights and to a concept of sovereignty as residing in the hands of those who 'know' and not in those of the people at large. It thus transgresses every one of the fundamental principles of democracy we identified in Chapter 2. It also points us towards a global concept of democracy, transcending national interests, as we shall see later.

Rationalist epistemology, then, however one views it, is anti-democratic in its political thrust. And it is that which renders it totally unacceptable as a basis both for democratic theory and for a theory of education in a democratic society.

We will need to unpack the details of this more thoroughly in later chapters. What we need to note here, however, is the dangers which must result from the acceptance of such an epistemology, and thus from the work of Richard Peters (1965; 1966) and those other 'philosophers of education' who have attempted to resurrect Kantian rationalism within the context of education theory. For those dangers threaten not only education but also democracy itself. And, as we shall see, they offer justification for the establishment of a system of education which it is very difficult to reconcile with our notions of democratic living. We must briefly explore the main features of this argument now.

THE APPLICATION OF KANTIAN RATIONALISM TO THE EDUCATIONAL DEBATE

One of the most significant theoretical influences on the education debate, and indeed on educational practice, during the last two or three decades has been the reassertion of Kantian rationalism, first made by Richard Peters (1965; 1966). His major claims were that education is 'initiation into intrinsically worthwhile activities', and that the activities which qualify for this cachet can readily be determined by the application of a test of their rationality, their universalizability. In short, it is 'cognitive content' which is the test of intrinsic value, so that a subject hierarchy emerges, exactly like that of Plato, with the more abstract subjects at the top and the 'practical' subjects at the bottom.

In terms of the philosophical technique of conceptual enquiry, one may not wish to quarrel with the first of these assertions. For, as we saw in Chapter 3, there are many people who would wish to reserve the use of the term 'education' for those learning activities which are undertaken for their own value, and not use it of the kinds of learning which are engaged in for instrumental or utilitarian purposes, and which are better described as 'training' or 'instruction'. Certainly, there is a conceptual distinction here which it is important to maintain.

The second assertion, however, takes us well beyond what, again as we saw in Chapter 3, the technique of conceptual analysis permits, since it falls into the fallacy of essentialism and takes us into the realm of prescriptions, of the assertion of 'objective' value judgements, which twentieth-century philosophy has long eschewed. It offers us the kind of totalizing theory of knowledge whose dangers, political as well as intellectual, we saw in Chapter 3 postmodernism seeks to warn us of. And it does this by resurrecting, almost word for word, Kantian rationalism.

For Peters' 'transcendental argument' (1966) is little more than a reformulation of the Kantian argument as it applies in the sphere of values, and especially educational values. And it seeks to establish that values are not personal, private or subjective but, as Kant would have it, universal, public, objective and derived from rationality itself, 'public propositions in the form of abstract principles' (Peters, 1966, p. 114).

On this kind of argument, valuing is not a personal matter nor is one justified in coming to one's own conclusions on issues of value – be they aesthetic, moral or, indeed, educational or political. And activities have intrinsic value not because an individual chooses to engage in them for their own sake but in some objective, metaphysical sense. Valuing is a public exercise which involves using 'a public form of discourse' (op.cit., p. 115) and 'probing public propositions' (*ibid.*).

Furthermore, the acceptance of this public form of discourse implies not merely that we are able to communicate with other people; it also implies, indeed entails, that we accept the universal conclusions to which these probings lead, the public propositions which are the inevitable and unchallengeable results of this rational process. For the public debate, beginning from certain concepts which constitute what rationality itself is, will lead to conclusions, even in the realm of values, which will have an equally public, rational and thus universal character.

Again the fundamental flaw in this argument is the assumption that reasoning in the sphere of values is the same kind of intellectual activity as scientific reasoning, that enquiry into aesthetic, moral, educational, political and other values must 'ask and answer questions in the way that science does' (Wittgenstein, 1975, p. 18). As we saw in Chapter 3, however, value assertions are of a logically different kind and order from empirical assertions, so that they cannot be subject to the same forms of verification and, as we have also seen, perhaps not to *verification* at all.

Nevertheless, this argument, flawed as we can see it is, and out of tune with the mainstream of twentieth-century philosophy as we can also see it is, has, over the last two or three decades, exercised considerable influence on the theory and the practice of education, not only in the UK but also worldwide.

It is a major purpose of this book to argue that this approach to education, both in theory and in practice, is not only philosophically flawed and untenable but is also inimical to, and incompatible with, the development of any system of education which can hope to measure up to those criteria of democracy which earlier chapters have identified. And furthermore, it will be argued as a corollary of that, that a truly democratic system of education must resemble those very forms of education which this theory has been at pains to demolish – that concern for individual development, for example, which has been the undergirding of the approach to education in the early years in the UK for many years – rather than initiation into preselected subject-content.

The first major challenge to this theory, however, came not from within the 'philosophy of education' but from those 'new directions' in the sociology of education which have been a contrasting feature of education theory during the last two decades. In particular, there emerged the concept of 'the politics of knowledge' and, since this is the route through which a challenge to the rationalist view of knowledge has entered the education debate, as well as being an important forerunner of postmodern theory, we must take some time to note here its main thrusts.

THE POLITICS OF KNOWLEDGE

If one does not accept this rationalist view of knowledge, and especially of values, or any kind of positivist assertion in the social or moral sphere, one has to acknowledge that what currently passes for, or is claimed to be, knowledge is imperfect and uncertain. And further, one has to recognize that the values implicit in what currently passes for knowledge, or what is currently claimed to constitute 'true' knowledge, are also imperfect and uncertain, and that they have no objective status.

All current knowledge, therefore, along with those discourses in which it is enshrined, must be recognized as being ideological rather than objective 'truth'. And that, it is claimed, renders the passing on of such knowledge *via* the education system a highly questionable activity. It is in effect, and probably in intention too, a very powerful form of social control. As such, it is fundamentally anti-democratic. And it is so primarily because it presents knowledge as unchallengeable and unproblematic – the classic position of the rationalist.

If all knowledge is 'socially constructed', then the values implicit in that knowledge and, indeed, all value systems, must be seen as part of that social construct, as the subjective values of particular groups within any society. And the selection of that knowledge and those values for distribution through the education system must reflect the values, the ideology, of those making that selection. 'How a society selects, classifies, distributes, transmits and evaluates the educational knowledge it considers to be public, reflects both the distribution of power and the principles of social control' (Bernstein, 1972, p. 47).

Further, the ideology to be promulgated through the education system will be that of the dominant group within society, the group which controls the system and especially the school curriculum :

> Education in a class society is a political act having as its basis the protection of the interests of the ruling class. It is a mechanism (and that word hardly does it justice) for securing the continuation of the existing social relationships and for reinforcing the attitudes and beliefs that will help ensure that those social relationships will continue to be accepted. Education is thus more than a 'mechanism' – it is an ideological force of tremendous import.
>
> (Harris, 1979, p. 140)

The argument that knowledge, and the discourses in which it is enshrined, are 'socially constructed' is a strong one. We have seen the support it gets from those twentieth-century developments in epistemological inquiry we examined in Chapter 3, and from the many dimensions of postmodern thinking.

The extension of that argument to the claim that school subjects are also social constructs is equally cogent (Goodson, 1981; 1983; 1985a; 1985b; Goodson and Ball, 1984). For, apart from anything else, the studies on which that claim is based cast considerable doubt on the validity of the view that the organization of knowledge into subjects, and especially the form and the continued presence of these subjects on the school curriculum, can be explained, as the 'philosphers of education' would have it, in philosophical or epistemological terms, in terms of the properties of knowledge or forms of rationality or any other aspect of the nature of the subjects themselves. The sociological explanation, expressed in terms of political policies and pressures, is far more convincing and compelling.

It is in this light that we must view the selection of those subjects which constitute the newly established National Curriculum in England and Wales, to a discussion of which we must come in Chapter 7. For, as we shall see, the subjects which constitute that National Curriculum have been both selected and defined by political agencies. And so that National Curriculum is a perfect example of a curriculum whose implicit values reflect the ideology of the government agencies which planned it, although its fundamental utilitarian thrust is dressed up in, and concealed by, rationalist assertions or assumptions of its intrinsic value. The selection of school subjects, and of the curriculum content of those subjects, is a political act and must be seen as, at least in part, a device for establishing and maintaining political control.

When one considers further the impact on pupils of the values implicit in this choice of subjects and the content of those subjects, one sees even more clearly how this device maintains and extends the existing social order. For one can see, for example, that its impact on those pupils for whom the values implicit in this curriculum do not chime with those of their social or cultural background is an impact which is fundamentally alienating and thus inimical to the attainment of educational equality. One can see its effect, again particularly in relation to these same pupils, of reducing rather than enhancing their freedom of thought and action, for example by devaluing their cultural inheritance where this is different from what is accepted as 'the norm'. One can see it denying their rights as members of a democratic society, for example their right to have their own cultures accepted, and indeed respected, and their right to participate in the decison-making process within that society, since it places serious limitations on their educational development. In general, one can see the many ways in which it falls short of being a satisfactory form of education for a democratic society. To these shortcomings we must return in later chapters.

This constitutes the kind of 'instutionalization of values' which Ivan Illich (1971, p. 9) claims 'leads to ... social polarization and psychological impotence'. And it is this which has led him and others to suggest the abolition of schools, a 'deschooling of society'. For, on this analysis, formal schooling is having the effect of limiting the freedom of individuals, of denying them all routes to social progress or improvement, of turning them into what Paulo Freire (1972) calls 'dopes', whose curricula, and thus whose lives, are determined for them by others, and of maintaining those social inequalities which characterize even the most 'advanced' of present-day societies.

Again, therefore, we need to note that the fundamental claim is that those very elements we have defined earlier as constituting the essence of democracy are denied by a form of education in which one, the dominant, section of society selects and controls the curriculum content for everyone else, and thus effectively selects and controls their lives, and denies them that empowerment which, as we shall see in Chapter 5, is a *sine qua non* of education in a democratic society. Far from being a democratic form of education, then, whatever description is given to the society in which it is offered, it is the very antithesis of democracy, and in fact operates to destroy rather than to support or promote the development of democratic forms.

Those who have wielded power in those totalitarian political systems which rationalism has spawned have been well aware of this aspect of educational provision, and have recognized the importance of control of the school curriculum as a device for controlling society through the repression of unapproved, 'incorrect' political values. A tight hold on the education system has thus been a feature of all totalitarian societies, those fascist societies which the present century has seen in Germany, Italy, Spain and elsewhere, and those communist societies in eastern Europe, the USSR and communist China. And control of schools and other educational institutions has been as important a goal in all revolutionary contexts as control of the media of communication. In this respect, it is interesting to remember that the idea of a national curriculum was first mooted in the UK in the 1930s but was immediately rejected because of its totalitarian implications.

Threats to democracy also emerge, as we shall see when we come to an evaluation of the present National Curriculum for England and Wales in Chapter 7, from the strategies which have to be adopted to ensure the implementation of this kind of centrally determined and ideologically controlled curriculum. In fascist and communist societies, these have often been repressive, violent and even bloody. In societies which claim to be democratic and seek to maintain an appearance of being so, the stategies adopted must be less overt and outrageous; they nevertheless constitute an equal threat, perhaps even a more serious threat because less apparent, to the maintenance and development of democratic forms. The use of rhetoric and the control of discourse, for example, which are salient features of current strategies for implementing the National Curriculum in England and Wales, as we shall see in Chapter 7, are as effective in denying democratic principles and processes as more overt forms of oppression.

These features of a knowledge-based curriculum, then, are not only to be found in the curricula of totalitarian societies. Furthermore, they can be discerned in the effects of this form of curriculum even when they are expressly not its intention, even when in fact the concern is to promote a liberal, democratic form of upbringing. It has been argued, for example, by Walter Feinberg (1975, p. vi) that even if one accepts that American schooling is 'a liberal institution conceived by liberal theorists and carried out by liberal practitioners' (op.cit., p. v), 'from Kindergarten through graduate school [it] operates to reinforce certain basic aspects of the American political, economic and moral structure' (op.cit., p. vi). And we saw in Chapter 3 that, on one interpretation of postmodern theory, this must be the inevitable effect of the empowerment of ideologies through legitimated forms of discourse.

It is a major theme of this book, however, that, while this must be true, it is not insuperable. For the problem arises entirely because the curriculum is conceived in terms of its knowledge-content, so that curriculum planning is viewed solely as the selection and distribution of knowledge. That selection and distribution must be undertaken by someone, or some group of people, and will be done according to their own values. It is thus the values of those engaged in the selection process which will permeate the knowledge-content of the curriculum and be communicated, often unconsciously, to the recipients of this kind of curriculum. It is this that makes the selection of curriculum content by governmental agencies especially dangerous.

However, this is an inevitable consequence, not of all education and curriculum planning but merely of that form of both which is based on a predominantly rationalist or positivist approach to knowledge, whether overt and conscious or not, and a consequent view of the curriculum as a body of knowledge-content, along with an implicit system of values, to be transmitted to pupils, and further to be transmitted in a manner which discourages, or at least does not invite, challenge. It is a function of the way in which knowledge is conceived and the way in which curriculum is conceived. If it is to be avoided, therefore, this can only be by the reconceptualization of both.

This, it would seem, is what Freire had in mind when he suggested (1972) that the only way to protect individuals from the attempts of others to control their lives, and indeed the only way to protect democratic society itself, was to seek through education to provide pupils with the skills necessary to see their problems in a reflexive perspective and thus enable them to gain some control over their own destinies. This was the central thrust of Dewey's version of pragmatism – a complete reconceptualization of both knowledge and education to match a properly democratic view of society. And, for some, this is the central message of postmodernism for education, the need 'to formulate a critical pedagogy committed to the imperatives of empowering students and transforming the larger social order in the interests of a more just and equitable democracy' (McLaren, 1988, p. xi, referring to the work of Henry Giroux).

The time has now come, therefore, to consider in some detail what are the implications of a postmodern conception of knowledge for democracy and for the school curriculum in a democratic society.

POSTMODERNISM, DEMOCRACY AND EDUCATION

We have seen in Chapter 2 that the very essence of democracy is individual freedom and, further, that this means freedom of thought as well as freedom of action. And we have just seen why a rationalist epistemology cannot coexist with such a view of society. In simple terms, it cannot admit of, or allow for, variations of opinion in its comprehensive view of knowledge, and values, as ultimatedly fixed and certain. As we have seen more than once, therefore, it can only support a political theory of a totalitarian kind. A true democracy cannot exist in a context of non-problematic universals.

The essence of alternative forms of epistemology, on the other hand, is that they cannot view knowledge in this way as fixed, certain and unquestionable. For them, as we saw in Chapter 3, knowledge is essentially problematic. What counts as knowledge at any given time or, indeed, in any given place, is uncertain, provisional, tentative and open to constant challenge, critical questioning and resultant change and modification.

The first point to note about the implications of this for political organization is that there is nothing in this view of knowledge which offers grounds for dogmatism. For dogmatism implies certainty and assurance. And while it might be true that there are many people in any society (perhaps most of them in government or at least in some position of authority) who continue to take a dogmatic stance on many issues (not least those of a social, moral and political kind), this kind of stance cannot be compatible with the acceptance of a view of knowledge as problematic. It may be justified by the adoption of a rationalist epistemology, whether consciously or not, as, for example, with religious dogmatism. It may be a result of ignorance and a failure, or unwillingness, to think things through. It may be more sinister than either of these. Whatever its base, however, it will represent, as we have seen, the attempt to impose an ideology, to establish a particular discourse. And it is certainly not a view which can be held, nor a practice which can be justified, by those who proclaim a commitment to democracy. For democracy and dogmatism cannot coexist.

To accept the uncertainty and changingness of human knowledge, then, is to recognize the need for humility in the face of every question that faces humankind, whether personally or collectively. It is to acknowledge the possibility that one may be mistaken in one's opinion or judgement, and that other persons' views may be 'right'. And so it is also to concede that those with different views have as much right to those views as we have to ours, so that the views of others, unless they are quite bizarre and irrational, or at odds with the essence of democracy itself, are to be taken seriously and certainly recognized as having equal validity to our own.

Second, this recognition of the problematic nature of knowledge, if it will not permit of dogmatism, equally cannot allow the claim that the interests of the state, the nation, the collective are more important than those of the individual, or of individual groups within the collective. It thus implies a rejection of that nationalism which we noted earlier to be a product of rationalist and positivist views of society. And it points us towards that global concept of democracy which we must return to later.

We noted in Chapter 3 that one major thrust of the existentialist revolt against German idealism was a concern to reassert the rights and status of the individual against the collective. And we will see in the next section the view taken by Dewey of the essential interaction of the individual and the community, a major feature of his concept of democracy.

This view of knowledge, then, supports the notion we have adumbrated elsewhere, that another essential aspect of democracy is that it should seek to reconcile differences of view, opinion, culture, not by attempting to ensure that they all conform with some collective value system, but by seeking to enable them to coexist in mutual tolerance and even support.

This implies a view of society as held together by what Émile Durkheim called 'organic solidarity' rather than 'mechanical solidarity'. The concept of organic solidarity is intended to explain those societies in which the form of social integration is one which emphasizes the differences between people and groups rather than the similarities, whereas 'mechanical solidarity refers to social integration at the level of shared beliefs' (Bernstein, 1967). The shift from the latter to the former kind of social integration reflects a move towards greater democratization of societies, towards an opening up of many social structures, towards what Basil Bernstein (op.cit.) has called an 'open society'.

Conversely, a shift in the opposite direction, towards an attempt to establish and impose a system of shared beliefs, which many would wish to argue is what we are currently witnessing, reflects a movement away from the open society, and thus away from proper forms of democracy.

The implications of this for current educational policies we will need to return to in later chapters. Here we must simply note that an acceptance of the problematic nature of knowledge must lead us to this notion of an open society. And it must cast doubt on the intellectual (let alone the moral) justification for any attempt to re-establish or maintain a form of society which is to be held together by the acceptance of a common set of beliefs, an acceptance which, in a pluralist society, can only be secured by the firm imposition of the values of the dominant group on the rest. Such an attempt has been called a policy of 'back to basics'. It is intellectually flawed in its inability, or unwillingness, to recognize the significance of those intellectual developments of the twentieth century which were explored in Chapter 3. And it is morally flawed in its similar inability or unwillingness to acknowledge the significance and the legitimacy of moral diversity and cultural pluralism.

Furthermore, it is a policy which transgresses against another of those elements we have earlier identified as fundamental to democracy, that of equality. For the failure to recognize differences between individuals and groups within society must lead to inequalities of opportunity through the maintenance of existing social structures. In Durkheim's terms, mechanical solidarity is characterized by the *ascription* of social roles, whereas in a society which emphasizes individual differences, social roles are *achieved*. Mechanical solidarity cannot accommodate changes in the social structure; it is of the essence of organic solidarity that it is readily able to do so.

A society in which organic solidarity is the basis of social integration, then, will be characterized by a high level of individuality, a diversity of values, a cultural pluralism, a greater sense of individual freedom and enlarged scope for social mobility and equality. In short, it will be an open, democratic society, and its basis must be a view of knowledge and of values as problematic. Furthermore, such a society or form of political organization is entailed by this kind of view of knowledge since, as we have seen, to accept this view of knowledge is to surrender all claims to intellectual, aesthetic, social, moral or political dogmatism. Any shift towards this kind of society, then is a shift towards increased democratization. Conversely, any move away from it is the reverse.

Furthermore, there must be a consistency between the form of social integration sought for a society and that planned for all the social institutions within that society. An open, democratic society will therefore need an open, democratic education system or, to put it more cogently, any society which claims to be open and democratic must accept the logic of being required to establish social institutions which reflect the same open form of democracy. Again, we will need to return to this point when we discuss what might constitute such an open, democratic education system. Let us for the present merely note that it is this kind of society and this kind of education system to which a recognition of the problematic nature of human knowledge, especially in the area of human values, must lead us.

We noted, however, at the end of our brief discussion of postmodernism in Chapter 3, that not all of those theorists who have adumbrated postmodern theories have accepted this connection. For we saw there that, on some interpretations, a postmodern perspective is seen as leading to the politics of the far right, and has been adduced in support of these. In particular, the individualism to which postmodernism must lead is seen as implying competition between individuals rather than collaboration, self-assertion rather than commitment to a 'public good'.

For a major feature of postmodern theory is the notion of 'difference'. Such a notion clearly must loom large as a necessary corollary of that rejection of absolutes which we noted in Chapter 3. 'The world finds itself increasingly in a crisis of difference, and we can no longer sanctimoniously count on a harmonious society that simply embraces a dominant status quo and its values and norms' (Kanpol, 1992, p. 217). Furthermore, 'we can no longer consider schools as places where there is no crisis, conflict or contradiction' (*ibid.*). Difference, then, is a central feature of that chaotic vision of the world which we have noted before. And all differences must be accepted, since postmodernism, as we have seen, has rejected any universal basis for distinguishing between them :

> The active processes by which we construct and interpret systems of belief or value are infinitely variable and highly contingent. This contingency is thought to undercut any purely intellectual, internal justification for epistemic, moral, or political claims. Any such justification is rejected as simply the special pleading of a particular group seeking to promote a

discursive order that legitimates their own advantages and privileges by promoting a specific basis of justification as the best one; any ultimate claim to 'rightness' is a ploy to discourage further investigation or to allow investigation only on one's terms, and thus is seen as restrictive.

(Burbules and Rice, 1991, pp. 393–4)

In short, 'there is no clear reason to grant any one special significance or value over others' (op.cit., p. 396).

It will be clear, then, how such a view can lead to an inability to justify the claims of democracy or to grant it any special significance over other theories of social organization. And it will be equally clear how postmodernism can be adduced to support right-wing political views, advocating that we should celebrate difference and 'encourage the multiplicity of as many voices and perspectives as possible, without seeking to reconcile them or combine them into a single, consistent, unified account' (op.cit., p. 394).

Such an interpretation, however, renders all discussion of democracy otiose. And, perhaps more seriously, it renders all discussion of social planning, as an activity which must conform to certain moral principles, equally otiose. For, however it may be presented, it represents a nihilistic, even anarchic, rejection of value systems of all kinds, or at least a view of them as mere social constructs, forms of discourse.

On this kind of interpretation of postmodernism, then, democracy, along with all of those elements our earlier chapters identified as central to it, is seen as 'the political framework of modernity' (Turner, 1990, p. 10), a totalizing theory, a form of discourse, of the kind that postmodernism challenges and rejects. In this light, therefore, it has been adduced to oppose democratic theory and to support those right-wing political policies and practices which emphasize individuality, competitiveness and, in general, a rejection of all kinds of moral and social imperative.

This problem, however, arises only if democratic theory is seen as a totalizing theory which purports to offer some kind of eternal 'truth', or only if the attempt 'to combine them [the differences] into a single, consistent, unified account' (Burbules and Rice, 1991, p. 394) takes the form of seeking to reduce them to a common system. For then, quite properly, it is to be seen as an ideology masquerading as something more substantial, an answer rather than a series of questions.

At no stage, however, throughout our discussion of democratic theory, has the attempt been made to present it as anything other than an ideology, a social construct, a particular form of discourse. Indeed, it has been stressed that it must be recognized as such, that it is a system of moral and social values which may be accepted or rejected. The concern has been merely to identify its essential elements as a moral and social system and to demonstrate what a commitment to such a system entails.

There is nothing in such an approach which contradicts the basic tenets of postmodern theory. If there is a commitment to the democratic moral system, to the discourse of democracy, it is because the further step which has been taken is to suggest that, in a social and political world conceived by postmodernism as characterized by difference, by competing discourses and struggles for political power, there would seem to be attractions in a social theory which, while not laying any claim to ultimate 'truth', nor seeking to impose any one particular ideology, nevertheless seeks to reconcile moral, social and cultural differences, to promote the empowerment of all and to create a context for continuing change and development. This, however, represents a moral stance not a claim for objective certainty.

It becomes necessary too, if one wishes to promote this view of the main thrust of postmodernism, to regard it as *after* modernism rather than as *anti*-modernism. 'Postmodernism must extend and broaden the most democratic claims of modernism' (Giroux, 1988a, p. 26). The attempt must be 'to reappropriate and expand modernist concepts such as democracy, liberty, rights, citizenship, and so forth' (Burbules and Rice, 1991, p. 398). It represents a reconceptualization rather than a rejection of these concepts.

Interpreted in this way, the postmodern perspective can be adduced, with equal if not greater force, in support of the attempt to construct, or reconstruct, a workable moral and social system, rather than to endorse the rejection of all morality. 'We must seek to connect postmodernism's notions of culture, difference and subjectivity with modernist concerns such as the language of public life, thus reaffirming a public philosophy that broadens and deepens individual liberties and rights' (Sholle, 1992, p. 275, citing Giroux and Aronowitz, 1991). And Sholle (*ibid.*) goes on to quote the claim of Giroux (1991, p. 6) that 'at stake here is an attempt to provide a political and theoretical discourse which can . . . develop a project in which a politics of difference can emerge within a shared discourse of democratic public life'.

On this kind of interpretation, postmodernism may even be seen as a prerequisite of democracy. At the very least, it must be recognized that an acceptance of the problematic nature of human knowledge is such a prerequisite. For one cannot, with intellectual honesty and integrity, claim to be committed to democratic forms of social living while rejecting all notion of plurality of values, aesthetic, cultural, social and moral. If a 'back to basics' policy involves a return to a form of mechanical solidarity based on an acceptance of one moral, social and cultural system, then it is *ipso facto* non-democratic.

In such a context, then, education must seek to celebrate difference, to empower individuals but at the same time to enable them to recognize the significance of community. 'The common normative core both of education and democracy can then be developed within a theory of intersubjectively reflected learning processes which are constitutive for a public sphere of social learning, criticism and autonomy, all of which may then be defined collectively as well as individually' (Peukertruth, 1993, p. 167). It might be further argued in support of this interpretation of postmodernism that this kind of social structure is entailed by the postmodern view of knowledge. For, if 'knowledge' is to be under constant challenge, it must always be open to critical appraisal, and subject to regular modification, change, reformulation, even reconceptualization. A free and open intellectual environment is thus essential. All forms of society other than the democratic – and, of course, the completely anarchic – are specifically planned to maintain their status quo, to inhibit change of all kinds, and especially change in values. Only a democratic society, again by definition, is accepting, indeed welcoming, of change.

This, in turn, as we shall see, also has crucial implications for the way in which education is planned, the approach to knowledge which is reflected in its policies and practices and the stance towards such knowledge which it invites. It is a major theme of this book that this view of knowledge as problematic must not only underpin democratic theory but it must also be reflected in the planning of any genuinely democratic system of education.

It is this view of democracy, both as requiring a recognition of the problem of human knowledge and as offering the only supportive environment for the continuous review of knowledge, which is fundamental to John Dewey's theories of knowledge, of society and of education. We must turn now, therefore, to that fuller discussion of his philosophy which we earlier suggested would become necessary.

PRAGMATISM AND DEMOCRACY

The prime reason why Dewey's philosophy offers us the ideal bridge from theories of knowledge to democratic theory and onwards to education theory is that, as we noted in Chapter 3, he himself saw these three areas of intellectual speculation as inextricably intertwined.

We shall see shortly the links he saw between his epistemological position and democratic theory. It is worth noting also at the outset, however, that, unlike many or even most of those who have engaged in the educational debate, at whatever level, he recognized the crucial significance of what is being argued here, and has been argued elsewhere (Kelly, 1986), namely that any worthwhile discussion of education must begin with and from a critique of knowledge.

Indeed, for him philosophical and educational speculation were not to be distinguished. For 'the most penetrating definition of philosophy which can be given is ... that it is the theory of education in its most general phases' (Dewey, 1916, Chap. 24, Sec. 2). And the reason he gives for claiming this is that 'education offers a vantage ground from which to penetrate to the human, as distinct from the technical, significance of philosophical discussion' (*ibid.*).

It is for this reason that it is largely through the work of Dewey that a pragmatist epistemology has entered the education debate. We shall see later, however, that its significance has seldom been recognized, and that Dewey's work has too often been regarded merely as a theory of education, with no appreciation of the quite distinctive theory of knowledge on which it is based. And so it has too often also been debated and evaluated quite improperly and inappropriately from that rationalist perspective we have seen adopted by most 'philosophers of education'. It is to an exploration of the significance of that epistemological base that we must now turn.

While we must accept the caveat that Dewey's views changed in the course of his long life (Westbrook, 1991) – indeed, we have already noted the influence of Hegelianism which was the point from which his thinking started – we saw in Chapter 3 that it is possible to identify what are the main general features of that epistemological theory known as pragmatism and of Dewey's version of it. We noted its adoption of a broadly scientific definition of 'truth' as that which 'works', and of knowledge as an interconnected body of such 'truths'. We noted too the influence of Darwin's theory of evolution, which had led to an acceptance of the continually evolving nature of these 'truths' and a rejection of the certainties of rationalism, along with its assumptions about the ultimate perfection of human knowledge.

We saw further, however, that, especially for Dewey, the concern was to avoid the potential subjectivity of such an epistemology. For him, knowledge, although tentative, provisional and evolutionary, nevertheless is public. It is an agreed corpus of hypotheses which, in spite of being hypothetical, enjoy current, if temporary, acceptance and an objectivity, albeit in a modified sense. Lack of certainty of human knowledge need not necessarily lead to lack of agreement.

It is worth now adding to this the influence of the times and the society in which Dewey lived and worked, since it is this as much as any other factor which offers us an explanation of the view he took not only of knowledge and science but also of democracy.

Pragmatism has been fittingly described as 'in a real sense an expression of American culture' (Childs, 1956, p. 3). For, as Childs (*ibid.*) points out, the major figures of the pragmatist movement

> were all born in the America of the open frontier. During the course of their lives they witnessed the conquest of the West, and the transformation of this vast, virgin territory through the use of the resources of science and technology. During this period of rapid technological and social change, the American people were also involved in the massive experiment of establishing a continental system of government that would be of, by, and for the people.

Dewey thus lived through a time of massive change which was not only technological, scientific, industrial and economic; it was, as an inevitable consequence of these, also moral, social and political. Not only was scientific knowledge changing rapidly; values, standards and ways of life were also altering with almost equal rapidity.

In such a social context there was no possibility of holding on to, or proffering, any theory of the stability of knowledge or values, although we have noted before that predilection people seem to have for certainty even in the context of present-day society, in which change of this kind is even more rapid and dramatic than it was in Dewey's day.

Dewey, on the contrary, argued that, in the midst of such change, what was needed was a complete overhaul of our ways of thinking, a total reappraisal of our habits of thought. To him it made little sense to be attempting to tackle social, moral and political problems of the kind that were emerging, with the modes of thinking handed down from the ancient world. New patterns of thought needed to be evolved to meet these new problems. Moral, social and political problems also needed to be tackled not in the manner of the ancients but by the kinds of approach 'with which we operate our machines' (Nathanson, 1951, p. 86).

Here, then, is a total rejection of traditional forms of rationalist epistemology. We have noted before the weakness of his insistence on the need to address every kind of issue in a scientific manner. But, against that, we must note that, in his view, what a proper scientific approach requires is an acceptance that it must be open ended, tentative and susceptible to constant challenge and resultant adaptation.

It is important now to note what it was that pointed Dewey to democracy as the only form of political organization which matched the kind of social context just described. For, after all, an awareness of social change has led, and continues to lead, others to the opposite conclusion, and to embrace totalitarianism as a possible device for arresting such change.

Fundamentally, Dewey's view begins from an acceptance of the inevitability of evolution and change. It is not necessary to adopt the rationalist view of change as the slow unfolding of perfection in order to recognize it as an inevitable feature of the world around us, including the social world. This, after all, as we saw earlier, was what had prompted the epistemological debate in the first place, as those early philosophers sought to explain this undoubted phenomenon of human existence. To attempt to arrest change, therefore, is not a serious or viable option. And it is this that makes a nonsense of those political policies which seek to put back the clock, to return to 'the basics'.

Second, to accept that everything is in a state of evolution is to acknowledge that this is true of society itself as well as of everything else. Society itself is subject to this inevitable and unstoppable process. And, unless one is prepared to adopt the rationalist position that change in society, or the state, is occurring according to some preordained, or predetermined, or at least rational process, one must seek for a social theory, and a social system, which will accommodate such change.

Such a social theory must of course be opposed to totalitarianism, the prime concern of which is to discourage diversity and change, or at least only to support change which is proceding along predetermined lines since, as we have seen more than once, it is quite incapable of accommodating the chaotic scenario of postmodernism. And Dewey's definition of democracy may be seen in the largely negative light of an absence of totalitarianism. For his view of democracy is that it is a term which can only be used to describe a society which is open to and, indeed, welcoming of, continuous evolution and change.

He is not prepared to define it in terms of particular kinds of political procedure since these, like all else, must be open to change and evolution:

> The very idea of democracy, the meaning of democracy, must be continually explored afresh; it has to be constantly discovered and rediscovered, remade and reorganized; while the political and economic and social institutions in which it is embodied have to be remade and reorganized to meet the changes that are going on in the development of new needs on the part of human beings and new resources for satisfying those needs.
>
> (Dewey, 1916)

A democratic society, then, on this definition is one which facilitates continued change and evolution in all aspects of its life and in every one of its social institutions. It is 'the political expression of the functioning of experimental method' (Rosenthal, 1993, p. 384).

It is also a society which, in order to facilitate this kind of continuing evolution, must promote free and regular interaction between its members. As we saw in the quotation at the beginning of Chapter 2, it was Dewey's view that 'a democracy is more than a form of government; it is primarily a mode of associated living, of conjoint communicated experience' (Dewey, 1916, Chap. 7, Sec. 2).

However, this emphasis on the importance of community does not lead to any loss of significance for the individual since, in Dewey's view, 'our individuality ... is achieved through association and by embracing our connectedness to each other' (Feinberg, 1993, p. 198). And 'social development is possible only through the dynamic interaction of this social dimension with the unique, creative individual' (Rosenthal, op.cit., p. 385).

In 'My Pedagogic Creed', Dewey himself tells us

> I believe that the individual who is to be educated is a social individual, and that society is an organic union of individuals. If we eliminate the social factor from the child we are left only with an abstraction; if we eliminate the individual factor from society, we are left only with an inert and lifeless mass.

We have seen that this issue of individual and community is also crucial to interpretations of postmodernism, especially in relation to its implications for democratic theory. It is an issue which surfaces in areas of educational practice such as that of multicultural policies where, in many countries, as Sandra Rosenthal (1993, p. 377) says of America, we have been moving 'from the ideal of the grand melting pot to that of the grand accumulation of aggregates'. Both of these extremes, however, as she goes on to claim, are 'destructive of the dynamics of true community' (*ibid.*), and neither is 'called for by the insights of Dewey's pragmatism' (*ibid.*). What is needed, and what was Dewey's ideal, is that 'the uniqueness of diverse cultures, as representative of the individual perspective, must be maintained not through separation from, but through a dynamic interplay with, the common perspective, bringing about a resultant enrichment of each' (*ibid.*).

There are many ways, then, in which Dewey's pragmatism offers a more attractive theory of knowledge, society and, as we shall see, education than that rationalist theory which it seeks to replace in all of these fields. For it is a theory which acknowledges, explains and facilitates those changes and developments in human knowledge, especially in the scientific sphere, which we have seen a view of human knowledge as problematic makes necessary. It is a theory which recognizes the importance of the individual but is able to reconcile this individualism with membership of a larger group or groups; and it does this not by denying individuality and demanding that it be dissolved into the collective, but by requiring every individual to accept a share in, and a joint responsibility for, the continued evolution of every social institution. It is, therefore, a theory which offers a basis, a recipe, for 'a society which controls its own evolution' (Rosenthal, op.cit., p. 384).

Finally, as we shall see, it is a theory which provides a more satisfactory basis for the planning of education in any society which purports to be democratic, and which claims to be manifesting those principles which we saw in Chapter 2 are the essential elements of democracy – individual freedom, equality, the guarantee of human rights and a share in the popular sovereignty.

It was asserted earlier that, in Dewey's pragmatism, theories of knowledge, democracy and education are inextricably intertwined. This view of democracy, therefore, is not only the focus of his social theory but it is also the key to an understanding of what he has to say about education. For if society is to be organized in such a way as to facilitate the evolution of knowledge, and indeed its own development, through the productive interaction of its members, it will require a particular form of education, one which is geared to this evolutionary theory of knowledge. And, conversely, that form of education will require the provision of a democratic social setting if it is to flourish and to promote the continuing evolution of knowledge.

A brief exploration of Dewey's views on education, then, will both further elucidate his theories of knowledge and of democracy and lead us naturally on to that discussion of the implications of democratic theory for both the theory and the practice of education which the final section of this book will seek to provide.

PRAGMATISM AND EDUCATION

For the pragmatist, education cannot be a process by which the young are presented with 'knowledge' in a manner which suggests to them that, because it is 'school' knowledge, or because it has been ordained by the government, or because of the authority of the person or body offering it to them, or for any other reason, it is unchallengeable and must be accepted without question.

Whatever 'knowledge' pupils are offered they must be encouraged to recognize as problematic. And the most important things they must learn through their education are, first, that the validity of knowledge does not derive from its source and, second, that their central task is to learn to question and challenge all the 'knowledge' they are presented with. In short, they must learn how to view the world, in all its aspects, from a questioning perspective. 'Education is not fundamentally the transmission of information but rather development of the skills of experimental inquiry' (Rosenthal, *ibid.*).

Further, they must learn that it may be necessary to jettison even well entrenched beliefs if these prove unable to satisfy the appropriate tests of their validity. For it is, after all, by this process of rejection that much scientific and technological advance has been facilitated in recent times, by falsification rather than verification.

Such a view of education and of the school curriculum entails a complete reconceptualization of both. For what is now central to both is a set of procedures rather than a collection of subjects or bodies of knowledge. And the educative process now becomes not one whose prime concern is the transmission and assimilation of 'knowledge' but one whose focus is the development of certain intellectual capacities and, in particular, the capacity to challenge the assertions of others, especially when these assertions are couched in absolutist terms or forms. It is the kind of empowerment we have seen Freire and others advocating and which we have already suggested is an essential purpose of education in a democratic society.

In Dewey's view, these capacities can only be effectively developed if education and the curriculum are conceived in terms not of their content but in terms of experience. For the kind of development which is envisaged cannot be brought about by the assimilation of knowledge; it can only be attained by using, testing and developing knowledge in the process of solving real problems – in short, by addressing a problem, framing a hypothetical solution and then testing that hypothesis to see if it 'works'.

Educational or curriculum planning, therefore, must start not from a statement of the bodies of knowledge to be acquired by the pupil but with a consideration of the devices and strategies to be employed in order to make this kind of experience available to every pupil in the most effective form. For education is not the assimilation of whatever at any given time happens to be the currently accepted corpus of human knowledge; it is the process by which one learns to challenge and test that corpus. Notable among these strategies and devices have been those methods of 'enquiry' or 'discovery' which have been advocated by those wishing to promote this kind of approach to education, and which have tended to be the focus for many of its critics.

It follows from this that the test of the effectiveness of this form of education is not a measurement of the amount of information which has been assimilated and retained; it is an assessment of the extent of the development which has occurred. Growth, therefore, becomes the only criterion by which we can evaluate educational progress. It has to be evaluated as a process, and not in terms of extrinsic objectives achieved or knowledge-content assimilated.

And it follows further that, within this theory of the continuous evolution of all aspects of existence, this process of growth cannot be seen as having a finite end. One of Dewey's criticisms of traditional approaches to education is that 'growth is seen as *having* an end, instead of *being* an end' (1916, Chap. 4, Sec. 3.1.). It is not, therefore, a process which is limited to education or the years of formal schooling; the whole point is that it is seen as the proper way of life for the evolving human being so that, in a sense, education must be seen as a lifelong process, a continuing process of challenge and questioning. 'The educational process has no end beyond itself; it is its own end' (*ibid.*).

One can see why this theory of education has not always been popular with politicians or with others – 'ecclesiastical, nationalistic, militaristic, economic, and racial – who assume that they are the trustees of immutable beliefs and practices, and who therefore seek to abridge the right of the people to inquire into certain departments of life' (Childs, 1956, p. 286). In postmodern terms, these are the wielders, the manipulators, of power and the legitimators of discourse. And one can now see some of the reasons for that holding on to outmoded rationalist theories which we have noted before. We have here also one clear explanation of the campaign which has been mounted against 'progressivism' as it was developing in the primary schools of the UK, and of why that campaign has been firmly located on the political right.

We must note, however, that there is a clear case for saying that to be opposed to this form of education is to be opposed to democracy itself. For we have seen the ways in which it might be claimed that the kind of open and constantly questioning approach to human knowledge which is the essence of this view is also a major element of democracy. Conversely, we have seen how the imposition of values, through the selection and distribution of knowledge, and the legitimation of discourse, can be, has been and continues to be used as a device for social control by whatever is the dominant group in a society; and we have recognized this as the very antithesis of democracy. And we have noted Paolo Freire's proposed solution to this, namely to use the education system as a device for providing pupils with that reflexive perspective which will give them some control over their own destinies, to offer them empowerment.

It is precisely this that the pragmatists' form of education is seeking to achieve. And it is that, as much as any other feature of it, which makes it a powerful statement of what education should look like in a democratic society. It must be stressed once again, however, that it entails a complete reconceptualization of education and of the curriculum, to match that reconceptualization of knowledge which is characteristic of pragmatism, and indeed of postmodernism.

There continue to be those, as we have just seen, however, for whom the creation of a population educated to take nothing on trust, to challenge what they are offered as absolutes, to think for themselves and to assert their own opinions, preferences and values is a source of concern rather than of delight. And 'many of the current attacks on the new education are inspired by groups who fear a theory and program of education that is committed to the nurture of consistent experimental and democratic attitudes in the young' (Childs, *ibid.*). In short, and not to put too fine a point on it, there are those who have their own vested interests in undermining democratic processes or in keeping them to the minimum consonant with that show of democracy which they recognize the need to maintain.

It is worth noting, however, that the criticisms which have been offered in the attempt to discredit this theory of education have seldom carried much substance. Even the more serious attempts at criticism have too often failed to appreciate the level at which the attack should be mounted or, more precisely, the appropriate target for the attack. There have been many criticisms, both of pragmatism and of that 'progressive' form of education and curriculum which has been derived from it, which, as was suggested above, have felt it adequate to address it simply as a theory of education, and have failed to recognize that its base is in a theory of knowledge, and a social theory, quite distinct from, and incompatible with, that perspective from which their criticisms have been mounted (Blenkin and Kelly, 1981; Kelly, 1986). This may be likened to engaging in criticism of poetry by the rules of prose, or of rugby football by the rules of 'soccer'. It is to regard difference of code as merely a difference of style. It might now also be seen as comparable to offering a critique of postmodernism from a modernist perspective.

This fallacious procedure has been most evident in the criticisms which have been offered of 'discovery' or 'inquiry' approaches to education. For such criticism has assumed that the advocacy of these was no more than a recommendation for a teaching/learning methodology, a device for the effective transmission of those bodies of knowledge which a rationalist epistemology insists that children must acquire, those intrinsically worthwhile bodies of knowledge we discussed earlier (Dearden, 1976). The criticism has thus usually taken the form of pointing out that to learn all of these things by discovery or individual enquiry is a lengthy and inefficient process, and that, as a consequence, many important areas of knowledge are often omitted from a child's education.

Such criticism is quite naive and again misses the point. For it fails to recognize the reconceptualization of education and curriculum which these approaches are seeking to reflect, that reconceptualization which is the inevitable consequence of the different epistemological base from which these theories start. As a critique of pragmatism, then, or even of these approaches, it is quite, and literally, meaningless, and carries no weight at all.

In the same way, criticisms of the concepts of growth and experience as the central concerns of education have too often missed the point and failed, again usually because they are entrenched in a rationalist concept of objectively worthwhile knowledge, to recognize the significance of the reconceptualization of education as process. Suggestions that any kind of growth will do, that any kind of experience is acceptable, that a *laissez-faire* policy must inevitably follow, since the pragmatist will allow no absolute value system within which an evaluation of kinds of growth or kinds of experience can be made, again miss the point. For Dewey makes it quite clear that the criteria of evaluation lie in the process itself and not in what it is being directed towards, that, as we have seen, growth does not *have* an end, it *is* an end. Again, therefore, it is the reconceptualization which is crucial.

Criticisms of this kind, however motivated, do at least have the merit of attempting to take up the issue in philosophical terms. There have been other criticisms of this approach to education, especially those right-wing attacks on that form of education which has been dubbed 'progressive', which have not even made the attempt at offering reasoned argument but have resorted merely to rhetoric, and particularly to that 'discourse of derision' (Ball, 1990) which consists of nothing more than attempts to 'rubbish' the opposition.

It is of course of some interest in the context of our present discussion to find that there are those who, in the twentieth century, will rubbish a theory for being *progressive*. But the fact that there are makes our point for us better than reasoned argument, since it alerts us to the kinds of threat to democracy which continue to be ever present.

It also goes some way to explaining why, despite the intellectual developments we have explored in this and previous chapters, the main thrust of educational policies continues to be traditional and fundamentally absolutist – a 'back to basics' style of planning which, as we can now see, must be grounded either in ignorance or in fear and apprehension, and a desire to impede the development of genuinely democratic structures.

What this chapter has sought to demonstrate is that such policies are essentially anti-democratic. The next section of this book will seek to elaborate on that claim by considering what criteria education in a democracy must satisfy and evaluating current policies and practices in some detail in the light of those criteria.

SUMMARY AND CONCLUSIONS TO PART 2

This chapter has sought to build on the exploration of the problem of knowledge which was undertaken in Chapter 3 by identifying the implications for democratic theory of the theories of knowledge examined there. It has also, and inevitably, begun to identify in broad terms their implications for the development of a democratic form of education.

We first considered the kind of society which seems to be an inevitable result of the adoption of a view of knowledge as fixed, as objective, as, at least in the long term, certain and unquestionable. And we concluded that, as had been foreshadowed in our discussion of metaphysical theories of the state in Chapter 1, such a view of knowledge cannot be reconciled with those principles of democratic living we had identified in Chapter 2. For it offers no scope for individual opinion or for those cultural differences which we had claimed are of the essence of democracy, especially in the context of modern, complex and pluralist societies.

We were also forced to the conclusion that a system of education which is predicated on this kind of view of knowledge, as we saw most current systems are, must also, and for the same reasons, be anti-democratic. And we noted the claims of those who have sought to alert us to 'the politics of knowledge' that to plan an education system in terms of certain bodies of knowledge to be distributed, transmitted and assimilated is to use that system as a means of social and political control. It is in fact to use the education system in exactly the same way as totalitarian governments can be seen to have done, albeit in a less overt manner, to manipulate a society in the interests of the dominant group, that group which has control of the system.

This is a practice which transgresses every principle of democracy our earlier chapters have identified. For it limits the freedom of the individual; it denies equality and social mobility; it infringes human rights; it erodes the notion of popular sovereignty; and it reveals a form of government which is concerned with its own interests and does not accept the responsibility to rule in the best interests of the people as a whole.

We then turned to a discussion of the political implications of those alternative theories of knowledge which Chapter 3 explored. We noted that, on one kind of interpretation, postmodernism, rejecting as it does all forms of totalizing theory, can be seen as supporting the demolition of all moral and social systems. Such an interpretation, we saw, renders any discussion of the moral system of democracy impossible, since society must now be seen as no more than an anarchic collection of competing ideologies. It was argued, however, that, on a different and, it was suggested, more plausible, interpretation, postmodernism might be seen as supporting democratic theory.

On such an interpretation, postmodernism, and indeed all views of knowledge which begin from a less confident and dogmatic view of knowledge, cannot but recognize the need for an openness in society. And that openness is necessary because of that lack of dogmatism, because of the need to create a social and political environment in which 'knowledge' can genuinely be challenged and, when appropriate, modified and changed, and because of the importance of a social and political context which can accommodate difference.

Further, when we turned our attention to the question of what kind of education system such a society would require, we found that this could only be an education system which was itself open in the same way. For, first, there can be no more justification for dogmatism in education than in any other aspect of society. Second, in the face of this kind of tentative and hypothetical knowledge, pupils must not merely be required to assimilate what currently counts as knowledge, they must learn above all things to challenge, to evaluate and, if necessary, to change it. And, third, they must learn to tolerate, even to embrace, difference – social, cultural, moral and political.

This we noted in turn entails a complete reconceptualization of education and curriculum, to match that new view of human knowledge which is its base. It is not merely a change of educational methods; it is a more substantial change in the way in which education is conceived. It is, however, a change that, it was claimed, is necessitated by an acceptance of the uncertain and problematic nature of human knowledge. And, we concluded, for much the same reasons, it is a change which is required by any genuine commitment to democracy.

We finally noted that these changes have been, and continue to be, opposed in many quarters, particularly by those who, for whatever reason, find it difficult to live with the idea of a society in which everyone is encouraged to challenge what he or she is offered as 'received wisdom' and to think for him or herself. Such opposition, however, it was claimed, is not merely to be seen as opposition to a particular form of education theory. It is opposition to democracy itself.

We now turn in our final part to consider some specific examples of this. For there we will seek to elaborate on the principles which must undergird policies and practices for education in a democratic society, and to evaluate current practices against the criteria, the template, we will have developed. This will provide us with an approach from two directions, the positive and the negative, to the question of what a properly democratic system of education might look like.

PART 3:

Democracy and Education

5

EDUCATION IN A DEMOCRATIC SOCIETY: BASIC PRINCIPLES

Dialogue is the only way, not only in the vital question of political order, but in all the expressions of our being. Only by virtue of faith, however, does Dialogue have power and meaning: by faith in humankind and in their possibilities, by faith that I can only become truly myself when other people also become themselves.

(Freire, 1976, p. 45)

One of the major tasks which education must perform in a democratic society is the proper preparation of young citizens for the roles and responsibilities they must be ready to take on when they reach maturity. An exploration of how that task might be approached and accomplished will be the subject of Chapter 8.

There is much more than that, however, to education in a democratic society. For we must not merely teach young people to play their parts, we must do so within a context which reflects the fundamental principles of that democratic form of social living for which we are preparing them. It is perhaps putting it too glibly and simplisticly to express this by saying that we must practise what we preach. But that is certainly a part of it, since no one, and especially not children, will accept moral preaching which is not backed by moral practice.

More important, however, is the point, which we have already made on several occasions, that it is not enough for democratic institutions and policies to be planned and framed by democratically elected governments, or even by majority vote. For a society will not be truly democratic if the basic principles of democracy are not reflected in every one of its social institutions. And the major threat to the maintenance and development of democratic social systems comes from a failure to ensure an adherence to these principles in every area of social living, and not merely in the election of government.

Those basic principles we sought to identify in Part 1. And we stressed there what seemed to be the minimum requirements of any concept of democracy, the most basic of its underlying principles.

In general terms, we suggested that any society with claims to being democratic must be based on a positive view of human nature as, if not perfectible, at least capable of reaching decisions which are in the general interest rather than merely expressions of personal desire and/or sectional interests, and of recognizing that general interest as being supreme. We concluded from this that the main task of government in such a society is to reconcile the conflicting interests of the many different groups within society and to support the development of a moral system which is based on some notion of collective responsibility and mutual interdependence.

From that position, we noted Aristotle's claim that society exists not just to support and protect the lives of its citizens but also to promote 'the good life', and in Chapter 4 we saw Dewey's definition of a democratic society as one 'which makes provision for participation in its good of all its members on equal terms' (1916, Chap. 7, Summary). And we suggested that this must be a major characteristic of any society which might be called democratic. Its concern must be positively to enrich the life of every citizen and not merely to offer protection from the potential incursions of others into individual freedom. Furthermore as a corollary of this, we noted in Chapter 2 the Roman concept of *virtus*, the notion that those elected to office in a democratic society have a moral obligation to fulfil the duties of office, in so far as they are able, in the best interests of the society or community as a whole. And we finally considered in more specific detail the four major principles which seemed to emerge from, and indeed to underpin, this kind of moral commitment – the equality of all citizens, the protection of human rights, individual freedom within a social context and the maintenance of popular sovereignty.

It was noted that these principles are often in conflict with each other and will need to be reconciled. That we saw as the prime task of good government. We stressed, however, that the justification for any such act of reconciliation must be derived from the principles themselves and can never be based on sectional interests.

This part now turns the spotlight directly onto that social institution we call education. For there, perhaps more than anywhere else, it is vital that our democratic principles pervade, in order that those principles be clearly communicated to the rising generation of future citizens, and moreover that they be so communicated through practice as well as preaching.

We have noted before the crucial role which education plays in the maintenance and development of any kind of political system. This has been fully appreciated by those who have wished to establish and maintain totalitarian systems. And it is no less central to the preservation of democracy. It was not a coincidence that Rousseau published his *Émile* and his *Social Contract* in the same year (1762), and he himself drew attention to the fact that the two works belonged together (Peukertruth, 1993). And it is important to note at the outset of this discussion that, as a general principle, 'how serious we are about democracy is revealed in how serious we are about education' (Peukertruth, op.cit., p. 167).

The intention now, therefore, is to explore in greater detail what those democratic principles we have identified imply for both the theory and the practice of education in a democratic society, so that we can go on to consider some of the practices which put them at risk and thus endanger the continuation of democracy itself. And, at the same time, in pursuance of that parallel theme of the book, a further concern will be to analyse the implications for the theory and the practice of education in a democratic society of the problem of knowledge which we discussed in Part 2. In short, having identified the main essentials of the knowledge debate in Chapter 3, and having begun to recognize the implications of that debate both for democracy and for education in Chapter 4, we will now focus more closely, and in greater detail, on the specifics of this issue.

There are two main reason for this. First, knowledge is the very stuff of education; it is impossible to conceive of, or to plan, any educational activity without recognizing the central role that some kind of knowledge-based transaction must play in it. Second, as we saw in Chapter 4, the potential for an undermining of democratic principles, whether by accident or design, through the systems devised for those knowledge-based transactions and for the distribution of knowledge is immeasurable. And we must recognize that this is one of the most serious, because one of the most insidious, sources of threat to the continued development of democratic forms of social living.

And so, in considering some of the more general features of education in a democratic society and some of the more general threats to it, we must also extend the discussion of the last chapter into a more detailed exploration of the implications of the knowledge debate for the theory and the practice of democratic forms of education.

With these two general themes in mind, then, the fundamental principles of democratic living and the implications of a postmodern perpective on human knowledge, we must now explore what our discussion so far implies for the planning and the practice of education in a democratic society.

In doing so, we must begin by again stressing a general point. Much of what follows, like much of what has gone before, may be seen as so 'idealistic' as to be unrealistic. It has been stressed on several occasions, however, that what this book sets out to do is deliberately idealistic, since its main concern is to analyse the notion of democracy as an ideal construct and to delineate those ideals which underpin a commitment to democratic forms of social organization.

It is recognized that, in the 'real world', societies which claim to be democratic will be seen to fall far short of these ideals. The main purposes of identifying them, however, are, first, to be able to judge how far short of them they fall and, second and much the more important, to be able to ascertain whether they are seriously seeking to attain them or not. For it has been claimed several times that a major threat to the maintenance and development of democratic structures is the failure to appreciate in detail what are the essential characteristics of such structures, what are the criteria which they must be seeking to satisfy. And it is plain that, if they are not constantly reminded of these criteria, governments of whatever stripe will find it relatively easy, as they clearly do, to ignore them in the framing of policies.

Furthermore, it has also been emphasized on several occasions that to be committed to democracy as a form of social organization is to be committed to several, quite specific, value positions, that democracy is a moral and not merely a political concept. And while it has also been made clear that it is not the purpose of this book either to present arguments in support of these value positions or to persuade anyone to adopt them, it has also been stressed throughout that the book's main purpose is to elucidate what those value positions are, what a commitment to democracy entails, so that, if we are so committed, as we saw in our Introduction Plato suggests, our 'behaviour will reflect the principles of that city and no other'.

We have also seen that pre-eminent among those value positions, indeed a common denominator of them, is a positive view of human nature, a faith in human nature. And the point we must note here, at the very beginning of our search for the basic principles of education in a democratic society, is that this is an underlying feature of all of them, a *sine qua non*, without which, as the Latin makes clear, the other principles would be meaningless and empty.

FAITH IN HUMAN NATURE

There is no point or purpose in discussing education in a democratic society, or indeed of speaking of democracy itself, unless one starts with this kind of faith in human nature. This is well expressed in the quotation from Paulo Freire at the head of this chapter. The kind of free interchange between human beings he terms 'Dialogue' has no meaning except within the kind of framework offered by 'faith in humankind and in their possibilities' (op.cit., p. 45), possibilities which may of course go well beyond actualities.

And what is of further importance in that same quotation is the assertion that such faith is accompanied by 'faith that I can only become truly myself when other people also become themselves' (*ibid*). For that sums up the fundamental value which those who are truly committed to democratic forms must embrace, since it entails all of those characteristics of democracy we have identified earlier – a respect for the rights of others, a belief in individual freedom, a commitment to social equality and an acceptance of the right to self-determination through some form of popular sovereignty. And beyond that it emphasizes that an adherence to these values not only makes social living possible but it also makes it an enriching experience.

All these ideals then are predicated on a view of, and faith in, human nature as capable of recognizing and endeavouring to adhere to these principles, even though that view may need to be tempered by the awareness that human beings will often, perhaps regularly, fall short of those ideals. This general acceptance of a faith in the potentiality of humankind must be seen to underpin all of the principles of education in a democratic society this chapter will seek to identify. And it must also be seen as justifying the statement of what may appear to be unrealistic social aims and purposes. For if we come to regard those aims and purposes as unrealistic, we must concede that democracy itself is unrealistic also.

EDUCATION AS A HUMAN RIGHT

The first point to be made, as we begin our attempt to relate those general principles of democracy which we have identified to the practice of education, is that, if, as Dewey asserts (1916, Chap. 7, Summary), a part of the essence of democracy is that it 'makes provision for participation in its good of all its members on equal terms', the provision of education to the citizens of a democratic society must be seen as an obligation on the part of society and not as some kind of act of generosity on the part of government, or of any other agency. 'A true community . . . , to maintain itself as a community, requires universal education' (Rosenthal, 1993, p. 385).

And so, whatever the motivations of those who originally established state systems of education – and the case for regarding these as being primarily utilitarian and economic is strong (Gordon and Lawton, 1978) – the maintenance of them in a democratic society is justified entirely by the principles of democracy itself. 'To the father's duty to his son and the rich man's charity to his neighbours has been added the state's duty to its future citizens' (CACE, 1959, p. 54).

Furthermore, at a very basic and practical level, it makes no sense to place responsibility for government in the hands of every citizen without making adequate provision for every citizen to be educated to participate in government. For, as Wilfred Carr (1991a, p. 185) expresses it, 'the primary role of education in a democracy is to provide all its future members with the opportunity to develop those intellectual and moral qualities which meaningful participation in democratic life requires'. Or, to put it differently, to argue against the making of such provision is to admit that one does not regard popular sovereignty as either a political or a moral reality.

The contradiction, which Carr also draws to our attention, 'between the obvious need for members of a democracy to publicly debate issues of general public concern and the conspicuous failure of our society to provide the kind of education which genuine participation in such debate presupposes' (op.cit., p. 183), must raise questions not only about how serious the planners of current policies are about education but also, by inference, how serious they are about democracy.

The provision of education is both a moral and a practical imperative in a democratic society. For it is entailed both by the value system which the concept of democracy encapsulates and by the practical demands of preparing all citizens for appropriate forms of participation in government. Views of education, educational ideologies, which would exclude the idea of universal provision, then, are not compatible with any coherent notion of democracy. For not only do they ignore the moral imperative but they are also essentially advocating either that the governance of society be placed in the hands of a populace largely unprepared to conduct it sensibly or that it be left by default to a privileged few. In neither case are we being offered a sound theory of democratic government.

Denis Lawton (1989, p. 7), as we saw in Chapter 2, identifies 'four ideological positions concerning the debate between those who would plan education and those who would leave education to market forces'. The case being made here goes beyond that identification, and claims that to leave education to market forces is to adopt an ideology which is at odds with democratic theory. For it is to regard individual freedom as the only value and to ignore the need to reconcile the demands of freedom with those of the other, equally important, principles of democracy we have identified.

As has been pointed out on more than one occasion, to adopt such an ideology is a perfectly rational thing to do. What is not rational, or acceptable, is to lay claim at the same time to being an adherent of democracy. For adherence to a democratic ideology must commit one to far more than a theory of 'market forces' and, in particular, it must include an obligation to provide education as a human right. At the very least it must entail a recognition that a democratic society requires educated citizens. All of the positions Lawton (1989) delineates are identifiable educational ideologies. All of them are easy to discern in the current attitudes and policies of individuals and of governments. Only the last of them, however, that of 'the comprehensive planners', is in tune with those principles of democracy we have identified.

Many reasons are offered in support of their positions by those who are adherents of the other views. Policies of 'self-help' and independence, an unwillingness to interfere with individual freedom, a desire to keep public expenditure to a minimum, even a fear that to educate the masses beyond a certain level is to invite social unrest, all of these are advanced as reasons for not making a full and proper educational provision for all children and young people.

They are all of them legitimate arguments. They must be recognized, however, as also being essentially undemocratic, even anti-democratic, since they are at odds with the fundamental principles of democratic living, in particular because they do not recognize that basic obligation to educate everyone towards an active participation in democratic life. And, further, they must be seen as undermining the foundations of democratic living since, whatever their claims, they must contribute to the erosion of all those features which make a society democratic – equality of opportunity, the protection of human rights, the promotion of the freedom of every individual and full participation in the governance of society.

It is not enough for an education system in a democratic society merely to provide opportunity, even equal opportunity, for all children to have access to whatever is on offer – access to 'the ladder of opportunity'. There is a further obligation to ensure that what is on offer is appropriate for all children. And that in turn means that there must be a variety of provision designed to meet a range of different needs – a 'broad highway' rather than a narrow set of tramlines.

This further necessitates a recognition that the focus of educational provision must be as much on the advantages it can, and should, offer to each individual child as on the benefits which might accrue from the provision of education to society itself.

This point was made strongly and powerfully as long ago as 1959 in the UK in the report of the Crowther committee (CACE, 1959). That report identified what it described as the 'burdens and benefits' of an education system. 'It is partly a burden on the national income, partly a means of sustaining it' (op.cit., para. 87). In other words, an education system must be planned not only in terms of the economic advantages society gets out of it but also in terms of what it must be prepared to put into it for the benefit of the pupils, and ultimately of course for the benefit of the quality of life for every citizen. For, as the report also asserts, 'education is at one and the same time both a basic human right and a necessary individual contribution to society' (op.cit. para. 82); 'education is a national investment' (op.cit., para. 83) but it is also 'the right of every boy and girl' (*ibid.*); and 'that right exists regardless of whether, in each individual case, there will be any return' (*ibid.*).

Furthermore, the report declares an unwillingness to disentangle these two purposes of education, telling us (op.cit., para. 86):

> Both are worthy and compelling, and we accept them both. Primacy must be given to the human rights of the individual boy or girl. But we do not believe that the pursuit of national efficiency can be ranked much lower – not least because without it the human rights themselves will not be secure ... There are indeed parts of everybody's education which have no economic value, and there is nobody whose education is entirely without it.

The report justifies its concern with the notion of educational provision as a human right on the grounds that 'education is one of the social services of the welfare state' (op.cit., para. 83). What we have discovered about the basic principles of democracy, however, must take us beyond that. For we have established that those principles require us to ensure that every citizen in a democratic society is provided with an education which will prepare him or her for a life of full participation in that society. And the 'return' to society from such educational provision is not merely economic (although we must not lose sight of the importance of that); that 'return' consists also, and equally, in the enrichment of the life of society which a properly educated citizenry must bring, and indeed of the maintenance of democracy itself:

> A rational society is one in which education is self-evidently a public good rather than a private utility and hence a society which regards the

need to educate all its future members to participate in debates about the future shape of their society as a moral imperative quite independent of instrumental considerations or utilitarian concerns.

(Carr, 1991a, p. 189, referring to Gutmann, 1987)

EQUALITY OF ENTITLEMENT

Another way of expressing this human right to education, another dimension of this principle of educational planning in a democratic society, is the claim that, in such a society, all pupils have an equal right to appropriate educational provision. A commitment to democracy entails a corresponding commitment to a democratic rather than a meritocratic concept of equality, to egalitarianism rather than to élitism. It commits us to the provision of a form of curriculum which will be appropriate to all pupils and not merely to those whose abilities, preferences, values and social/ethnic, cultural background predispose them towards the kind of curriculum which might be devised with nothing beyond the economic advantages of society in view. It demands a curriculum which goes far beyond the 'basics' (whatever they might be). It necessitates a curriculum whose prime purpose will be to support the development of all pupils on all fronts – moral, social and political as well as intellectual. For this is what is involved in a recognition of education as a human right and not either as a privilege or as a device for social engineering.

In a democratic society we must see education from the perspective of that group of people Raymond Williams (1961) described as the 'public educators', those concerned to ensure the provision of appropriate educational opportunities for all, rather than from the perspective of his 'industrial trainers', satisfied with the production of a trained workforce and a parallel 'gentling of the masses', or even from that of his 'old humanists' who want to ensure the maintenance of the 'traditional' culture. Democratic principles, as we have seen, require that we view and plan education as Denis Lawton's 'comprehensive planners' advise (Lawton, 1989).

In a democratic society, then, education must be seen as a human right, as the entitlement of every child and, what is more important if only because more difficult to attain, it must be planned and implemented in such a manner as to reflect this. In essence, as we have seen before and must explore in detail again, this means that we must conceptualize curriculum as process rather than as content and education as development rather than as the assimilation of knowledge.

For we will not be able to achieve this equality of entitlement or ensure the protection of the human right to education of every child if we seek to do so by requiring every pupil to assimilate the same bodies of knowledge. Such an approach to curriculum planning is not only simplistic and naive but it is also dangerous in so far as it threatens the very democratic principles we are in process of identifying.

For it is not only a prime example of that use of the distribution of knowledge as a form of social and political control which we noted in Chapter 4, and thus reprehensible in the context of any kind of democratic moral system. It is also ineffective in practice as a means to the achievement of equality of entitlement, since its effect must be to alienate from educational opportunities large numbers of those pupils whose background and cultural origins, social or ethnic, render both the knowledge they are offered and the values implicit in that knowledge inappropriate to the kind of educational experiences they need as well as and, indeed, as a consequence of, being incompatible with what their own cultural background leads them to regard as important.

Quite massive evidence has been gleaned over the years by sociological studies which have revealed the scale, the nature and the causality of this kind of alienation. It is clear from that evidence that it is closely linked with social and ethnic background. What has perhaps been less clear, but is more important here, is the degree to which it is a function of the kind of curriculum which has been – and still often is – on offer. And it is not without significance that, with the extension of a content-based curriculum to the early years of education in England and Wales, as a result of the Education Act 1988 and its National Curriculum, it is now becoming a phenomenon of some significance there too (Barrett, 1989). A curriculum which has these effects cannot be regarded as an appropriate curriculum for a democratic society.

It is for this reason that it is being claimed here that we need a reconceptualization of curriculum if we are to produce a curriculum that is consonant with democratic principles, and that such a reconceptualization, as we shall see when we explore it in greater detail later in this chapter, must involve a move away from viewing it, and planning it, in terms simply of its content. The Plowden Report (CACE, 1967) argued that equality of educational opportunity does not imply commonality of provision. And, as Mary Warnock points out (1977, p. 26), 'there is a difference between claiming that everyone has an equal right to education and saying that everyone has a right to equal education'. What is being claimed here is that commonality of provision offers only a facade of equality and is in practice positively detrimental to its attainment, so that a curriculum which seeks to provide no more than this kind of commonality is not an appropriate curriculum for a genuinely democratic society.

To promote a genuine form of equality of entitlement, which is what a democratic curriculum must seek to do, a curriculum must not only be common to all but it must also be 'genuinely suitable for all, not suitable only for the middle-class or most academic' (Warnock, op.cit., p. 84). And so 'a system must be devised so flexible that it can be made to accommodate everyone, whatever his [or her] ability, whatever his [or her] cultural background' (*ibid.*). And 'it is possible to devise a curriculum which is both common and non-middle class, adaptable for all, and within which no-one is doomed to failure or frustration' (*ibid.*).

What is being added to those claims here is the assertion that, in the light of all that was said about knowledge in Part 2, and in the light of that alienation we have just noted, such a flexible curriculum can only be devised if we move away from the idea that its planning must start from a consideration of its common content.

There are two important concomitants of this claim which we must note. The first of these is that to decide that some areas of knowledge, and thus certain kinds of aesthetic, moral and cultural values shall be transmitted to all pupils and thus by inference that other kinds shall not, is to be guilty of that intolerance and dogmatism which we have seen a commitment to democracy cannot permit. For such a commitment, as we have also seen, entails a tolerance of all shades of opinion, preference and values. And that tolerance must be displayed in a curriculum which seeks to accommodate and reconcile these differences – an 'open' curriculum for an 'open' society. A curriculum whose content is preselected by any section of society cannot, by definition, satisfy that requirement, so that it cannot be a democratic curriculum.

Second, this would further suggest that the underlying rationale of such a curriculum must be one of co-operation and collaboration rather than of competition – a unity in difference rather than a disunity through sameness. For competition must imply an intolerance of others' values and achievements, and this must be the result of a curriculum which by its very shape and form demonstrates the existence of a single dominant ideology. At the very least, such a curriculum must make the promotion of tolerance more difficult. To recognize someone as an individual is to encourage that person so to see others. Conversely, not to be so recognized is an invitation not to acknowledge, and thus not to tolerate, the individuality of others.

What is needed is an openness to difference, a celebration of diversity, although this can and should be accompanied by an awareness that these are, or can be, complementary rather than inimical to agreement in areas of common concern. For a successful form of democratic living requires not only that differences be accommodated and tolerated but also that concessions be made and agreement reached where this is necessary for harmonious coexistence. It requires the 'dynamic interaction of this social dimension with the unique, creative individual' (Rosenthal, 1993, p. 385) which we noted in our discussion of Dewey's concept of democracy in Chapter 4. And for both the acceptance, even the celebration, of difference and the resolution of disagreements, tolerance and a spirit of co-operation are essential.

A curriculum conceived and framed in this way then, and not merely by preselected subject-content, is the only route towards the kind of universal provision we are claiming democracy requires. It is the only way in which we can hope to secure that human right to education and that entitlement which are essential to the continuation of democratic forms of social living. And it is the only way in which we can genuinely seek to promote the kind of mutual tolerance and co-operation which are equally crucial to the development of a successful democratic system.

It is also supported, as we have seen, by the analysis of knowledge which we undertook in Part 2. For the entitlement which a democratic structure entails is not an entitlement to have imposed upon one that knowledge and those values which the dominant group in society determines; it is an entitlement to have one's capacities and capabilities developed to the point where one can reach one's own decisions and frame one's own values. In a democratic society the entitlement is to individual autonomy and empowerment.

INDIVIDUAL AUTONOMY AND EMPOWERMENT

The third principle of democratic educational planning we must note is that the human right and the entitlement we have just been exploring are at root a right and an entitlement to individual autonomy and empowerment. The concept of individual autonomy is complex. For at one level it might seem to suggest a form of freedom from restraints which is indistinguishable from complete licence, and irreconcilable with other democratic values, and thus to imply that even the mere requirement that children attend compulsory schooling infringes its essentials – that problem which, in Chapter 2, we saw John Stuart Mill wrestling with.

On the other hand, it has been regarded as an essential ingredient of moral behaviour. We have seen, in discussing Kant's moral theory, how important for him is the will of the individual and how crucial it is to the moral nature of any action that the individual should perform that action out of autonomous choice rather than out of obedience to some external law. In Kant's view it is vital that we give ourselves the laws we obey. And although we have seen good reason for rejecting his parallel view that, in determining these laws, we have no choice beyond adherence to some concept of universal rationality, it is difficult to reject the underlying notion that moral behaviour must in some sense be freely chosen. For without that kind of prerequisite it is difficult to make sense of any notion of moral responsibility.

Indeed, those studies of moral development which have been undertaken by major contributors to our understanding of human development, such as Piaget (1932) and Kohlberg (1966), have seen the process of moral development as proceeding through several stages, the last of which, the climax of moral development, is that of autonomous moral thinking.

We will need to consider this in greater detail when we consider the issues of moral education in Chapter 8. What we must note here, however, as a further principle of education in a democratic society is that neither Piaget nor Kohlberg see this process as a natural development; neither takes the view that human beings develop morally in the way in which they develop physically, i.e. with or without external help and support. Moral growth or development requires education if it is to result in moral autonomy. And, in their view, many people never reach the autonomous stage.

This suggests in turn that individual autonomy cannot be viewed in that simplistic form which sees it as mere licence to act in whatever way the law permits. It is a far more complex concept than that. The right to choose is of little value if one lacks the understanding to use it intelligently, after careful thought and in a properly informed manner.

And a democracy requires citizens whose choices and decisions are made in precisely this way – not 'off the tops of their heads' but after informed and thoughtful debate with themselves and with others. A democracy can only operate effectively if its citizens not only have adequate opportunity for that debate or dialogue we have seen is crucial to its existence but also have the capability to use that opportunity as effectively as possible. It is impossible to deny, therefore, that a democracy needs citizens who are moral beings in the fullest sense of that term, and whose education has assisted them to achieve that status.

We will consider in more detail in Chapter 8 how children might be assisted to acquire that capability. What we must note here is that another fundamental principle of education in a democratic society is that all children have a right to the kind of education which seeks to develop their capacity for autonomous thinking and decision-making.

A second dimension of this which we must note is that the development of this capacity for autonomous thinking is a major part of that process of individual empowerment which we have also seen to be a crucial function of education in a democratic context. We noted in Chapter 4 that the restrictions on the development of individual autonomy, which it has been claimed are the inevitable accompaniment of the imposition of a curriculum whose content is determined by the dominant group within a society, can only be avoided by either 'deschooling' society or by planning curricula in a form and manner which will promote rather than obviate individual autonomy, which will empower rather than inhibit the individual pupil.

This we are now asserting to be an essential characteristic of any curriculum which lays claim to being appropriate for a democratic society. For, as we also noted in Chapter 4, the concept of democracy obliges us to be 'committed to the imperatives of empowering students and transforming the larger social order in the interests of a more just and equitable democracy' (McLaren, 1988, p. xi, referring to the work of Giroux).

Far from being designed to pacify and silence future citizens, to 'gentle the masses', education and curriculum in a democratic society must be centrally concerned with their emancipation. The masters of Imperial Rome were more than familiar with the powers and advantages (to them) of *panis circique* (bread and circuses), well aware that, if the populace was well fed and regularly entertained, it was likely to offer little resistance to all but the most outrageous of their political decisions. Such policies are the antithesis of democracy.

There are of course modern versions of 'bread and circuses' to be found, in particular, in certain sections of the communications media; and these must be recognized as a threat to democratic procedures. Above all, however, they must be recognized as having no place in educational provision. For it is not the role of education in a democratic society to foster passivity or apathy in the citizens of the future. On the contrary, educational provision must be positively designed to achieve the opposite, to encourage and promote questioning, challenge, critique, dialogue and debate. For the concern must be to release pupils from the chains of ignorance and apathy, to emancipate them, to empower them to take a proper share in the control of their own destinies and that of their society.

In part, education must do this because, in a democratic society, it is predicated on a view of individual autonomy and freedom. In part too, however, it must do it in an attempt to ensure that active participation in decision-making and/or the evaluation of social policies which we have seen to be essential to the maintenance and development of democratic structures. For as we saw Pericles asserting 2000 years ago, in a democracy the person who takes no interest in public affairs is to be considered not merely impractical but useless, as indeed he or she must be if unwilling to take any share in the government of society, and thus in the direction of his or her own destiny. The creation of a form of curriculum which will genuinely support the development of individual autonomy and the empowerment of future citizens, then, is one of the implications of the basic principle of individual freedom for the planning of education in a democratic context.

We have seen, however, on more than one occasion that a curriculum framed in terms only of its knowledge-content cannot support these aims, nor indeed any of the other aims we have identified. And we have suggested, therefore, that if the curriculum is to be able to do so, a different conceptual base for curriculum planning is needed, a reconceptualization of what we mean by curriculum, the purpose of which we can now see is to ensure that the curriculum we offer is compatible with the principles of democracy.

It is to a fuller consideration of what this entails that we now turn.

A RECONCEPTUALIZATION OF CURRICULUM

Fundamentally, the problem we have identified arises not merely from the control of curriculum content and the dogmatic dictation of what that content shall be but also, and more significantly, from the very conception of curriculum in terms solely of its content. We have noted before that education must involve some kind of engagement with knowledge. The problem we are facing here is that which arises when that engagement is seen simply in terms of the transmission (by the teacher) and the assimilation (by the pupil) of predetermined bodies of knowledge-content.

The solution to the problem must, therefore, lie, as we saw when discussing Dewey's theory of education in Chapter 4, in a more sophisticated analysis of that engagement. In short, it must lie in a conceptualizing of curriculum in terms of the *process* of learning rather than its content, and of education as *human development* rather than as the assimilation of knowledge. It is perhaps worth noting in this respect that both 'curriculum' and 'education' are terms whose etymological roots are verbal rather than substantive.

The first aspect of this which we must explore is that which relates to what we said in Chapter 4 about the concept of the 'open society' (Bernstein, 1967). The open society is characterized by what we saw Durkheim had called 'organic solidarity', a form of social integration which emphasizes differences between individuals rather than similarities, acknowledges diversity of values and views social roles as achieved rather than as ascribed.

What we must note now is that such an open society requires open schools or, more specifically, an open curriculum. What is needed, if the education system is to mirror the open nature of the democratic society, is a shift 'from a pedagogy which . . . was concerned with the learning of standard operations tied to specific contexts – to a pedagogy which emphasizes the exploration of principles; from schools which emphasize the teacher as a solution-giver to schools which emphasize the teacher as a problem poser or creator' (Bernstein, 1967). Open, democratic societies, for reasons we have noted on more than one occasion, require this kind of open school and open curriculum. And this in turn necessitates many changes in the way in which education is planned and implemented.

It necessitates, first of all, as Bernstein is suggesting, a significant change in the role of the teacher, and especially in patterns of authority in schools, a shift 'to more personalized forms of control where teachers and taught confront each other as individuals. The forms of social control appeal less to shared values, group loyalties and involvements; they are based rather upon the recognition of differences between individuals' (op.cit.).

The teacher's authority must be employed to support the development of the pupils' own powers of reasoning and to promote their ability to think for themselves and to reach their own conclusions, not to dictate those conclusions to them. For a central concern of education in a democratic society, as we have seen, is the promotion of personal autonomy. The teacher must be *an* authority rather than *in* authority. Or to use another kind of analysis of authority, that of Etzioni (1961), the only justifiable form of authority for the teacher to employ is authority which is 'normative' rather than 'calculative' or 'coercive'. And education, as Freire claimed, must be viewed as 'dialogue'.

A further reason for this shift is again that twentieth-century view of knowledge, which we explored in Chapter 3, and the concomitant claim that intolerance and dogmatism are out and that freedom of thought must be promoted from the earliest possible moment. It is here that the need for a reconceptualization of curriculum becomes apparent. And it also becomes clear that the kind of reconceptualization which is needed is that which, as we saw in Chapter 4, Dewey, operating from the same premises, advocated. For education must now become a matter of growth and development through experience; and the curriculum must be framed in terms of principles and processes, 'areas of experience' (DES, 1977), those experiences which might promote such growth and development, and not in terms of bodies of obsolescent knowledge to be assimilated – in terms of process rather than content. Pupils need to be assisted to learn to develop their own knowledge, understandings and, above all, values, not merely to swallow whole those of others, and especially not those of people whose aim it is to exercise control over their thinking.

This view of curriculum has also gained immense support from recent studies of child development, particularly those which have focused on the early cognitive development of neonates. These studies have led to what has been called a 'quiet revolution' (Bruner and Haste, 1987, p. 1). For detailed studies of the behaviour of neonates (Lewin, 1975; Bower, 1977; Bruner, 1981) have shown that, from the very point of birth, human beings seek to manipulate and control their environment, including the other human beings in that environment. From the very beginning, then, human beings are using and developing skills to act intelligently and to take control of their environment, and thus of their own lives.

It is argued, therefore, that education must be seen as the process of supporting the individual human being in developing these skills, since the only other purpose it could have would be to inhibit that development. And this in turn means, first, assisting in the development of modes of representation and understanding, different strategies for understanding the world, thinking about it and manipulating it, supporting the child in structuring his or her own knowledge; and, second, doing this in the context of the culture of the child's environment, helping the child to learn 'how to negotiate meaning in a manner congruent with the requirements of the culture' (Bruner and Haste, *ibid*.). The modes of representation are public modes. This further demands that we see education as an active process rather than as the passive assimilation of preselected bodies of knowledge.

And, finally, we should note Eliot Eisner's (1982) charge that current forms of education in western cultures are having the opposite effect and are counterproductive to the development of children's cognitive powers, since they reduce the opportunities for developing the ability to represent a wide range of sensory experience and thus for conceptualizing such experience. His concern is that we should start our educational planning from a more sophisticated view of human development. This important line of research reinforces our case not only for a reconceptualization of curriculum but also for the form we are claiming it must take.

There are several cogent reasons, therefore, why a democratic society requires a curriculum planned not as a vehicle for the transmission of subject-content but as a device for supporting individual development. Those reasons derive from the earlier points we have made in this chapter, those principles of education in a democratic society which we have already identified. For this is the only kind of curriculum which will offer genuine entitlement, and equality of entitlement, to all; and which will seek to empower and promote individual autonomy. It is also the only form of curriculum which will support and reflect that openness towards knowledge which is demanded not only by any concept of democracy but also by an acknowledgement of the problematic nature of human knowledge.

For the principle of education for autonomy and empowerment not only requires a reconceptualization of curriculum; nor does it only presuppose an acceptance of the uncertainty of all forms of human knowledge; it also has implications for the way in which 'knowledge' is handled in society. To argue that education and the school curriculum must be concerned to assist in the making of informed decisions, and to empower everyone to take responsibility for such decisions, is to imply further that the necessary information must be available and that all citizens should have access to it. And an acceptance of the problematic nature of knowledge reinforces the claim that they should be able in every sense – politically free and intellectually capable – to question and challenge the 'knowledge' and information they are offered.

This takes us on to our next major principle of educational planning in a democratic society – freedom and openness in the face of knowledge.

OPENNESS IN THE FACE OF KNOWLEDGE

This principle derives from what we have noted in earlier chapters concerning not only the importance of individual freedom but also the evolution of knowledge and the consequent need to create a social climate which will be supportive to both.

For openness in the face of knowledge, as we have seen in earlier chapters, is essential not only for the maintenance and development of democratic social forms but it is also equally important for the continued development of human understanding itself. 'The rational development of knowledge and the effective operation of democracy *both* depend on the existence of an informed and critical community, i.e. a community which has been "educated" in the analytical skills which will enable them to evaluate and compare rival sets of assertions, arguments and "facts"' (Winter, 1991, p. 468).

In Part 2 it was argued that a rationalist perspective on knowledge is incompatible with a concept of democracy. For such a view of knowledge cannot accommodate differences of opinion or of values, aesthetic, moral, cultural and even, ultimately, political. It cannot thus accommodate questioning and challenge to the prevailing orthodoxy. Nor can it lead in practice to any form of social or cultural equality, since there can be no equality, even of respect, in a context where one version of knowledge, values and culture is deemed to be superior to all others and, as a result, is imposed on every member of society through the education system and all other related social institutions. It leads inexorably, therefore, to that linking of knowledge with political power which we saw postmodernism has alerted us to. And Chapter 4 further sought to demonstrate why, as a consequence, a rationalist epistemology is incompatible with the creation of a democratic system of education.

Democracy, therefore, it was argued, implies a view of knowledge as uncertain, tentative, provisional, evolutionary and subject to constant challenge, questioning and possible modification and change. And this is especially important to appreciate in the field of values since, even if one can expect a reasonable, albeit provisional, consensus of opinion on matters scientific, a public acceptance of an agreed corpus of current knowledge and understandings, there can be no comparable expectation in the realm of human values.

Such an expectation in that area cannot be sustained for a moment once one contemplates the wide variety of value positions that people, individually and in groups, quite reasonably take on a range of moral issues, on some of which even the churches are divided, and the similar range of cultural differences to be seen in modern pluralist societies. Indeed, it was argued earlier that it is this very variety which makes life interesting, which enriches life for everyone, which constitutes one of the major attractions of democracy, but which also makes the practice of democracy, the task of fairly and justly reconciling these differences, immeasurably difficult.

We noted, therefore, in Chapter 4 that the fundamental principles of democracy, supported by this view of knowledge and values, entail that no one may legitimately be intolerant or dogmatic over particular areas of knowledge, and especially over particular value stances. They also entail the right of every member of society and every constituent group within society to freedom of opinion and of values.

We saw, however, when we considered the principle of individual autonomy earlier in this chapter, that the exercise of that freedom of opinion and values is not, or should not be, a random matter. There is a crucial difference between an informed opinion and one reached 'off the top of one's head'. And it was suggested there that the preparation of future citizens to make such informed opinions is a major task for the education system in a democratic society.

We must now note the other side of that coin. For if the citizens of a democratic society are to be enabled to reach informed opinions, decisions and evaluations of public policies, they need not only to have been educated so to do but they also need access to such 'knowledge', understanding and information as is necessary for doing so. Freedom of access to such 'knowledge', understanding and information is crucial. And its justification comes from two sources. For, as we have seen, such freedom is required, first, by the view of human knowledge which is the essence of the postmodern perspective, and the resultant need to oppose the use of knowledge and the discourses in which it is enshrined as tools for the exercise of political power. And, second, it is also essential for the proper exercise by the individual of his or her democratic rights.

This is also a further aspect of another point which has been made on more than one occasion, that democracy entails more than a periodic election of a government which then has *carte blanche* to govern as it will, that relapse into slavery of which we have seen Rousseau accuses the British constitution. For in a democratic society, an informed citizenry is entitled to clear reasons for the framing of any set of policies and to access to the knowledge, the understanding, the information and indeed the choices upon which such policies are based. For without that it is in no position to make a proper evaluation of those policies. And it is entitled to be permitted, indeed encouraged, to make such evaluations rather than to be kept in the dark and 'sold' policies by the use of rhetoric and other devices more appropriate to the work of barrow boys or girls and travelling salespersons. Freedom of access to public knowledge (except of course at times of dire national emergency) is a *sine qua non* of democracy.

The corollary of this is that for any group or body, even the elected government, to seek to exercise control over the distribution of knowledge, or to limit and suppress that distribution by denying access to what should be public information, is anti-democratic and must ultimately lead to the demise of democratic forms. For to attempt this, whether consciously or not, is to embrace an intolerant and dogmatic perspective on knowledge; and that, as we have seen, is in essence totalitarian and quite incompatible with both democracy and twentieth-century views of human knowledge. In fact, it is one of the most characteristic and recognizable strategies for the kind of political control which is exercised in totalitarian societies. Recourse to secrecy by a democratically elected government can never be condoned in areas of social policy, even if under certain circumstances it may be acceptable in foreign policy, since it is not only undemocratic; it is also a positive threat to the maintenance and development of democracy.

This is why the freedom of the press, and of the other media of mass communication, although too often abused and used irresponsibly, is a crucial safeguard for democracy. This is why the existence of a financially, and politically, independent radio and television network is similarly important. And this is why freedom of knowledge and information within education is equally central to the maintenance and the continuing development of democratic forms.

This freedom of knowledge and information within education has long been protected by procedures to support academic freedom within university systems and, to a lesser extent, by a minimizing of political control over the school curriculum, especially in the UK. We must move on, therefore, to a brief consideration of academic freedom before we turn our attention, in Chapters 6 and 7, to the ways in which both of these sources of protection have been considerably diminished by the trend of recent policies for education.

Higher education is the sector of society where the responsibility for protecting the kind of openness in the face of knowledge a democratic society requires most obviously resides. For it is here that most of the activities concerned with research and the development of knowledge and understanding occur. It is thus here that we can most productively focus our discussion of academic freedom.

Exploration of the issue of academic freedom in higher education will also take us from our theoretical discussion of the underlying principles of education in a democratic society towards the consideration of some of the realities of current practices in this field which will be the concern of Chapters 6 and 7. For it is impossible to go any further in exploring the ideal without facing up to the reality.

ACADEMIC FREEDOM AND ACADEMIC AUTONOMY

The claim was made by Newman (1859) in the middle of the last century that universities should be places for the pursuit of knowledge for its own sake. That view still persists in many places, although it has been considerably eroded in recent times. For there has been a massive shift in recent years in the curriculum of higher education, as indeed of education generally, towards a utilitarian and vocational emphasis. And this has happened in response to the demand, supported by government, that the public money spent on higher education should yield some tangible return in the form of young people who have been assisted towards the development of a range of useful knowledge, skills and understanding which they will then be able to employ to the benefit of society at large. The shift, then, has been towards the Crowther Report's view of education as a 'national investment' and away from its parallel concern with education as a human right (CACE, 1959).

It would be foolish to take a stance that is completely opposed to this. For there is no doubt that complex, developed, modern technological societies do require this kind of continuous supply of highly trained and skilled persons. What must be argued alongside this, however, is the (not incompatible) point that a postmodern view of knowledge and a commitment to democracy together require that this should not be all that higher education seeks to achieve nor, indeed, should it be all that students at that level acquire.

For we have seen already that technological advances themselves have most often come from challenge to existing orthodoxies, so that even at the utilitarian, instrumental level of economic advantage, it must pay to *educate* rather then merely to *train* the next generation, to develop a modern equivalent of what the Crowther Report (CACE, 1959) described as 'general mechanical ability' rather than merely to induct students into those currently accepted skills, knowledge and understandings which we know to be obsolescent. Or, to express it in the words of the Robbins Report (Committee on Higher Education, 1963, p. 8), 'we do not believe that modern societies can achieve their aims of economic growth and higher cultural standards without making the most of the talents of their citizens . . . But beyond that, education ministers intimately to ultimate ends, in developing man's capacity to understand, to contemplate and to create'.

More importantly, however, the very notion of democracy requires that students, of whatever areas of knowledge, be encouraged to address that knowledge from a questioning perspective, to challenge what currently counts as knowledge and especially to debate the values implicit in it. And so, even in areas where the main point of study may be deemed to be extrinsic to the activity itself, it is vital that that knowledge be addressed in its own right – not merely in terms of what it is *for*, but also in respect of what it *is*.

Even in these areas, then, academic freedom is crucial for both teacher and taught, since it is the only route to securing a context in which knowledge can develop and the student can acquire those habits of scepticism and challenge which are essential to all in a democratic society.

Next we must note that it is now widely accepted that universities have two main and inter-related functions – teaching and research. Indeed, in the UK they are now financed under separate funding mechanisms in respect of these two functions. And again an acceptance both of the problematic nature of human knowledge and of the basic principles of democracy require that in respect of both of these functions there should be complete academic freedom, for both teacher/researchers and students.

Furthermore, the form of academic freedom which is essential is that defined in the Robbins Report (Committee on Higher Education, 1963, p. 229): 'The concept of academic freedom entertained in most western countries has two aspects, personal and institutional. It involves the relationships of the individual teacher to his colleagues, his pupils and his institution. It involves the relations of academic institutions to society and the institutions of government.' This entails, therefore, academic freedom for individuals and academic autonomy for institutions.

In principle, then, the notion that there should be any form of political control over what is taught, what is learnt or what is researched is, for reasons we have explored fully, incompatible with any concept of democracy. Indeed, I have argued elsewhere (Kelly, 1993, p. 129) that

> if John Locke had appreciated, as with hindsight we can today, the full significance of the empiricist epistemology to whose foundation he contributed so much, it is certain that he would have included a politically independent university system (if not a politically independent education system) as one of those 'checks and balances' which he regarded as essential for the maintenance of a democratic [or at least a liberal] constitution, a check on political control of equal importance to, if rather different from, that offered by the politically independent judiciary he did advise.

Where knowledge is uncertain and tentative, and values are recognized as subjective, as 'socially constructed', a context in which knowledge can evolve and in which all shades of value and opinion can find tolerance is essential.

Governments do of course have a proper concern with education, including higher education. They are the guardians of the taxpayers' money and have a responsibility to see that it is not 'wasted' or used 'unwisely'. And there is no doubt that many of the current changes we are witnessing in the higher education systems of the UK and elsewhere are prompted by an intention to effect financial savings.

However, governments do not, or should not, have sole responsibility for defining 'waste' or 'wisdom' in this context (or, indeed, in any other), or for determining the nature or the extent of the financial savings to be made. These must be, in so far as they can be, collective decisions, and taken only after properly expert and professional input to the decision-making process. And the first criterion must be the maintenance and development of democratic procedures. To use responsibility for the allocation of public finance as a subtle device for control of the curriculum, of both teaching and research, is a highly insidious and dangerous form of that use of knowledge as control we discussed in Chapter 4. And its effect, as we also noted there, is to diminish rather than to promote the democratic health of society.

Postmodernism requires, and democracy demands, that universities be conceived and managed as politically independent centres for the fearless and impersonal pursuit of knowledge and understanding in all spheres, and especially in those spheres whose value content makes them more problematic and thus more susceptible to abuse and manipulation.

Furthermore, democratic societies require such institutions, managed in this way, as a *sine qua non* of their very existence. For as we have seen, it is of the essence of a democratic society that it should continually develop, and such development is only possible via the evolution of knowledge and understanding. And that evolution of knowledge and understanding in turn requires the kind of constant challenge, critique, debate and dialogue which is the *raison d'être* of an academically free university system.

Academic independence, then, is not only important to universities and the academics working in them but it is also important for society itself. And the case for it which is being made here is not for 'a kind of moral supremacy to be claimed and secured by the academic community against its host society' (Barnett, 1988, p. 89). It is not 'an attempt by a small, though not unimportant, community to carve out special privileges for itself' (op.cit., p. 90). Indeed, as Barnett goes on to argue, 'academic freedom cannot, in a modern society, represent some kind of *carte blanche* for members of the academic profession', and any inquiry into its nature must be undertaken in the context of 'the interconnections between higher education and the wider society' (op.cit., p. 96). The point being made here is that pre-eminent among those interconnections must be the contribution which the existence of academic freedom and autonomy makes to an openness of knowledge and information, to the freedom of values and opinion and thus to the very essence of democracy.

Academic independence is essential both for the continued development of human knowledge and understanding and for the democratic health of society. We have seen how the kind of open, questioning approach to knowledge it facilitates has been the single most important factor in that technological advance which has characterized the twentieth century. We have seen the many ways in which it is entailed by postmodern perspectives on human knowledge and particularly on human values. And we can now see that it is a crucial element in the maintenance and development of democratic structures.

It is thus a further fundamental principle of education in a democratic society that openness of knowledge must be promoted and freedom of opinion not only permitted but also encouraged and supported. And that support in turn must come through both an open availability of knowledge, understanding and information and a free context for the generation of new forms of knowledge and understanding. It is that which makes academic freedom an essential prerequisite of democracy, and which makes a politically independent system of higher education one of the greatest safeguards we might find against its overthrow.

It is, however, a safeguard which is becoming increasingly less secure in many current societies. And its slow erosion is constituting an ever-growing threat to the maintenance of democratic structures in those societies. It is for this reason that it was suggested earlier that a discussion of academic freedom would take us into an evaluation, against the principles we have now identified, of current policies for education, especially in the UK. That evaluation will be the concern of the chapters which follow, where we will see the effects of this erosion of academic, and indeed intellectual, freedom in greater detail.

Our quest for the fundamental principles of educational planning in a democracy began with a reaffirmation of that faith in the potentialities of human nature which we have on several occasions asserted to be a basic presupposition of democracy itself. And it is on that same note that this chapter must end.

For every principle it has adumbrated is derived from the assumption that human beings can take responsibility for their own collective destinies and, as the corollary of that, that in any society which claims to be founded on a commitment to their doing so, they must be supported in this by an appropriate form of educational provision.

How appropriate current provision is when evaluated against these principles it will be the task of our next chapters to investigate.

6

CURRENT TRENDS AND POLICIES IN HIGHER EDUCATION

Freedom of institutions as well as individual freedom is an essential constituent of a free society and the tradition of academic freedom in this country has deep roots in the whole history of our people. We are convinced also that such freedom is a necessary condition of the highest efficiency and the proper progress of academic institutions, and that encroachments upon their liberty, in the supposed interests of greater efficiency, would in fact diminish their efficiency and stultify their development.

(Committee on Higher Education, 1963, pp. 228–9)

Chapter 5 attempted to identify what should be the underlying principles of educational provision in a democratic society. It suggested that among the most important of these is not merely a recognition that in such a society there is an obligation to provide an education for all future citizens but a further acknowledgement that the form of education provided must offer genuine equality of entitlement to all pupils, and that such entitlement is to a curriculum which seeks to promote in them the ability to think for themselves and to reach their own conclusions.

And it was also claimed that an essential prerequisite of such a form of education is an intellectual and social context characterized by an openness in the face of knowledge and a lack of dogmatism in relation to any particular belief or set of beliefs. This, as we have seen in earlier chapters, is also a conclusion one must come to if one accepts a view of human knowledge as problematic and, especially, if one further acknowledges the force of the postmodernist linking of 'knowledge' with political power. That chapter then went on to consider the important contribution which must be made to the creation of such an open intellectual context by the establishment and maintenance of an appropriate system of higher education. In particular, it stressed the importance of the preservation and protection of academic freedom, as a safeguard against the manipulation of society through the control of knowledge as well as in order to provide a suitable context for its continued development.

We now set out to evaluate how far current trends and policies for education measure up to these requirements, how far they satisfy our democratic criteria. It is here, then, that we take that template we have fashioned out of our idealist principles and apply it to the reality of current practices.

In this chapter, we look at higher education. For Chapter 5 made out a strong case for the existence of an appropriate form of higher education, a system which is academically free and politically independent, as a major safeguard of democracy. And it will be apparent that, if democratic principles are not reflected in that sector, there is little hope of our finding them anywhere else.

First, however, it will be helpful if we attempt to pick out some general trends which are to be seen in current educational policies at every level. For the identification of these will provide a backcloth against which to examine the more detailed features of those policies for both higher education and the school curriculum which have recently been established in the UK.

CURRENT TRENDS: AN OVERVIEW

In general terms it can be argued, with some conviction and with some weighty evidence, as this and subsequent chapters will show, that the major trend in educational provision, in most developed countries, has, in recent years, been away from rather than towards the realization of those ideals and principles which the earlier chapters of this book have been concerned to identify. Thus at least as far as education is concerned, democracy is not advancing, it is on the retreat; and there is every justification for the claim of this book that it needs to be cherished and protected. 'The public debate on education, and all things social, has shifted profoundly to the right' (Apple, 1990, p. 378) and there has been what Michael Apple in the same article, writing of the scene in the USA, describes as a 'conservative restoration'.

This shift has been characterized by a rejection of the notion of education as an individual human right; an emphasis on the instrumental and utilitarian dimensions of learning and research; a concern to encourage people to learn to compete rather than to collaborate; a loss of any sense that social policy should be based on ideals; and a corresponding stress on the short-term expedient. In general, in many societies moral considerations have given way to the mechanistic, and social concerns to the political. And there has been a resultant reduction not only in the quality of life for most citizens but also in the degree to which such societies can claim to be genuine democracies.

It is less easy to locate the reasons for this shift than it is to identify its major features and the evidence for its occurrence. One reason must be the world wide economic recession and the consequent problems of funding educational provision on the scale which the principles of democracy we have identified would seem to require. In many places, however, this has been exacerbated by an unwillingness to fund education (and other forms of social provision, such as the health service) to an appropriate level, a preference for spending public money on other things or, worse, on reducing taxes in order to permit some members of a society to increase their personal wealth rather than limiting that process in the interests of ensuring adequate provision for every citizen. Certainly in the UK during a period when the level of funding for, and thus the quality of, educational provision has fallen significantly, the individual wealth holdings of those in the higher echelons of society has increased to a similarly significant degree.

Economic recession cannot, therefore, of itself be responsible for the shift we have witnessed. An unwillingness to find the funding for adequate provision has been a more significant factor. And the economic doctrine has been successfully translated into the 'language of experience, moral imperative and common sense' (Apple, *ibid.*). This is clearly illustrated by those proposals we noted in Chapter 5 for the privatizing of educational provision or limiting it to 'the basics' or attempting no more than to provide a 'ladder of opportunity' to the more privileged members of society – those ideological positions we saw Denis Lawton (1989) has identified as significant features of current views on education, not only in the UK but also elsewhere. It was argued in Chapter 5 that such views are incompatible with any principles of democracy, and that they threaten the continuation of democratic forms. We must note here, however, that, whether that is the case or not, they have been gathering momentum.

And so the first general feature of current trends in educational policies we must note is a shift away from the view of educational provision as a human right in a democracy, as an entitlement for every individual *qua* individual, as 'the right of every boy and girl' which we have seen the Crowther Report (CACE, 1959, para. 83) advocating, and towards Crowther's other educational aim, education as a 'national investment'.

Moreover, that national investment is usually conceived in a very simplistic and limited form, as an economic investment only and not as an investment for the improved quality of social living. Even where the slogan, 'Investment in People', is bandied about, it is clear that people are to be invested in as potential producers rather than as persons, as potential economic units rather than as individual human beings.

There are several further features of this shift worthy of note. First, a move towards seeing educational provision almost solely as a national investment involves also coming to regard it in instrumental terms. The kinds of study, research and learning which then come to be valued are those which can be seen to have some kind of economic 'pay-off'. This is certainly the case in relation to the school curriculum, as we shall see in Chapter 7, and there are many 'signs that higher education is being broached by the means-end thinking of the wider society' (Barnett, 1988, p. 89). This puts at risk the notion of education, or of any kind of activity, undertaken for its own sake, and promotes the idea that all things are to be evaluated in terms of what they are *for* rather than of what they *are*.

In the context of education this deprives us of that important distinction we have noted before between education itself and instruction or training. Perhaps more importantly, however, it not only reflects but also promotes within society at large an instrumentalism which threatens the quality of life by assessing the value of everything by reference to what it leads to and never facing the question of what might be of long-term intrinsic value. It thus leads to what Enoch Powell (1985) once called 'a modern barbarism'.

Another way of expressing this is to say that it is an approach to social policy which removes all ideals and replaces them with considerations only of the expedient. And while some may wish to argue that it thus has the merits of being realistic, others would still wish to claim that such realism is hollow without the underpinning of a set of aims or goals, values or principles. More importantly, as we have seen before, democracy itself is an ideal, a system of moral principles, so that to advocate and undertake social planning on the *ad hoc* basis of immediate expediency rather than in accordance with a set of principles is to deny democracy also.

For, fundamentally, such an approach denies all considerations of morality. It asks 'How can we achieve our goals?' without ever addressing the prior question of whether those goals are worth achieving or even acknowledging that there exist considerations of a moral kind. Thus questions of the kind which we have argued are central to the planning of a democratic society are not recognized as moral questions but are viewed as technical rather than as moral, and are approached in a mechanistic or technocratic manner, as questions of means rather than of ends. And social issues become political issues, a matter of what is politic, even a matter of what will lead to political survival, rather than what is right for society. More specifically, every aspect of society is viewed from a commercial perspective, every activity within society is evaluated on some industrial model of productivity, and competition has become the salient feature even of those areas of human coexistence where co-operation is clearly far more appropriate.

This is a category error of the first order, and it is thus leading to much conceptual confusion. More importantly, however, it is also leading to serious reductions in the quality of provision in most areas of social service; to a corresponding loss in the quality of life for most members of society, not only those who have greatest need of this provision but also all of those who find it uncongenial to live in an atmosphere of continuous rivalry, conflict and underprivilege (i.e. all but the most socially and morally insensitive); and to that shift away from democratic forms of social living which this book is concerned to warn of.

For democracy is not a competitive matter. And democratic forms of education are certainly not areas for competition. The market-place economy view of education is thus inappropriate and especially at odds with democratic principles. For

Education . . . is acquired by a structure of appropriation that does not exclude others from its possession. On the contrary, education is furthered the more it is shared, and the more there is free and open access to all of its accumulation. That is why learning which is not conveyed to others is deemed 'lost', 'wasted' or 'dead'. In direct opposition to market exchanges, educational exchanges flourish most with the unpaid gifts of others and develop the more they are *not* mediated by private possession and profit.

(McMurtry, 1991, p. 212)

As John McMurtry argues, there are fundamental contradictions between the market and the education models. The imposition of the market model, the stressing of an economic view of education, at any level, including that of higher education, puts at risk not only education itself but also democratic structures. For the model sets up a value system within the education service which is incompatible with those structures and incapable of supporting the development either of the structures themselves or of a citizenry appropriately prepared to operate them. It offers a form of 'education' which specifically is not concerned with the development of critical capacities in the learner, and thus 'must leave society in a very real sense without its capacity to think' (op.cit., 214).

As McMurtry goes on to demonstrate, however, this is precisely what we are currently witnessing in the framing of educational policies. In the interests of competing effectively in the international market-place, the curriculum at every level is increasingly being viewed in utilitarian and instrumental terms. 'What was traditionally education's by-product function is now proclaimed as its ultimate goal' (op.cit., p. 210).

And so, 'we face the prospect of an inevitable transformation of our educational process into an organ of the captalist market' (op.cit., p. 214). This 'implies the negation of education as such' (op.cit., p. 216). And, 'if it is permitted to continue . . . it must end in the destruction of education itself' (*ibid.*). To these claims we must add that this must also lead to a transformation of that educational process into one which is anti-democratic, and to the negation and ultimate destruction of democracy.

It was suggested earlier that the reasons for this major social shift are difficult to locate. One reason as was suggested there, is certainly that economic recesssion which has been a feature of world economies in recent years, or rather the ways in which many developed societies have chosen to respond to that recession.

A further and extremely serious hypothesis which must be considered, however, is that the world has moved on 50 years from the forms of totalitarianism which characterized fascist regimes in Hitler's Germany, in Mussolini's Italy and in Franco's Spain. It is even moving away from the totalitarianism of communist Russia and perhaps also China. Memories of the excesses of those regimes may thus be fading, and perhaps in particular memories of the ways in which they manipulated education to promote their anti-democratic purposes. And that means not only that people in general are less concerned about the prospect of their returning but also, and more seriously, that advantage can be taken of this by those who wish to see them return.

It is no exaggeration, therefore, to speak, as Fred Inglis (1989, p. 128) does, of 'a new Fascism' which he suggests, among other features, is 'crudely militaristic', 'authoritarian with hostile class interests' and in which 'the militarism and authoritarianism invoke stridently anti-socialist and anachronistically nationalist emotions in their support'. In support of this claim he cites the fact that, in manipulating education in England and Wales to support this ideology, 'he [the Secretary of State] and the Prime Minister have removed the teachers' negotiating rights and, simply and coercively, sought to instal them as the mouthpieces of the new curriculum, the automatic measurers of achievement in relation to manpower planning, and the unarmed custodians of the rising underclass (op.cit., p. 129).

In this context it is not surprising to find that these policies are also characterized by a return to absolutism, a reaffirmation of rationalist theories of universal values and a corresponding rejection of twentieth-century views of the problematic nature of human knowledge and values. There is nowhere any acknowledgement that these policies are based on ideological positions, that their underpinning values are not everyone's values, that they are not universal or God-given, that they represent not *the* viewpoint but only *a* viewpoint and that, further, the viewpoint they represent is fundamentally at odds with democratic theory itself. They reflect 'a canon of unquestioned cultural texts as opposed to an openness to varied ethnic, gender and subcultural voices' (Sholle, 1992, p. 281). They thus demonstrate, better than any academic paper, the force of what postmodernism is proclaiming about knowledge, discourse and political power.

It has been argued throughout this book that democracy will always be at risk and must thus be constantly cherished and protected. There can be no better evidence of this than what is currently happening in social policy generally, and in educational policies in particular. These phenomena can be observed in most developed countries, whether they call themselves democracies or not. They are a major feature of current educational policies in the UK, as we shall see as we turn now, and in our next chapter, to a consideration of how those policies measure up to the principles of educational provision in a democratic society we have identified.

ACADEMIC FREEDOM AND ACADEMIC AUTONOMY: CURRENT TRENDS

We concluded our discussion of the importance of academic independence to the democratic health of society in the last chapter by suggesting that we would need to explore in this chapter the ways in which it has been, and is being, eroded. The point had been made that academic freedom is not to be seen as a privilege enjoyed by those who work in university institutions but as a responsibility they hold on behalf of society for the protection of that openness in the face of knowledge which is essential to the development both of knowledge itself and of democracy. There are important 'interconnections between higher education and the wider society' (Barnett, 1988, p. 96), and this is perhaps the most important.

There are, however, other kinds of interconnection, and the influences work in both directions. For 'being an institution *of* its host society, higher education is also subject to the dominant values of that society. And so we see . . . the signs that higher education is being breached by the means-end thinking characteristic of the wider society' (Barnett, op.cit., p. 89). And the threats to the maintenance of a form of higher education which is characterized by academic freedom and autonomy are increasing, especially as economic factors seem to be convincing many people that it is an unaffordable luxury.

As Malcolm Tight (1988, p. 2) says:

> We read, for example, of the stultifying consequences of the central direction and control of academic life in Czechoslovakia; of the pressures placed on academics who express contrary views to those of the government in Singapore; and of the controversies surrounding the participation of delegates from South Africa in international conferences. And, most recently of all (at least at the time of writing – March 1988), there has been extensive reporting and analysis of the possible impact of the current Education Reform Bill on higher education.

What is perhaps of more concern since it is seriously damaging to the democratic health of society is that, where these principles are being eroded, too often this is not being done by open democratic discussion – of priorities, of preferences, of the appropriate bases for the allocation of funds to competing interests – but by stealth. For most change in policies is now brought about by such devices as the manipulation and centralized control of funding machinery, the establishment of (in themselves highly costly) mechanisms for the control of expenditure, the institution of bureaucratic rather than democratic systems of accountability and, above all, that use of rhetoric and the control of discourse, especially that discourse of derision (Ball, 1990) which we have noted elsewhere, that has in recent years become an increasingly common, and highly disturbing, feature of political control even in societies whose claims to being democratic are vociferously reiterated.

One of the first steps taken towards the erosion of these principles of academic freedom in the UK was the abolition of 'tenure' for academics working in university institutions. Tenure is the guarantee of continuation in one's post unless one is guilty of some act of gross moral turpitude. It was devised as a major plank in the base of academic freedom, since its main significance was that an academic could not be fired for pursuing studies or research which might be regarded as politically unacceptable or 'incorrect', nor could he or she be prevented in this way from expressing opinions which might not be to the taste of the politicians or even the policy-makers. It thus ensured the existence of the challenge, critique, dialogue and debate which an open democracy requires.

Conversely, its loss has meant that there is no longer this safeguard. And the result has been an understandable reluctance on the part of many academics to overstep the mark by challenging 'authority', not least because, in some cases where that step has been taken, there have been sackings. It must be acknowledged that some of the more public, and more outrageous, of these have been the subject of later reinstatements. That in itself, however, merely reinforces the point being made.

It is also worthy of note that one of the devices employed for justifying the abolition of tenure was the claim (on little evidence) that many academics were abusing the protection it gave them, not to research and publish freely but to live feckless and unproductive lives at the public expense. This is a very good example of the discourse of derision in action. For it precedes by 'rubbishing' that which it wishes to destroy (whom the politicians wish to destroy they first make look silly or incompetent or irresponsible), feels no need to offer evidence in support of its criticisms and thus creates a climate in which action on its part seems not only justified but also necessary. To justify change one must first demonstrate a deficit. To justify 'mending' something one must first show that it is 'broken'.

There may of course have been some examples of this kind of abuse. As the Robbins Report (Committee on Higher Education, 1963, p. 229) said, 'freedom of this sort may sometimes lend itself to abuses'. However, as the report went on to say (*ibid.*), 'the danger of such abuses is much less than the danger of trying to eliminate them by general restriction of individual liberty'.

Furthermore, the argument that tenure has been abolished in order to avoid wastage of public money hardly holds when one weighs the cost of the elaborate bureaucracies which have been created to provide checks on the activities of academics in universities – costs which are comparable to those expended on checking the activities of those engaged professionally in the health service. For it is clear that in higher education, indeed in education generally as in the health service, the cost of those bureaucracies far excedes any savings they may be making in checking wastage, let alone their cost in terms of what they are doing to inhibit academic freedom and thus the development of democracy. The cost of administering institutions of higher education has, as a result of developments such as these, rocketed in recent years. Preventing wastage is only the stated intention; the real thrust is towards increasing administrative, and thus political, control. Quality assurance is another piece of such rhetoric, providing again a pretext for political interference in academic autonomy, as the issuing of *The Charter for Higher Education* by the Department for Education indicates.

The only argument for the erosion of academic freedom through the abolition of tenure and, indeed, for other forms of political control of higher education which might be felt to carry weight in the context of a democratic society, is the argument from public accountability. Accountability is an important mechanism in democratic societies. In ancient Athenian democracy, for example, it was a more important democratic principle and safeguard against malpractice than even the popular vote; and the holder of any political office could, on completion of his term of office, be arraigned before a jury of citizens and required to give an account of decisions taken; that jury would then decide whether to accept the account or to decree some form of punishment – a fine, exile or even death. This is another feature of democracy which is sadly absent from most current practice.

Public accountability, however, has to be clearly distinguished from political control. Its concern must be to ensure the best possible practice not to control that practice. It is thus essentially a *post hoc* or *post eventum* activity. Furthermore, the procedures adopted for ensuring accountability must be appropriate. They must be *democratic* rather than *bureaucratic*.

Bureaucratic procedures for accountability are a form of 'management by objectives' (Atkin, 1979); their central concern is with the results obtained for the money spent; they are systems of 'payment by results'; they require accountability only to the controlling bodies; they are thus instrumental, economic and political; and they offer only a very crude model of what accountability in a democratic society should or might be.

Democratic accountability, on the other hand, is accountability 'to diverse constituencies rather than to the agglomerate constituency of the public alone' (Sockett, 1976, p. 42). It is concerned with quality of performance rather than merely results. It thus begins from, and is based on, procedural principles rather than objectives. In education it is accountability 'for adherence to principles of practice rather than for results embodied in pupil performance' (*ibid.*). It is thus, as the terminology implies, the only form of accountability which is compatible with democratic principles.

In the context of higher education, a bureaucratic form of accountability restricts the activity to a concern with outputs – the teaching of students and the productivity of research. It leaves untouched, and thus puts at risk, that major function of universities we have identified – the protection of freedom of and openness of knowledge.

The argument from public accountability, then, does not provide a justifica-tion for the erosion of academic freedom or the withdrawal of academic tenure. It merely requires the offering of accounts of the ways in which that freedom has been used. And that is a very different matter. A properly democratic form of accountability is not incompatible with the existence of academic tenure nor does it require that it be abolished

Once tenure had been abolished, however, it became possible to fire staff. And this in turn made possible the second step towards the establishment of external control of higher education in the UK – control through funding mechanisms and the allocation of target intakes. Institutions are now funded according to the numbers of students they have in each subject area, and that funding is related to the numbers of students they are permitted to have in each subject area. Thus student numbers, and by inference the range of subjects to be offered, are controlled by the politicians through the civil service and related forms of bureaucracy. This has enabled the politicians to ensure that the money allocated to universities will be used, in the main, to support those subjects which it wants to have supported and, conversely, not to promote those it has little interest in or even has an interest in discouraging. Thus, for example, humanities subjects are grossly underfunded and, indeed, several departments of philosophy have closed, while business studies flourish.

Again, it is worth noting that this is a worldwide scenario. John McMurtry (1991, pp. 216–7) quotes evidence from various countries of this kind of process in action. In Britain 'some University grants were reduced to less than 50% ... Humanities departments have been particularly hard hit – Philosophy lost between 30% and 40% of its positions. At least twelve British Universities have now no philosophy department at all' (Graham, 1989). In Canada, the Conservative government announced cuts in the funding of universities for the period 1990–5 to a sum 'much greater than the operating budgets of universities in Newfoundland, Nova Scotia, Ontario, Alberta and British Columbia' (Stutt, 1990). And, in the USA,

> Columbia University has dispensed with its geography and linguistic programs. Johns Hopkins cut back on spending for arts and sciences, and Washington University in St Louis dismantled its well-regarded sociology department ... A recent survey by the Association of American Universities indicated that at least 60 per cent of AAU institutions were 'consolidating, eliminating or reducing academic departments'.
> (Minsky and Noble, 1989, p. 496)

What is of significance here is, first, that these changes reflect that shift towards the economic, market-place model we discussed in the previous section, away from the educational model and consequently away from forms of educational provision which are supportive of democracy; towards viewing universities in terms only of what they can produce rather than also of their wider contribution to the democratic health of society.

And, second, in keeping with that model, the changes have been brought about by mechanisms of external control, which have seriously eroded the academic autonomy of university institutions, and not by any process of debate or dialogue which one could readily describe as democratic. In both respects it is not without relevance that the subjects which have suffered as a direct result of these policies and processes are, for the most part, those very subjects which it might be claimed are most conductive to the development of a free-thinking, questioning and critical approach to knowledge in their students.

Not only, then, do these policies and the means by which they have been implemented fail to measure up to our criteria of democracy but they can also be recognized as positively, and perhaps deliberately, inimical to the maintenance and continued development of democracy, and especially to that academic independence we have claimed to be essential to it.

Again we must note that the only argument in support of these policies which might be felt to carry weight is that which was offered in 1976 by James Callaghan, as Prime Minister, in his famous speech at Ruskin College. For in that speech he castigated the education system, and especially schools, for failing to promote the teaching and learning of economically useful subjects and placing far too much emphasis on the humanities and social sciences. This criticism then provided the base on which subsequent governments, most notably that of Margaret Thatcher, were able to transfer responsibility for economic failure by attributing it to educationists and teachers, and to advocate on those grounds that marginalization of professional expertise which we must discuss later in this chapter and the parallel institution of external political controls of educational policy and practice.

Whether there is evidence for this claim that the education system is responsible for the present poor economic health of society or whether it is merely being made a scape-goat for governmental incompetence is one issue here. The second and, in the context of this book, more important issue, however, is that the attempt to solve the problem by eroding academic independence and professional responsibility, through ever-tighter forms of political control, is incompatible with the principles we are arguing must underpin the government of any society which claims to be democratic. And so that process must be recognized as a further manifestation of that 'conservative restoration' (Apple, 1990) which we noted earlier.

Similar moves towards political control can be discerned in the new mechanisms for the funding of research in the UK. For whereas academics, through their institutions, were once provided with a proportion of their salary for their research activities, whatever these might be, that funding now comes from two quite different sources. First, there are regular evaluations of research productivity and, although these are currently (but not it seems for very much longer) conducted by the academics themselves, the real decisions concerning the allocations of funding are made by the policy-makers in their distribution of resources to individual subjects. Second, there is further funding through research councils which provide resources only for those projects they regard as worth while. In both cases, therefore, the crucial decisions are made at a political level. Again the rhetoric is that of avoiding wastage; again the reality is that of political control.

This is manifestly the case where the research funding comes from government departments especially, in the UK, the Department for Education and the Home Office. For increasingly such research is controlled by those government departments themselves rather than by the researchers. Publication of findings, for example, is at the discretion of those government agencies, and researchers must sign an agreement not to publish without official permission as a condition of receiving funding for the research. Again, therefore, we note the extension of political control over the distribution of knowledge and information. Such research must come up with the 'right answers' or be consigned to oblivion. And, sadly, the most blatant examples of these practices are to be found in the research which has been commissioned into education, and especially the National Curriculum.

There is a further dimension of the current mechanisms for the funding of research in the UK which is worthy of note, since it represents another threat to democratic principles. For access to that funding has now become a matter of competition, almost of professional survival. Researchers must now bid against each other for financial support for their research.

It might be argued of course that this should ensure that the money available is used to support the most productive or valuable research. Its actual effects, however, go far beyond this. For not only are decisions concerning the productivity and value of particular research activities now placed, as we have just seen, in the hands of the politicians and their aides, more importantly academic research has now become a matter for competition rather than collaboration. Academic researchers have now every motivation not to share their findings with colleagues working in the same fields but to keep it to themselves in order to enhance their own chances of receiving further funding. An 'arms round work' attitude, reminiscent of the worst 'swots' one knew at school, is now prevalent.

There are two serious consequences of this. First, its effect is to slow down the development of knowledge and understanding. And it is not difficult to find current examples (even in the field of medical research, where advances can actually save lives) of parallel research projects which could clearly gain much from collaboration but which are encouraged by the system to compete with each other.

Second, it is a practice which, as we have seen, transgresses a basic principle of democratic living. For it discourages that openness in the face of knowledge which we have claimed is an essential ingredient of democracy, and especially of education in a democratic society. It inhibits that free access to knowledge and information which we have seen is also an important ingredient. It bars the way to dialogue and debate, to a sharing of understandings. And it denies the principle that a democratic society exists to promote the good of all of its members.

It is also a good example of the effects of that category error, of regarding education as a commercial/industrial activity, which we suggested earlier was leading to conceptual confusion and a loss of quality. For it reveals some of the results of allowing educational decisions to be made in response to 'market forces' when education is not a market-place activity.

Current policies for higher education, then, represent not only a massive erosion of academic freedom and autonomy but they also, as a consequence, have serious implications for basic democratic principles. Indeed, throughout current policies in the UK there is hardly a democratic principle in sight. All have been lost in a set of practices which cannot be distinguished, except in terms of their stealth and surreptitiousness, from those one has become accustomed to seeing in overtly totalitarian contexts. There could be no better illustration of the central message of the politics of knowledge and of postmodernism, that society is manipulated by its dominant group through the control of the distribution of knowledge, the legitimation of discourse and the imposition of ideology. And the ideology in this case is that of self-help and competitiveness, neither of which can readily be seen as compatible with democracy.

The only protection society has against this process, as we have seen, is the maintenance and protection of academic freedom and autonomy. And that requires a politically independent system of higher education. There is no doubt, however, that both academic freedom and political independence are being rapidly eroded by current policies. And so, if we are right in our assertion that openness in the face of knowledge and a willingness to modify one's views, and thus one's policies, in the light of developing knowledge are essential prerequisites of democracy, we must acknowledge that in many societies which currently claim to be democratic these essentials are to be found ever less frequently.

These problems are highlighted, and indeed exacerbated, when one looks at the sector of higher education which is concerned with the preparation of those who are to teach in the school system of a democratic society. We must look briefly at this aspect of higher education before we move on, in Chapter 7, to consider the implications of what we have said about democracy and knowledge for the ways in which school systems must be evaluated in democratic contexts.

THE PREPARATION OF TEACHERS

It might be argued that the main reason for locating courses for the preparation of schoolteachers in university institutions is to enable them to develop within a context in which academic freedom is part of the air they breathe. Certainly, it must be argued that that is the only context for the education of teachers for a democratic society, since it is that very openness in the face of knowledge and tolerance of the opinions of others that academic freedom is concerned to safeguard which is the essence of what they should be seeking to communicate to their pupils.

For teaching is not, or at least in a democratic setting should not be, a matter merely of transmitting knowledge to the next generation. If there is more to teaching than that, then there is more to the preparation of teachers than merely providing them with the knowledge-content to transmit and the methodological skills to transmit it most effectively, more to being a teacher than being 'a carrier of knowledge with transmission skills' (Goddard, 1985, p. 35). A democratic society needs teachers whose own approach to knowledge and to education reflects those democratic principles which education in a democratic society must communicate to the next generation.

And so to prepare teachers by giving them bodies of politically correct and/or economically useful knowledge and then *training* them to *deliver* it not only falls short of those democratic principles we have identified but it is also, beyond that, a positive threat to those principles. For it is a process which is designed not only to turn them into mindless operatives but, far more seriously, also to make them agents for the uncritical dissemination of the ideology of others, and for the implementation of those forms of social control which are exercised through the distribution of knowledge, 'mouthpieces of the new curriculum . . . and unarmed custodians of the rising underclass' (Inglis, 1989, p. 129).

Teachers in a democratic society must, above all else, be assisted to recognize the problematic nature of knowledge, of values and thus of the practice of education itself. They must learn the importance of constantly evaluating their own practice in terms not only of its methods but also of its goals. They must be constantly aware of the need to question and assess not merely the effectiveness with which they are 'delivering' a curriculum but also the value of the curriculum they are seeking to 'deliver'. And these two kinds of evaluation are conceptually quite different (White, 1971), and require different kinds of skill, technique and understanding.

They must be helped also to recognize the social and political significance of education in a democratic society. And this means that their study of educational practices, their own and those of others, must go well beyond description to analysis and critique. They need to acknowledge the value dimension of educational practice, the fact that it is always a matter of choices, and that those values and those choices are not the objects of a scientific or positivist form of study but are much more problematic than that, so that they need to be approached without dogmatism and with a genuine openness. In short, they must be made aware of the full significance for educational practice of the twentieth-century debate concerning human knowledge. And the study of education must include the application of a postmodern perspective to the educational debate.

This is the essence of the notion of the teacher as a 'reflective practitioner' or, as Lawrence Stenhouse (1975) expressed it, the 'teacher as researcher'. For as he also said (op.cit., p. 143), 'it is not enough that teachers' work should be studied; they need to study it themselves'. I have argued elsewhere (Kelly, 1993) that this is the only route to a proper integration of the theory and the practice of education. Of far more importance is the fact that it is the only route to a properly democratic form of education. For if teachers are not merely to be the agents through whose activities the values of the dominant group in society are imposed on the rising generation, they must learn to reflect on their practice, and to do so in the widest possible terms in order to embrace all its implications. They must also of course have the professional freedom to translate these reflections into practice. And they must be assisted to develop that professional understanding of education as a social institution which will enable them, as professionals, to provide society with the kind of expert input to its decision-making which, as we shall see later, should be an important part of the role of every professional in a democracy.

If teachers are to be prepared for their task in this way, then the courses which are so to prepare them must, as was suggested above, be located in the kind of university institution which is characterized by academic freedom as we have defined it.

This point was stressed specifically in relation to the preparation of teachers by the Robbins Committee (Committee on Higher Education, 1963, p. 231):

> It is fundamental that an institution should be able to prescribe the requirements of its courses and the combinations permitted. We know of no argument that would justify the imposition of external control from the centre in this respect, though it is obviously essential that the universities should consider carefully any representations made to them, for example, about the type of course best suited to various kinds of future teacher. Liberty to experiment with content and method is one of the surest guarantees of efficiency and discovery.

Conversely, however – and this is the current reality in England and Wales – we must note that, if the courses they are offered are not designed to develop in them the kinds of questioning approach to knowledge and values which is essential to democratic existence, then the case for locating courses of what must now become teacher *training* in universities falls.

Indeed, it might be argued that in the UK the fact that many such courses are located in universities gave the politicians the entree they wanted to all aspects of the universities' work and thus they acted as a kind of Trojan horse through which universities have been invaded and their academic autonomy seriously eroded (Kelly, 1993). It may be worth briefly tracing the processes by which this has occurred. For again they reveal some of those insidious threats to democracy we are seeking to identify.

A massive overproduction of teachers in the early 1970s in England and Wales (a result of an equally massive bloomer by civil servants who had expanded the intake into teacher education courses only a few years earlier) led to the institution of controls over intake into courses, not only in terms of student numbers but also in terms of the distribution of these numbers between subjects and age-phase specialisms.

It might of course be argued that, if teacher education were conceived in the terms outlined above, it would not have the kind of specific training character which would make it any more unsuited to other kinds of career than any other non-vocational study, since properly *educated* young people are as much needed in other areas of life as they are in teaching. And further, many of the skills developed by intending teachers have a wider application than the school classroom. However, it is not desirable to entice into specific, career-related areas of study large numbers of students for whom it is known that there will be no future in that area, so that to introduce some form of control over the numbers entering these courses seemed in the circumstances not unreasonable.

Unfortunately (although fortune played less a part in this process than deliberate design), control did not end there. For within a decade it had been extended to include the form and content of courses as well. And that control was immediately exercised to stress their subject-content and methodological elements, and to diminish the attention given to the development of those critical, evaluative skills and understandings which it was suggested earlier are the essential prerequisites for teaching in a democratic society. Again, therefore, we have a set of policies and practices which are fundamentally inimical to democracy.

Nor were the procedures which were established to implement this control any less undemocratic than the policies themselves. A national body, the Council for the Accreditation of Teacher Education (CATE), was created whose task it was to grant accreditation to courses, i.e. to license them as courses leading to the award of the status of qualified teacher (QT status), only if those courses were deemed to have met its criteria of approval. Those criteria, which were highly detailed and rigid, including, for example, explicit requirements of the hourages to be devoted to the major activities of the courses, were determined by the politicians, albeit 'with the advice of CATE' (a by now well-known rhetorical technique), and with very little if any input from the professionals, other than a few tame ones. That this was a device for effecting the changes the politicians wanted, rather than the mechanism for monitoring and improving 'quality' which it was claimed to be, is apparent from the limited scale of the involvement of the professionals in the work of this group, and the extent to which professional comment and advice were ignored.

The work of CATE was facilitated by inspections of courses conducted by Her Majesty's Inspectorate, in addition to, and as supplementary to, the details of those courses submitted by the institutions which provided them. These inspections too left much to be desired in terms of democratic principles, since their aim was not to advise on the development of these courses according to educational criteria but to convert them into what the politicians wanted them to be. Their 'evaluations', therefore, were not undertaken in terms of the principles upon which the courses had originally been constructed, nor in terms of how effectively those principles were being put into practice, nor even by reference to any alternative set of principles framed on educational grounds. All such principles had to be destroyed and replaced by a new political ideology, a new discourse. And this was done not by debating the prevailing principles on which teacher education was planned, since this would have placed them at a considerable disadvantage, but by taking it as read that they were fundamentally misconceived and must be ousted.

This they did by basing their 'evaluations' entirely on the criteria set by the politicians through CATE, as though these were self-evident and God-given (as for them they probably were). However, this was never openly admitted. The claim that was always made was that they were operating as the kind of independent guardians of quality which Her Majesty's Inspectors are supposed to be – and once were. However, even when directly faced by the question, they would not declare what their own criteria of quality, the basis of their evaluations, were.

To undertake an evaluation without clear criteria is of course an extremely odd thing to do – both professionally and intellectually. To undertake an evaluation with criteria one is not prepared to make plain, however, is not so much odd as sinister, and quite incompatible with democratic principles. It is also clear evidence that the main purpose of the activity was political control rather than educational advancement. It was thus an exercise that was intellectually dishonest, professionally unacceptable and politically sinister, and which did no credit to, and left one with no respect, personal or professional, for those who were its voluntary agents.

In this way, in England and Wales during the last decade or so, the training of teachers has become a political rather than a professional activity, as the politicians have achieved a tight control over the ways in which teachers are prepared. And they have used that control to shift the focus of courses of teacher preparation away from those critical studies, which we suggested earlier are central to the education of teachers for a democratic society, towards much more intellectually limited forms of training for what are clearly seen as the limited tasks of knowledge transmission.

One extremely serious loss that has resulted from this process is that of the study of child development from the preparation of teachers to work with very young children in nursery, first and infant schools. It would seem self-evident that what such teachers need above all things is an understanding of young children, far more, for example, than they need to be expert in one of the subjects of the National Curriculum. Yet in the interests of ensuring that they acquire that subject expertise, the study of child development has virtually disappeared from their courses of preparation.

The evidence for the importance of high-quality education in the early years is massive (Sylva, 1992). And one project which is currently seeking to identify the main constituents of quality in early years provision, the Early Childhood Education Research Project based at Goldsmiths' College, London, has already found that an understanding of child development is ranked as the most important of these qualities by every kind of professional working with young children. Yet that is the very aspect of courses of preparation for teachers of the very young which has had to be jettisoned. Again, therefore, we note the rejection of professional advice, the discouragement of critical challenge and the imposition of a particular political orthodoxy, a new discourse.

It is worth further noting that this process has again been assisted by the use of 'discourses of derision', a 'rubbishing' of the 'woolly minded' academics who would see the processes of education in a democratic society as far more subtle and demanding than mere instruction – the creation of an apparent deficit to justify the sweeping changes which have been undertaken.

And the final effect of this process has been that the training of teachers has been reduced to an activity which, it can now be claimed, no longer requires a university setting but which is best done 'on the job', in the classroom, since it no longer requires reflective thought but merely an operative's skills.

It is more than likely, therefore, that courses of teacher preparation in England and Wales will soon no longer be located in university institutions.

At the time of writing, the House of Lords has rejected that clause in the current education bill which would permit schools to award qualified teacher status (QTS) with no input from institutions of higher education. This it did on the grounds that a university ambience is essential for the development of future teachers. There must be serious doubts, however, concerning for how long the universities themselves will regard it as appropriate to offer and validate the kinds of courses intending teachers are now required to follow, and to accept the further erosion of their academic freedom which the political control of these courses involves. Either way, one extremely important mechanism for the protection, maintenance and development of democracy will have been totally destroyed.

As a postscript to this, we should also note that the intention is now to create a Teacher Training Agency (TTA), which will not only take over the control of initial courses of teacher training but will also, it is currently proposed, again through the funding mechanisms, extend that control to courses of further study for teachers and even to the choice of topics for individual research in education. This will further remove the study of education from its university context by setting it apart for purposes of funding and control of curriculum. It will also further reduce the scope for any kind of objective, critical evaluation of educational practice. And that of course is the intention, whatever the rhetorical accompaniment.

Thus courses for intending teachers in the UK are now producing teachers who, in hardly any respect, measure up to those principles we identified earlier as being essential criteria for the assessment of the suitability of teachers for a democratic society. In fact they are producing, or at least being required and expected to produce, teachers who, it might be argued, are totally unsuitable for that role.

Moreover, those courses of further education for teachers which have for the last several years sought to redress the balance, if only for a very small proportion of the teaching profession, are now themselves to come under this process of political control. And, finally, those restraints which we saw earlier have been placed on research activities and which, as we noted, have been particularly restrictive in the field of educational research, are now to be extended to inhibit educational research at every level, even that of the individual doctorate.

It can now be seen how teacher education has provided the Trojan horse inside which the vandals (if the historical elision can be permitted) have entered the university system. And there is an important warning there for the rest of that system.

What must be stressed here, however, is that it all adds up to a considerable threat to democracy. For not only are the bastions of higher education and academic freedom under seige but we have already lost the battle to ensure that schools are provided with the kind of teacher who can support the development in the next generation of a proper democratic awareness.

The process that has just been described is of course a process of deprofessionalization. It is a process by which teachers in every sector of the education service in England and Wales have seen their professional status reduced and, more importantly, their influence on social policies in education minimized. And this is part of a more general process of deprofessionalization which extends to every profession, most notably perhaps to that of medicine.

We noted earlier that a justification for this has been offered in the form of attributing the nation's economic failure to the inadequacies of the teaching profession. We must finally note, however, that, whether such an attribution is valid or not, the process not only contributes to the erosion of democratic principles, as we noted there; it also has the effect of denying society access to the kind of professional expertise it needs in order to make and evaluate policies from a position of informed understanding. In fact it has the further effect of creating a situation in which such professional expertise is not only rejected; it also actually ceases to be available. For its development will have been brought to a complete halt.

It is thus a good example of the attempt to arrest development which characterizes much current public policy, perhaps especially in the field of education but in many other fields, such as health and welfare. It seems that it is only in the spheres of technology, economics and the generation of wealth that progress is welcomed. Elsewhere, and especially in education, to be 'progressive' is to offend.

One of the main devices for arresting this kind of development in education, then, has been the rejection of professional opinion in the framing of educational policies. And so we must finally explore here the question of the proper role for the professional in a democratic society.

THE ROLE OF THE PROFESSIONAL
IN A DEMOCRATIC SOCIETY

We have seen Plato's hostility to democracy; and we have also seen that it is prompted in large part by his view that the management of a society is too complex a task to be left to people who lack the knowledge and the skills to carry it out effectively. He offers us the analogy of the navigation of a ship, and suggests that it would be foolhardy for the passengers on a ship to commence their voyage by voting who was to be the captain and navigator.

That analogy is too simple, however. For the major, if not the only, value issue in relation to the navigation of a ship is the question of where we want it navigated to. And it is not difficult to conceive of a situation in which that decision is made by the passengers in a properly democratic manner, while the navigator's expertise is used to put the decision into effect.

There are several points to be seen in this analogy which have a direct bearing on what might be an appropriate role for the professional, the intellectual, the holder of expertise, in a democratic society.

First, as we have seen on more than one occasion, the value issues which permeate political decison-making go well beyond mere questions of destination or goals. And those value issues are matters of opinion and preference; they are not matters of expertise. Social policies are matters not of science but of values, of ideology. And there are no experts in this field. Indeed, we have constantly seen the dangers which follow, especially to democracy itself, from the assumption that there are, from positivist approaches to social 'science', for example. If the ship of state has professional navigators they will take it where they want it to go. And the whole point of democracy is to avoid that.

Second, however, there are comparable dangers in leaving all to the amateurs. For there are many kinds of expertise needed in the planning of social policies. Nor is it the case that this expertise is only required at the stage of implementation. Again Plato's analogy of the ship is too simplistic and does not allow for the complexity of policy-making. We may indeed feel that the decisions concerning the direction in the which things should go ought to be taken democratically, but it is important, as we have already noted, that such decisions be reached on the basis of maximum information and understanding. And it should be the role of those people who have relevant professional understanding to make it available to assist in the decision-making process, and not merely to wait in silence until policies have been made for them to implement. For there is no other way of ensuring that those policies are as sound as they can be made.

Furthermore, again as we have noted before, in a context where all decisions must reflect the ideologies of those who make them, it becomes crucial that adequate reasons, justifications and explanations be advanced in support of them. And those reasons, justifications and explanations must have a clearly enunciated theoretical base. It thus reveals both an intellectual inadequacy and (at best) a political naivety or (at worst) a disturbing dishonesty to advocate the rejection of theoretical considerations in favour of something called practicality. For as we have claimed in relation to the preparation of teachers, in any sphere practice without theory is impossible; and, in the political sphere, practice without a sound, clearly thought-out and openly stated theory is sinister and dangerous.

If, then, policy decisions are to be informed decisions, if they are to be based on a sound consideration of relevant knowledge and understanding, if they are to be accompanied by properly detailed reasons, justifications and explanations, they must take full advantage of what can be discovered from those who have relevant professional expertise. It is not the role of the professional in a democratic society to take decisions for the rest of us; it is not for teachers to dictate the form of the education system nor doctors that of the health service. 'The function of the intellectual is not, in the first place, to be a prophet who compels all people to step in line' (Sholle, 1992, p. 278, quoting Foucault's view). It is an extreme form of foolishness, however, if in planning the education or health services we refuse to consult those with professional expertise or to listen to their advice. It is an even worse form of foolishness, bordering on the criminal, if we positively reject that advice.

For even if it is done in the name of democracy, as it often is, it is at root anti-democratic.

It is the role of the professions in a democratic society to ensure that democratic choices are as fully informed as they can be and that they are made with a full awareness of their theoretical, practical, even ideological implications. They have a responsibility for ensuring that policies are made on the basis of the fullest possible information and, equally importantly, that every citizen has access to that information in order to be able to evaluate those policies. For as we have seen, an effective democracy requires an informed and emancipated citizenry.

And a major part of this is the duty to support the citizenry in their resistance to the efforts of those who would seek to deny them this access to further understanding in order to be able to impose their authority on them. For this reason, the education of teachers, and that of every other professional, should include not merely a practical training but an adequate preparation for this wider role. For in a democratic context they should be expected to advise society, at whatever level, on matters where policies must be developed, or evaluated, to assist in the process of ensuring that these policies are as sound as they can be made and, above all, to provide an assurance that such policies are genuinely the result of due democratic processes and not of the decisions – and the ideology – of a few, foisted on to the rest. Teachers in particular must be prepared not merely to do an effective job in their classrooms but also to provide society with this kind of professional expertise. For again it is an essential ingredient of democracy and a crucial device for its maintenance and protection.

Again, however, we are forced to note that a major trend of the last decade or so has been towards a progressive deprofessionalization. Most of the recent policy decisions which have been made in relation to the education system of the UK for example, have been made with little or no professional input and, indeed, with little or no genuine debate. In particular, when we consider in Chapter 7 against our democratic principles current policies for the school curriculum in England and Wales, we will see that the National Curriculum there has been constructed with little or no professional input. That lack, however justified, has inevitably led to mistakes which might have been avoided, to unnecessary wastage of public money and to serious inadequacies in provision. More seriously, however, it is also plain that it has contributed to a further erosion of democratic principles and of democracy itself. If this had been done simply out of error or a lack of due consideration, it would be serious enough. It is plain, however, that it is a result of a deliberate policy of deprofessionalization so that it is also highly sinister to those who have the interests of democracy at heart.

For, first, it is not just that the advice of educationists has not been sought; it has been positively rejected. There is hardly a serious educationist, for example, who did not warn of the major inadequacies of the National Curriculum for England and Wales. Yet their views were ignored and rubbished by that process of derision we have noted before, and they were excluded from any role they might have been expected to play in the framing of the new curricular policies. Indeed, the whole teaching profession has been, and continues to be, denigrated and put down by the present government.

Second, it is not only the teaching profession which has been so treated. The medical profession has also been most effectively marginalized in relation to the framing of policies for health. And attempts have even been made to erode that political independence of the legal profession, the judiciary, which, from the time of John Locke, has been asserted as a major safeguard against the erosion of liberal, democratic principles.

Again, we must also note that this reflects a worldwide trend. Reports on 'Curriculum theorizing and the state', published in the *Journal of Curriculum Studies* (1990, Vol. 22, no. 4, pp. 377–400), for example, paint a similar picture for the education systems of the USA, Spain and Australia, as well as for England and Wales. And again we must note that the stated 'rationale' behind this trend everywhere is that economic, commercial model of education which we have seen is not only inappropriate to educational planning but, more seriously, also anti-democratic in its import. For the major reason why governments do not want the advice of the professions is that professional advice will always be concerned to ensure the highest quality of provision, whether it be in health, education, social work or the administration of justice. And high-quality provision is expensive. It is not politically expedient, however, to declare this as one's reason for rejecting such advice. It is more expedient to denigrate the professions, to accuse them of wasting public money, of being responsible for economic failure, of being idle or even, to use one of the favourite terms of abuse, of being 'ideological', and to use that as an excuse for doing the planning oneself or of handing the task over to 'right thinking' laypersons.

For a corresponding feature of the management of all social services in recent years has been the increasing involvement, especially at the managerial level, of non-professionals. This has even led to the appointment of inspectors of schools from whom no previous experience in education has been required or expected.

To involve members of society at large in decision-making is clearly right in a democratic society, as we have already suggested. To give them authority to over-ride professional advice, however, and even to make judgements concerning professional performance, for reasons we have also discussed, can only be justified by the desire to save money and/or to exercise political control, and to do this at the expense of quality. For it can hardly be claimed that what has arguably been the least competent sector of many developed societies in recent times, namely those industrialists and business persons whose efforts have led to the kind of economic recession which is at the root of the whole problem, are *ipso facto* more competent than the professional experts to take on the running of other major areas of social living.

Again, therefore, we see further effects of the adoption of that commercial model of educational planning which we have argued is not only inappropriate to education but also detrimental to the maintenance of democracy. And we also see further evidence of that process of the de-democratization of society which is a major feature of current political trends.

To ignore the expertise of the professional is foolish. To do so deliberately and, further, to seek to discredit and so to reduce the quality of that expertise, even to the point of eliminating important elements from initial training courses for teachers, is criminal. For it is a crime against any society to deprive it of professional input to its policies; and it is a particular crime against democracy, every bit as serious as the worst forms of anti-intellectualism which characterized Maoist China.

And so again we must remind ourselves that it is not consonant with any principle of democracy to vote once every five years for a government and then to allow that government to make its own policies with neither aid nor professional advice. And when a government acts as though it has this kind of free hand, it places the future of democracy and its continuing development at risk.

The failure to make appropriate use of professional expertise, then, is another feature of current social policies which adds to the general picture of democracy in decline. It is also a major explanation not only of why the National Curriculum in England and Wales has failed so manifestly and miserably that it is currently being redesigned but also of why that curriculum must itself be seen as contributing to that decline. It is to a consideration of this and related issues that we turn in Chapter 7.

7

CURRENT TRENDS AND POLICIES
IN THE SCHOOL CURRICULUM

An education that makes complete sense must provide opportunity for personal fulfilment – for the good life as well as for good living.

(*Newsom Report, 1963, p. 117*)

When we turn to a consideration of the implications of democratic principles and of a postmodern perspective on human knowledge for the school curriculum, we find a similar picture to that we have just examined in higher education. Again it is the dictation of content and the discouragement of challenge to that content which combine to form the root problem. For as we saw in Chapter 4, to dictate what pupils must learn and assimilate is to impose on them what currently counts as knowledge, thus inhibiting the essential process of the evolution of human knowledge and, further, to indoctrinate them into the values implicit in the knowledge selected and, indeed, in the process of selection itself. It is thus to use education as a subtle form of social control and denial of individual empowerment. And so the development both of individual autonomy and of human knowledge itself is seriously inhibited.

It was for this reason that, as we also saw in Chapter 4, some writers have called for a deschooling of society to protect the rising generation from the limitations on their freedom of thought, and thus ultimately their freedom of action, which this kind of social control entails.

We also saw, however, that a less radical solution to this problem might lie in an approach to education which would explicitly seek to empower pupils by encouraging them to view the conditions of their lives from a 'reflexive' perspective (Freire, 1972). And, in Chapter 5, it was argued that the fostering of such empowerment must be a central purpose of education in a democratic society. We noted also, however, that such a solution would require a complete reconceptualization of curriculum, a redefinition that might match that reconceptualization of knowledge which is postmodernism and the kind of open society which is democracy. And it was further suggested in Chapter 5 that that reconceptualization involves a shift from regarding a curriculum as no more than a body of knowledge, a list of subjects and of subject syllabuses to be transmitted to pupils, towards seeing it in terms of the processes of individual development, a device for promoting the growth of autonomy and offering that empowerment which we have suggested education in a democratic society must be centrally concerned to support.

It is important to note that this, indeed, was the direction in which the school curriculum had been evolving for some time before that process was halted by those contrary trends we explored at the beginning of Chapter 6, that emphasis on commercialism, 'value for money' and economic utility. And it is important that we remind ourselves of the kinds of development which have been blocked by current policies, since these are as central to an evaluation of those policies as the stated aims of the policies themselves.

Before we attempt to evaluate current policies and practices, and in particular the National Curriculum that has been introduced in England and Wales, it is important to recognize that in many ways these have gone against the stream of educational development, which was taking us towards the kind of reconceptualization we have suggested democratic principles demand. And they have done so to such an extent that they can only be regarded as a deliberate attempt to halt the flow of that stream, and thus as a deliberate attempt not only to prevent any response from the education system to postmodernism but also to hold up the democratization of education.

They are thus a further manifestation of those political trends we identified at the beginning of Chapter 6 and saw reflected in current policies for higher education in the UK. For those trends, as we saw there, represent a 'conservative restoration' (Apple, 1990) and are leading most developed societies in the opposite direction from that which increased democratization requires, not only in the sphere of educational provision but also in social provision generally.

The effect and, indeed, the intention of the National Curriculum for England and Wales, for example, have been to retard any shift towards the realization of those principles of education in a democratic society which Chapter 5 sought to identify, or towards the reconceptualization of curriculum it has been argued that these entail. It has in many ways been an attempted culmination of those contrary trends we have also identified.

And it has blocked the implementation of these principles mainly through the concept of curriculum that is fundamental to it, its treatment of curriculum as conceptually indistinguishable from a syllabus or series of syllabuses, and its consequent failure to acknowledge the need for the kind of reconceptualization of curriculum which both democracy and postmodernism require. It is important to note first, however, that it has done this in spite of, or perhaps even because of, the emergence of clear trends in a contrary direction.

A RECONCEPTUALIZATION OF THE CURRICULUM IN PRACTICE

It was suggested in Chapter 5 that, when Bernstein (1967) writes of the shift to the open school, he writes of it as though it were actually happening. And, indeed, in many places and in many areas of educational provision, at that time it was happening.

We have made frequent references in earlier chapters to the statements and recommendations of a long line of official reports on education, in particular those of the Crowther, Newsom, Robbins and Plowden Committees, and we have noted the view of education to which they all subscribe. It is the kind of view which we have suggested a democratic society must be committed to. We should also note that those forms of teacher education which the establishment of CATE and its associated mechanisms was designed to destroy had developed in response to this kind of view, an attempt to produce the kinds of teacher that a democratic form of educational provision would require. Those reports, and indeed those forms of teacher education, were not always completely clear about the implications of what they were attempting to bring about for the way in which the curriculum is conceived. One of them, however, among the very earliest, was quite specific on this theme.

For the kind of open curriculum which it is being claimed that the open, democratic school needs is, in all respects, the curriculum which had been developing within primary education in the UK, and especially in the early years sector. And there could be no clearer statement of the basic principles of this concept of curriculum, for example, than that oft-quoted assertion of the Hadow Report on Primary Education (Board of Education, 1931, p. 93):

> The curriculum is to be thought of in terms of activity and experience rather than of knowledge to be acquired and facts to be stored. Its aim should be to develop in a child the fundamental human powers and to awaken him [or her] to the fundamental interests of civilized life so far as these powers and interests lie within the compass of childhood.

Given the frequency with which those words have been quoted, given the later support for that view of the primary curriculum which was offered by the Plowden Report (CACE, 1967), given the common tenor of the recommendations of all the other reports we have referred to, given the massive reinforcement of this approach to education, especially in the early years, which has been derived from extensive studies of human development during the last half century, and given the case which is being made out here for this form of curriculum as the only form which is compatible with postmodernism and with democracy, it is difficult, indeed impossible to claim that the reason why it has diminished rather than developed in recent years is an accident rather than the result of a deliberate policy to kill it off.

The main work of destruction has been undertaken by the politicians and their aides. And what we must note here is that it cannot be claimed that this has been done in the interests of democracy. On the contrary, an argument might more easily be developed to show that its effect, and its purpose, has been to undermine democratic processes. For it is clear that it has been undertaken in support of those alternative, anti-democratic ideologies which we have seen Denis Lawton (1989) has identified.

The developments we have just described have been largely confined to the primary curriculum, although similar attempts at redefining curriculum can be seen in secondary schools. Many of those schemes for integrated studies which were a feature of secondary schools in the UK in the wake of the raising of the school leaving-age to 16 in 1972, for example, were characterized by the kind of openness towards knowledge which is being advocated here as the only basis for a democratic curriculum (James, 1968). And in many schools where mixed-ability groupings were adopted in the 1970s and 1980s, this form of reorganization was accompanied by a freeing-up of the curriculum and the replacement of didactic teaching methods with schemes which offered more scope for individual inquiry (Kelly, 1974; 1975; 1978).

It is worth noting also that at both primary and secondary level these developments were prompted by a concern to ensure that there should be equality of opportunity and entitlement for all pupils regardless of their social or ethnic origin, although it cannot be denied that some of them were somewhat misguided in this respect.

In spite of these developments, however, the curriculum of most secondary schools continued to be framed by subjects and thus to be conceived in terms of the transmission of subject-content. However, there was developing even within those subject areas an awareness of the need to encourage critical inquiry and challenge on the part of pupils, to stimulate them to think for themselves, to promote some form of dialogue and to get away from the notion that education is a matter merely of assimilating the knowledge-content which is laid out before one, and meeting the demands of 'target-related assessment'. And there was clear evidence that many subjects were undergoing a process of redefinition, as subject-specialists re-examined both the subjects themselves and their role in education.

Perhaps the best illustration of this is to be found in some of the developments of recent years in assessment techniques, which have been modified and adjusted to match changes in how subjects and, indeed, the educational process itself, have come to be conceived. There have been important moves, for example, towards an attempt to assess the quality of pupils' thinking rather than merely the extent of their knowledge. In its later phases, the work of the government's own Assessment of Performance Unit (APU) can be seen to have been moving significantly in this direction (Kelly, 1987). And the development of systems of profiling, Records of Achievement (ROA), have reflected also a concern to delineate each pupil's abilities on a broad front rather than to seek to 'measure' short-term attainment.

There is a sense, then, in which Bernstein (1967) was right to believe that the shift towards the open school was under way. And what was happening in education must be recognized as part of that wider process of social evolution which it is the concern of democracy to facilitate. Education was responding to changes elsewhere in society, and especially to changes in views of knowledge and values.

Furthermore, this movement seemed to be given official sanction in a publication by members of Her Majesty's Inspectorate in 1977 (DES, 1977). For that publication suggested that the curriculum should be conceived and planned in terms of 'areas of experience', and it listed those areas in the form of eight adjectives – 'aesthetic/creative', 'ethical', 'linguistic', 'mathematical', 'physical', 'scientific', 'social/political' and 'spiritual' ('technological' was added later).

This was clearly an attempt to formalize the shift of emphasis in the curriculum, especially that of secondary schools which we have just identified, and to move closer to a reconceptualization of curriculum in terms not of knowledge but of experience, not of content but of process. And the use of adjectives to define and describe such a curriculum has its own significance, since it indicates that the curriculum is now to be viewed no longer in terms of its substantive content but in terms of something less concrete than that, perhaps more elusive but also with the potential to accommodate more variety and offer more freedom of manoeuvre for both teachers and pupils.

Discussions of a possible national curriculum for England and Wales were also under way at that time, and it was argued (Kelly, 1977) that this kind of statement of the common principles and processes of a national curriculum would be more in keeping with the way things had been developing and, indeed, with democratic principles, than a national curriculum framed in terms of subjects and syllabuses. This is the kind of national curriculum which has been established in some other countries, such as New Zealand, and it is clearly the only way of reconciling the need for some form of central oversight of educational provision with the principles of democracy.

One of the stated aims of the proposals for a national curriculum in England and Wales has been to ensure equality of entitlement, and this was also one of the main concerns behind the proposal for a curriculum planned by areas of experience. Indeed, the follow-up document to that of 1977 was called *Curriculum 11–16: Towards a Statement of Entitlement* (DES, 1984), and it outlined the steps which had been taken in several local authority areas to implement this new form of curriculum in the secondary schools.

A good deal of progress, then, was being made towards that reconceptualization of curriculum which it is being claimed a democratic society and a postmodern view of knowledge demand, and towards those changes in educational provision which this would require. In short, education was evolving and developing in phase with all other aspects of society, as we have seen within a democratic context it should be enabled to do. It would be wrong of course to claim that these were the conscious reasons for these developments. It is plain, however, that those responsible for them were seeking after precisely those things we are suggesting democracy and postmodernism require – a rejection of dogmatism and intolerance, a recognition of the plurality of values, an openness in the face of knowledge, an acceptance of the centrality of dialogue and, most consciously, an equality of opportunity and of entitlement for every young citizen.

At the same time, however, as we saw in Chapter 6, there were other pressures on education systems building up as a result of economic recession and decline. The oil crisis of the early 1970s both reduced the level of funding which governments were prepared to allocate to education and increased the pressures to devote that money to activities which would promote the economic health of society. The speech of Prime Minister James Callaghan at Ruskin College in 1976 made this quite explicit.

Such pressures could not be ignored, nor should they be, since the economic health of society is as crucial to the effectiveness of its education system as to any other dimension of its life. What has happened, however, is that, as we have seen, they have been allowed to dominate educational planning since that time to the exclusion of almost every other concern, except perhaps those 'law and order', social control issues which are now coming to the fore. And so what has come to take precedence, and largely to dominate educational provision, is that commercialism, concern for 'value for money' and economic utility which we identified at the beginning of Chapter 6 as the central features of recent trends at all levels of education systems.

In the event, that movement towards a greater democratization of education, which we have just noted, was seriously curtailed. And in England and Wales it has been halted by a set of policies, and especially the creation of a national curriculum, which are characterized by a rejection of all of that movement's major features, and which reaffirm, re-establish and reimpose the kind of curriculum all of these arguments and developments tell us needs to be replaced, if our system of education is to take account of twentieth-century views of knowledge and, especially, if it is to evince the characteristics which we have shown to be essential to education in a democratic society.

School subjects and, indeed, education itself, have again been redefined. This time, however, the process of redefinition has been undertaken by the politicians so that it has clearly been a political rather than an educational act. And it has taken the form of a return to positivism and thus to all of the political dangers we have seen that that presents. These policies must be seen as part of that process of 'conservative restoration' (Apple, 1990), as a deliberate attempt to return to 'traditional values' (i.e. the curriculum of the public and grammar schools at the beginning of the century), to bring to a halt, indeed to reverse, those developments we referred to earlier, and effectively to ensure that education should not be permitted to evolve, and should not be allowed to become democratized.

It is against this backcloth that we must evaluate the National Curriculum for England and Wales as a central element of current policies for the school curriculum there. Before we do so, however, there is one further theoretical issue that needs to be addressed. For the debate over how we are to conceptualize the school curriculum in a democratic society raises important questions concerning the appropriateness of any form of national curriculum in such a society. And so the concept of a national curriculum and the question of its compatibility with democratic principles needs to be reviewed very carefully before we can address and evaluate the actualities of current practice.

THE CONCEPT OF A NATIONAL CURRICULUM

The concept of a national curriculum needs to be explored and analysed most carefully within the context of a democratic society because it raises questions about the degree of governmental, and thus political, control of the school curriculum which is permissible within a society that purports to be democratic. *Prima facie* it smacks of totalitarianism, and it brings with it reminders of the extent to which totalitarian governments have used control of the school curriculum to achieve goals that are the direct converse of those which in Chapter 5 we identified as integral to any form of truly democratic curriculum.

On the other hand, a second reason why we must consider the concept of a national curriculum very carefully is that it might also be seen as a *sine qua non* of educational provision in a democracy. For if we were right in Chapter 5 to claim that access to education is the right of every young citizen in a democracy, a legal requirement such as that for the universal provision of a national curriculum would seem to be an essential device for ensuring that that claim is met.

It is for this reason that the notion of 'entitlement' has loomed large throughout the process of establishing the National Curriculum for England and Wales. And the idea of national legislation to ensure equality of entitlement has for a long time been a central feature of the case for central control of the school curriculum (White, 1973), since the offering of differentiated curricula to different 'kinds' of pupil has been seen as a form of 'education in obedience' (White, 1968), as providing a 'curriculum for inequality' (Shipman, 1971), and thus again as a denial of individual empowerment. We thus have an apparent dilemma. For on the one hand we have the claim that central control of the school curriculum is, or can be, inimical to the preservation and development of democracy; while, on the other hand, there is the argument that it is essential to its achievement.

Again, the problem derives from the way in which the school curriculum is conceptualized, so that again the solution to the apparent dilemma is to be found in a reconceptualization of curriculum as process. A national curriculum can be dictated by central government without transgression of democratic principles if it is framed in terms of the promotion of development through appropriate experiences, in terms of 'areas of experience' (DES, 1977; Kelly, 1977). Indeed, as we have seen, such a curriculum is the only device for securing a genuine equality of entitlement and thus of empowerment, so that it is essential to a democratic form of educational provision.

And, as we saw in Chapter 6, the argument that a national curriculum is necessary to ensure teacher accountability requires no more than that teachers be held accountable for adherence to procedural principles framed in these terms – accountability to ensure quality of professional practice rather than as a device for political control of that practice. Indeed, such a model of accountability, as we also saw, is the only form which is compatible with democracy.

To frame a national curriculum in terms of its constituent subjects and, worse, the content to be transmitted under those subject headings, on the other hand, is to put at risk every principle of democracy and of democratic education we have identified. And to hold teachers accountable for little more than the performance of their pupils in national tests of the assimilation of this subject-content is to reinforce that risk. It is a prime example of the politics of knowledge in action, of that linking of knowledge to political power which postmodernism asserts, and thus of the denial of genuine empowerment.

There is of course a pragmatic, economic argument (although it is far from convincing philosophically) for insisting that schools teach those subjects which are central to the health of a country's economy. This is one aspect of that trend towards economic utility in curriculum planning which we have already noted, and few would wish to take issue with it as one part of what the curriculum should be seeking to attain, although even here the manner in which these subjects are presented is crucial.

There are, however, at least two important caveats to be recognized. First, it is not possible to extend this argument to areas of the curriculum whose economic value is difficult, even impossible, to explicate. Thus while the teaching of mathematics, science and technology, provided that it is undertaken in an appropriate manner, may be justified on these grounds, the inclusion of subjects such as history and religious education, especially when their precise content is prescribed in great detail, cannot be so justified.

And, second, the insistence on this kind of national curriculum, even in those manifestly economic subjects, cannot be proclaimed as a form of entitlement. For the use of the term 'entitlement' implies that the underlying concern is with the advantage of the individual pupil. And the argument for the compulsory inclusion of economically useful subjects is clearly founded on what is seen as in the interests of the society as a whole.

There is thus a fundamental inconsistency in the attempt to offer a curriculum whose main concern is with the economic health of society as if its focus were the entitlement, and the empowerment, of the individual. The use of the term 'entitlement' in such a context can only be explained as a piece of rhetoric, designed to 'sell' the product, since it cannot be reconciled with the reality.

The concept of democracy, then, can support the provision of a national curriculum whose concern is with equality of entitlement. Such a national curriculum, however, to achieve this goal, must be framed in terms of 'areas of experience' rather than subjects, processes rather than content. Any other form of national curriculum, even if justified on economic grounds, must be recognized as placing democratic principles at risk.

There are thus three main features of the theoretical backcloth against which we now seek to evaluate the National Curriculum for England and Wales – that evolution of the curriculum towards a greater democratization which we identified earlier in this chapter; the conditions under which a national curriculum might be compatible with this; and the cogency of those pressures for economic utility which we discussed in Chapter 6.

THE NATIONAL CURRICULUM IN ENGLAND AND WALES

Put simply, the National Curriculum in England and Wales is everything a curriculum for a democratic society should not be. It envinces none of the principles we have identified as essential to education in a democratic context. It is framed entirely in terms of subjects and their knowledge-content. Its testing procedures emphasize the degree to which pupils have assimilated this content, and offer little encouragement for them to adopt a critical stance towards the knowledge they are being presented with. It is overtly competitive. And it manifestly fails, as it must fail, to provide that equality of entitlement which is essential to democracy (and which in fact is one of the National Curriculum's own watchwords). It is, as we have already suggested, an attempted culmination of those tendencies towards a 'conservative restoration' (Apple, 1990) which we noted in Chapter 6.

It was asserted by many within the teaching profession from the very outset that the National Curriculum was so flawed that it could not succeed (Lawton, 1987; Lawton and Chitty, 1988; Kelly, 1990). In the event it has lasted only six years from the date of the legislation by which it was established. For it is now being substantially reduced and revised. And there are aspects of it, such as the testing programme, which many teachers are refusing to operate. It has collapsed, however, mainly because of its apparent impracticability, the burden it has placed on teachers and taught alike, for example, and the sheer complexity of the structures required for its full implementation. Hence the current concern is merely to reduce its scale.

What is only slowly being recognized, but has not yet been publicly acknowledged, is that its major inadequacy is that it is fundamentally misconceived; it is at its very roots the wrong kind of curriculum for a democratic society. And it is that aspect of it which we must examine here. For through its own palpable unsuitability, it offers us the best possible guide in our search for what an appropriate curriculum for a democratic society might be.

The most obvious feature of the National Curriculum to be noted in our present context is its subject base, and its consequent content base. It adopts, or at least accepts, as we have seen, a positivist view of human knowledge. In this, as in many other respects, it is a throwback to an intellectual age which well predates postmodernism. Indeed, it has been claimed (Aldrich, 1988, p. 22) that 'the most striking feature of the . . . national curriculum is that it is at least 83 years old' in so far as it is in every major respect identical with the the curriculum for secondary grammar schools as prescribed in the regulations issued by the Board of Education in 1904. 'There is such a striking similarity between these . . . that it appears that one was simply copied from the other' (*ibid.*). The only significant difference is that that curriculum 'is now to be extended to primary and comprehensive secondary schools' (op.cit., p. 23).

The full significance of this is not to be found merely in the fact that this is the inevitable result of a policy which places responsibility for curriculum planning in the hands of amateurs, whose knowledge and understanding of education goes little beyond that derived from their own experience of it – in most cases in public or grammar schools. Nor is its significance only to be found in this further evidence that current policies seek to promote advances in every area of social living except education, that, while technology and the development of knowledge and understanding may be permitted to change all other aspects of life, education must remain unchanged, so that the worst offence a teacher or educator can commit is to be 'progressive'. These are of course serious causes for concern. The real significance, however, of this decision to go so far 'back to basics' as to ignore almost a century of development lies in the fact that it represents an attempt to impose the values which are implicit in that form of curriculum – those of the public and grammar schools of a hundred years ago – on the present population of a society which is very different in many respects, and particularly in its plurality of values, faiths and cultures.

And, further, the effect of this is to ossify the curriculum and to inhibit the development of knowledge. For while the content of the subjects the National Curriculum imposes may well be different from what they were in 1904, the way in which they and thus the curriculum as a whole are conceived has changed not at all. And the values implicit in those subjects remain unchanged. Education continues to be regarded as merely the transmission of knowledge, knowledge itself as non-problematic and the curriculum as a statement of the knowledge so to be transmitted. And the implicit values continue to remain hidden and unchallenged, especially by those who are to imbibe them. Thus those redefinitions of curriculum and of individual subjects, which we noted earlier, have been erased, and new (or old) definitions, reached by political fiat rather than after professionally informed debate, have been imposed.

In a number of respects, therefore, this kind of curriculum not only falls well short of being an appropriate curriculum for a democratic society; it can also be seen to be positively inimical to democratic forms of social living. And it is inimical to democracy precisely because it transgresses all those principles of democratic living we identified in earlier chapters and especially in Chapter 2, and all those principles of education in a democracy which we examined in Chapter 5. For rather than promoting the continued evolution of human knowledge, it creates barriers to that process. It makes no kind of attempt to reconcile different values, cultures and opinions, other than by attempting to over-ride them all by the imposition of a single system – that of the dominant group. It thus inhibits the development in individuals of the power to think for themselves, to reach their own opinions and in this way to prepare themselves for active participation in the governance of society, to play their part in the sovereignty of the people. And in giving prominence to one cultural system by holding it up as 'the model', it denies equality of opportunity and entitlement to those whose roots are embedded, by social class or ethnicity, in a different cultural milieu.

Most, if not all, of these inadequacies of course stem from the adoption of that economic, value-for-money, commercial, instrumental, utilitarian model of planning which we discussed in Chapter 6, where it was claimed that it is a model which is fundamentally incompatible with principles of democracy. If the central aim of the National Curriculum is to support the economy, along with the parallel but equally instrumental aim of social control, then this must, as we have seen, put at risk any deeper, more long-term educational aims, and especially that of equality of entitlement. And the extension of this policy to all areas of the school curriculum must, as we have also seen, threaten the essence of social democracy.

The official literature which has been produced to support the implementation of the National Curriculum does of course stress that it has a liberal dimension, that many of its component subjects are subjects which have traditionally been regarded as supportive of the liberal ideal (Carr, 1991a), in short, that those subjects have been chosen to promote the development of those capacities which we are claiming are essential for full participation in a democratic society. The detailed dictation of the content of these subjects, however, as we have seen, has an effect which is far from liberalizing.

And whether these claims to liberalism are genuine or not, we have seen that the National Curriculum has been presented to society in terms of its economic value – to society and to the individual. The emphasis throughout has been on market forces, not only in relation to the curriculum itself but also, and perhaps most obviously, in its associated administrative structures, such as the scheme for 'opting out' of local authority jurisdiction and, especially, the enforced publication of 'league tables' by schools, ostensibly to provide information for parents of potential pupils, but in essence to promote a form of commercial competitivism. The general ethos which permeates all these new policies is one of utility:

> It is thus unsurprising to note that those subjects which promote critical evaluation of contemporary society – subjects such as social studies and economics – are systematically neglected and that history, literature and the other liberal arts are organised in ways which minimise their political function and emphasise their market value. Nor is it surprising to find that the more vocationally-oriented subjects of the National Curriculum do not incorporate any critical questions

about the norms and values of 'the world of work'. Because, in a modern market democracy, education must subordinate democratic participation to market participation, the National Curriculum must not only depoliticise liberal education; it must also depoliticise vocational education.

(Carr, 1991a, p. 190, with reference also to Feinberg, 1983)

We see again, therefore, that the National Curriculum, whatever its supporting rhetoric, through its deference to and promotion of market forces must be fundamentally inimical to the achievement of longer-term educational goals, must in fact, as we have seen, negate those educational goals, and must, as a consequence, diminish opportunities for the provision of a proper form of democratic education. This is a further result of that category error of treating education as a commercial activity.

Finally, we must note that the extension of the policy of central dictation of curriculum content beyond those subjects where a pragmatic form of justification might be found in the economic needs of society takes us, as we saw at the beginning of this chapter, into the dangerous waters of totalitarianism. For in subjects such as history and religious education to dictate content is manifestly to impose values and beliefs in a manner that cannot be consonant with genuine democratic principles. And the current public debate over whose values and beliefs will dominate, what kind of history will be taught and which religious view imposed, illustrates this quite graphically. Again it is the politics of knowledge in action. And again the concern is manifestly to 'gentle the masses', to legitimate particular forms of discourse, to use knowledge as a tool of political control, rather than to empower individuals to act autonomously.

These criticisms of the National Curriculum for England and Wales apply not only to the National Curriculum as a whole, to its rigid division into subjects, to all the individual subjects of which it consists, and especially to those subjects in which cultural values, and differences of cultural values are most apparent but they also apply to the manner in which it has been implemented. For the process of its implementation has also left much to be desired in terms of democratic principles.

THE IMPLEMENTATION OF THE NATIONAL CURRICULUM IN ENGLAND AND WALES

There are three main aspects of the implementation of the National Curriculum in England and Wales which are worthy of note in our discussion of education in a democratic society. Two of these, the suppression of information and the lack of professional input, relate to general points we discussed in Chapter 5, so that they need little further elaboration here. The third, the use of rhetoric and the control of discourse, will need rather fuller exploration.

The suppression of information

Our earlier discussions of freedom as one of the fundamental principles of democracy, and of academic freedom as a necessary safeguard of democratic forms, led us to the conclusion that there is an obligation on any democratic government not only to provide all citizens with access to relevant information but also to offer adequate evidence and justification in terms of its own response to such information for all the decisions it makes on their behalf. In short, in a democratic society public policies should only be made after full, free and open debate, offering open access both to the evidence and to the policy-makers' thinking. On both counts, the implementation of the National Curriculum in England and Wales is revealed as seriously lacking.

For, first, as we saw in Chapter 6, there have been quite deliberate attempts to deny access to any evidence which is not felt to be supportive of government policies, in particular, as we also saw, by preventing researchers from revealing any results of their research which might suggest that those policies were not as well conceived as they might have been, or their effects other than those predicted for them.

There may well be contexts, even in a democratic society, where open access for all to certain kinds of information may not be in the immediate interests of the society as a whole. That is after all the purpose of legislation such as the Official Secrets Act, although we should perhaps note that this is not accepted practice in all democracies. Suppression of such access, however, like any other contravention of democratic principles, can only be justified if it can be shown to be to the advantage of democracy itself and to be in tune with, or even for the protection of, other principles of democratic living.

Policies for education, however, can never conceivably fall into this category. Education policies can only be a threat to national security and to the preservation of democracy when they are expressly not formulated on democratic principles. To suppress relevant information in this context, then, can never be a device for protecting democratic procedures; it must always on the contrary be a threat to their maintenance. This is the first of the ways in which the implementation of the National Curriculum can be seen to put democracy at risk.

The second aspect of this principle of open access to information, as we have seen, is the further inference that, in addition to such information being made available to all, it be used by those who make policies in the making of those policies. In other words, it requires that evidence and reasoned arguments be offered in support and justification of those policies. It demands that public policy be formed only after free and open debate on the part of all involved. Yet it is unsubstantiated assertions rather than such reasoned argument or evidence which has characterized the implementation of the National Curriculum, and 'debate' is a very odd, and totally rhetorical, term to apply to the processes which have accompanied it.

It was suggested a long time ago that there are three major strategies for effecting social change (Bennis, Benne and Chin, 1969). The 'empirical-rational' strategy requires that those wishing to bring about any change offer either empirical evidence or rational argument (or both) in support and justification of it. The 'normative-re-educative' strategy involves an attempt to persuade those who will be affected by the change to accept its worth, to embrace the values and norms implicit in it. The third strategy is that of 'power-coercion' which, as the term suggests, seeks to effect change by the exercise of power or force.

It will be apparent that only the first two of these can be compatible with the principles of democracy, and that the third is more readily associated with totalitarian forms of government. It will also be apparent, however, that it is the third which has been the main strategy employed for the implementation of the National Curriculum (Blenkin and Kelly, 1993; Kelly, 1994). For as we have seen, there has been little attempt to offer evidence or reasons in support of it. Indeed, we have just seen that every effort has been made to suppress evidence. And the major technique adopted has been a series of acts of legislation designed to compel acceptance and compliance.

Further, this legislation has been supported by financial sanctions, both covertly, through funding mechanisms, like those which we saw in Chapter 6 have been used to control the higher education sector, and overtly, through penalties of various kinds for various 'misdemeanours'. And the elaborate mechanisms for the testing of pupils, along with the publication of the resultant 'league tables' and other related features of a bureaucratic model of accountability, can only be seen as a device for the exercise of this kind of power-coercive control; it is in no sense a means towards genuine improvements in educational standards.

Indeed, evidence is now emerging that it has encouraged a form of competitivism which has led to a drop in the moral and professional standards of some teachers and headteachers, such as those who are falsifying their examination results by entering poorer candidates privately to ensure that their results do not affect the school's standing in the league tables. This is a form of behaviour which cannot have the best effects on the standards (certainly not if we include moral standards) of their pupils. 'Improvement in standards' is merely part of the rhetoric which we shall see has been employed in the attempt to gain acceptance for these policies.

There are of course limits to how far, in a society which is still said to be democratic, this kind of power-coercion can go without being revealed as totally undermining to democracy itself. And the revolt of teachers, parents and governors against some aspects of current policies, and most notably the testing programme, may illustrate that this point has been reached.

However, there are more subtle methods of power-coercion than legislation, sanctions and penalties. Most notably the use of rhetoric and the control of discourse represent a subtle attempt to change attitudes not only without evidence or reasoned argument but also without obvious compulsion. Again these devices are the more dangerous for being less immediately identifiable. They thus constitute another serious threat to democracy which we must shortly unearth.

First, however, we must briefly note the other major source of inadequacy, and threat to democratic forms, in the planning and implementation of the National Curriculum, the absence of professional input.

The absence of professional input

We noted in Chapter 6 the debate about the role of the professional in decision-making in a democratic society. We saw that, while it would not be consonant with democratic principles to permit professionals to dictate policies to society even within the sphere of their own professional expertise, it is foolish and equally at odds with those principles to ignore that expertise and, in quite properly, leaving decision-making to the citizenry as a whole, to deprive them of the understandings which the expertise of the professional can supply. Yet we have also seen that that is exactly the procedure adopted for the planning and implementation of the National Curriculum.

There can be only one explanation for this and that must be again a desire to suppress the knowledge and the understandings which that expertise would have supplied. For that 'conservative restoration', which we have seen Michael Apple (1990) speaks of as a worldwide trend, will not be forwarded if advice is sought from the very professionals who have taken education in directions from which the right wishes to withdraw it. And so, 'one of the conservative movement's major successes has been to marginalize a number of voices in education' (op.cit., p. 378), and one 'group of people who have lost even more of their already limited voice is curriculum scholars' (*ibid.*).

It is of course the case that many people take the view that education is not a matter of professional expertise in the way that, say, medicine or engineering are, and that the professional expertise of the teacher does not go beyond a knowledge of a curriculum subject and of the techniques of controlling pupils in order to teach them that subject. No one could have read the earlier chapters of this book, however, without realizing that the professional expertise of the teacher is far more significant than the mere skills of transmitting knowledge, nor without appreciating the kinds of understanding that expertise embraces. So that one has to be naive in the extreme to continue to regard educational planning as something which does not need that kind of input, and which can be effectively undertaken by laypersons.

However, our political masters and mistresses have ignored that expert input, and have placed responsibility for planning the National Curriculum in the hands of selected groups of laypersons. We have, therefore, to conclude either that they are thus evincing a form of naivety which makes them intellectually unfitted for government, or that they have a hidden agenda which they are not prepared to reveal to society at large and thus are unfit on moral grounds to take responsibility for government in a democratic society. For that hidden agenda, as we have seen over and again, can only be a concern to halt and reverse the democratization of education, and one device for achieving this, as we have also seen, is the deprofessionalization of teachers, and indeed of all 'intellectuals' and experts.

To take any decision in a democratic society without full regard for what can be learnt from the relevant experts is, at best, very foolish and, at worst, criminal, in the sense that it is a crime against democracy itself. And in the case of the kinds of educational policy we are considering, it is manifestly the latter.

The clearest evidence of this is the necessity it creates for the adoption of power-coercive devices in the attempt to ensure implementation. And the most insidious and, as far as democracy is concerned, threatening of the devices which have been employed in the attempt to establish the National Curriculum has been the use of rhetoric and the control of discourse. It is to a consideration of this that we now turn.

Rhetoric and the control of discourse

Rhetoric was once regarded as an essential part of a liberal education. It was one of the seven elements of the curriculum advocated by the Roman educationist, Quintilian. And it was reaffirmed by writers such as Thomas Elyot in the sixteenth century, when Quintilian's *Institutes* was rediscovered. It thus has not always had the pejorative meaning it is usually given today.

It does not follow from that, however, that its meaning has changed in any substantial way. It is merely an interesting example of change in social and political values. For what rhetoric denoted for those such as Quintilian and Elyot who advocated it was a device for influencing and persuading others. And it is not difficult to understand why this was regarded as an important part of education when education was available only to those whose birth and background marked them out (the males at least) as men whose role in life it would be to control and govern others.

A major part of the education of such people, then, was a training in the skills of oratory, the development of the techniques of persuasion, not merely by reasoned argument but also by the skilled deployment of words. It was of course expected, certainly in Roman times, that these techniques would be used for the good of the community as a whole, that that *virtus*, which we noted in Chapter 2 was demanded of every political figure in Rome, would in fact be displayed by all. And so the Roman philosopher, Cato, could define the educated orator as 'a good man skilled in the art of speaking'. There was, however, no guarantee of this, no assurance that he would be a good man, since there was little genuine accountability to ensure it.

Rhetoric, then, has always been the skill of persuading others to accept one's decisions and judgements. All that seems to have changed is the notion, which we have seen ran parallel to this in Roman thinking, that it should be used for the benefit of those others. However, with or without this corollary, it is plain to see that this kind of activity has no place in a democracy. For, to put it bluntly, it is a device for fooling people – fooling them into voting for one, fooling them into blindly accepting one's policies, fooling them into buying one's products, fooling them into doing whatever one wants them to do, whether this is in their interests or not.

As such, it is of course the stock-in-trade of the politician, the advertiser and many other agencies in society. This, however, still does not make it an acceptable feature of democracy. Indeed, if we have been right to claim that full access to information, the justification of policy decisions and open debate are essential characteristics of any democracy, then we must acknowledge that rhetoric is hostile to the preservation of those characteristics and thus to the maintenance and development of democracy.

One cannot ban rhetoric from a democratic society. A major task for education in such a society, however, is to arm pupils against it, to prepare them to recognize it for what it is and to see beyond it. This is part of that process of empowerment we suggested in Chapter 5 is a crucial purpose of education in a democratic society. And it must follow from this that to use rhetoric to bring about change in education, and to establish policies for education, is particularly inappropriate and out of phase with democratic principles. It is one thing for politicians to resort to rhetoric to gain power or to retain their power. There is a sense in which we all expect this and have learnt to live with it, mainly by never believing a word they utter. It is quite unacceptable, however, and completely out of line with democratic principles, for rhetorical devices to be used to 'sell' and to implement official policies.

Yet, again, we must note that this is the major device which has been used, alongside the more overtly coercive measures of the law and its sanctions, to establish and implement current policies for education in the UK. It has taken three main forms (Blenkin and Kelly, 1993; Kelly, 1994).

First, there is that basic rhetorical device, the use of 'buzz' words, words with warm and persuasive connotations. The Education Act 1988 is not just an Education Act, it is the Education *Reform* Act. The National Curriculum is described there, and elsewhere in the official documentation, as an 'entitlement' curriculum, as a 'good and relevant' curriculum, as a 'broad and balanced' curriculum, which will 'raise standards', meet the 'particular needs' of every pupil, and provide 'continuity' and 'progression'. Clearly, the message is that it will reach the parts other curricula cannot reach.

And one notes too the skill with which such terms have been hijacked from the discourse of those who have used them to promote diametrically different approaches to education (Blenkin and Kelly, 1993). For 'entitlement', 'relevance', 'balance', 'needs', 'continuity', 'progression' and many related terms were once part of the discourse of those who sought to promote rather than to thwart the development of democratic forms of education – those, for example, who have been advocates of education as development, of learner-centred approaches, and those who have contributed to those redefinitions of education, of curriculum and of individual subjects which we saw earlier were major features of the ways in which educational thinking was developing before these policies brought such developments to a halt. The hijacking of these terms by the political right has not only provided them with a range of useful and effective 'buzz' words but it has also deprived the opposition of the essence of its own discourse.

One looks in vain, however, in the promotional documentation for any definition of these highly elusive terms. And one looks in vain for the evidence that the curriculum which has been created will in fact, or is even likely to, bring about the marvellous results claimed and predicted.

It is clear, therefore, that these claims are no more than rhetorical devices designed to 'sell' the policies to an unsuspecting public. And as in all such cases, the fact that rhetoric is the device employed suggests that the reality is very different.

The second major device we must note is the use, or rather the misuse, of metaphor. Metaphor enriches language and is thus a figure of speech to be welcomed. A particular metaphor, however, can insinuate itself into our thinking until we no longer recognize it as a metaphor. And so, as Elliot Eisner (1982, p. 6) has said, metaphors 'also have a cost. That cost resides in the ways in which they shape our conception of the problems we study'.

What must be added to this is that the cost also resides in the fact that the metaphor can be used as a rhetorical tool to shape those conceptions quite deliberately. For a metaphor, or a 'metaphoric model' (Ortony, 1979), can be devised and propagated to change not only the way in which we talk about some aspect of society but also the way in which we regard it, the value perspective from which we view it. And argument from analogy being such an easy kind of fallacy for anyone to slip into, once a metaphoric model or system has been established, it is difficult not to be carried along by it into false kinds of reasoning. And again we have no better example of this than the way in which metaphor has been used to change the perspectives from which people view education and prepare them for an acceptance of the values implicit in the new educational policies.

The metaphor that has been foisted on the world of education in recent years is that of commerce and industry. 'The language of educational purpose has undergone a sea-shift of transformation into business terminology and the going discourse of the corporate culture' (McMurtry, 1991, p. 211). The language of education is now littered with terms such as 'products', 'providers', 'customers', 'clients', 'machinery', 'mechanisms', 'managers', 'curriculum delivery', 'quality control' and so on. As Martin Lawn (1990, p. 388) has expressed it:

> The language with which schools are to be described is no longer a private educational or curriculum language, made up from its own reference points; it is now the language of the city pages and business news. Enterprise, enterpreneurship, cost-centres, incentive contracts and privatization are now all educational terms. The language of the previous

decade and of the post-war decades has been expunged from the record.

This is further evidence of that category error we have noted before, that treatment of education as a form of industry, the imposition of an economic model on educational planning, which we have suggested is not only conceptually confused and confusing but also damaging in its practical effects, inimical to both education itself and to democracy. We can now see how that model has been engineered and how its imposition has been effected.

For once that language and that metaphoric system have been accepted, the model of education which they reflect, and the value system which they encapsulate, are imbibed along with them. And so we slip the more readily into a view of the education service as product oriented, as instrumental, as competitive, as 'a national investment' rather than 'the right of every boy and girl' (CACE, 1959), as concerned primarily with output rather than with the safeguarding of human rights, as élitist rather than egalitarian, as mechanical or technical rather than moral, as to be evaluated in terms of cost-effectiveness rather than educational quality. In short, it is a metaphoric system which not only undermines democracy by its attempt to by-pass our thought processes but it does so also by smuggling into those thought processes a set of social values and a model of education which are themselves inimical to democracy.

This kind of control of discourse is a subtle form of censorship, then. And such censorship is at its most dangerous when it becomes what Richard Hoggart (1992, p. 260), in discussing censorship and the media, has called 'the most difficult of all kinds of censorship: self-censorship'. This is the kind of censorship which results when we accept the controls placed on our thinking and our action, adopt the discourse which is officially legitimated, and abandon the values we once adhered to for no better reason than that they are now no longer 'fashionable', i.e. no longer officially approved, 'expunged from the record'. As Hoggart goes on to say (op.cit., pp. 260–1):

> You would not perhaps yield to explicit directives or bullying, and they are rarely needed. You do begin instinctively to evade issues, opinions, positions not acceptable to those above or the body of those out there. All this is hugely practised in totalitarian states; but like persistent bad drains it also haunts open societies.

We must go further here and say that it is a practice which not only haunts open societies; it also threatens their very openness.

The imposition of that industrial/commercial metaphor which we have just noted on the thinking, and thus the practice too, of those concerned with education at all levels is a prime example not only of the legitimation of discourse or a subtle form of censorship but also of the ways in which such censorship can quickly become self-censorship. For that metaphor, and its implicit values – of competition, productivity, value for money and so on – has come to dominate discussions of education, and educational practice. And so, 'it is difficult to avoid the conclusion that the educational process has been so persuasively subordinated to the aims and practices of business that its agents can no longer comprehend their vocation in any other terms' (McMurtry, 1991, p. 211).

And those who still seek to adhere to earlier educational values find it increasingly difficult to assert these, not least because many who would do so have experienced attempts to silence them, either by that process of 'rubbishing' we have noted before or, in some cases, by positive directives to remain silent, as in those many cases where headteachers and other teachers have been forbidden to share with parents any doubts they may have about the experiences their pupils are having, or missing, as a result of these new policies.

Education, however, is not, or at least in a democratic society should not be, an industrial process. Educational institutions are not, or again should not be, factories. To look for efficiency in the work of such institutions is perfectly legitimate. To define efficiency in this context in industrial terms is manifestly erroneous and, for those reasons we have elaborated, hostile to both education itself and to democracy. The criteria by which the work of any educational institution must be evaluated are far more sophisticated than efficiency of output and cost-effectiveness. The industrial metaphor, however, seeks to make us view and evaluate those institutions differently. As such it undermines democratic principles both in the values it seeks to propagate and in the manner in which it seeks to propagate them.

This attempt to impose the metaphor of industry and commerce on the education system is a good example of the third aspect of the devices adopted for the implementation of current policies which we must note – the legitimation of discourse. We saw in Chapter 3 what postmodernism is seeking to tell us concerning the role of discourse within society. And the importance of discourse in setting the rules for, and the parameters of, our thinking and thus our actions has been strongly emphasized. We also noted there the claim that we are all the product of the discourses within which we operate, so that the manipulation and the legitimation of discourse has come to be seen as an important device by which social control through the distribution of knowledge is effected. The strategies employed for the implementation of current policies in the UK offer a rich example of this process, not least in the establishment of that commercial discourse we have just considered.

It has been argued (Cherryholmes, 1987, p. 301) that the rules of discursive practices 'govern what can be said and what must remain unsaid . . . [and] identify who can speak with authority and who must listen', so that 'dominant discourses determine what counts as true, important, relevant and what gets spoken' (*ibid*).

In the UK over the last decade or so this process can be observed in action from both perspectives – determining both 'what can be said' and 'what must remain unsaid'. For, first, as we have seen, the discourse which was prevalent within the educational debate in the 1960s and most of the 1970s, that which we have seen reflected in those developments we noted earlier in this chapter, has been ousted, expunged. What we might call the 'Plowden discourse', for example, in primary education has been discredited and every attempt has been made to destroy it, to remove it from the educational debate, to confine it to the category of 'what must remain unsaid'. We saw above that Martin Lawn (1990, p. 388) draws our attention to the fact that 'the language of the previous decade and of the post-war decades has been expunged from the records'. And with it has gone its underlying model of education.

These attempts to erase that discourse and thus that approach to education, however, have not taken the form of reasoned arguments against it or in support of an alternative view. They have merely proceeded by that process of 'rubbishing' which we have seen Stephen Ball (1990) has termed 'discourses of derision'. And so approaches to education and curriculum based on the 'Plowden discourse' are discredited as 'outmoded', as 'old hat', as 'unfashionable', as inappropriate to the 1990s. And the intention is that they be supplanted by approaches based on the new dominant discourse, the new, approved version of 'what can be said', that encapsulated in the industrial metaphor and the economic model we examined earlier.

And in association with this there has emerged a new group of people 'who can speak with authority' on educational matters, the politicians and the 'educrats' rather than the teachers or the educationists, whose expertise, as we have seen, has been excluded from the policy-making process.

The effect of this manipulation of discourse has been to reinforce the effects of the use of rhetoric and the industrial metaphor we considered earlier. For it has brought about that significant shift in the intellectual categories within which we debate and plan educational provision, which we noted in Chapter 6. The moral category has been replaced by the mechanistic; the social by the political; the ideal by the expedient; the co-operative by the competitive; and, again, education as a 'human right' by education as a 'national investment' (CACE, 1959). And all this, as we have seen, adds up to a serious threat to democracy.

It also represents again the use of a device which makes it unnecessary to produce evidence or reasoned arguments for that change. The change is effected by stealth and not through open debate. And the fact that this is so again raises questions not only concerning the legitimacy of the procedure but also about the motivations of those adopting it.

Again, therefore, we have a serious threat to the maintenance and development of democracy. And we have discovered further evidence in support of the claims of postmodernism that knowledge and discourse are used as political tools, as devices for effecting massive and unpopular change by subtle, power-coercive means, so that again we note the denial of all opportunity for the kind of open debate which we have seen on more than one occasion the principles of democracy demand. Not only, then, are current policies for the school curriculum in England and Wales themselves a threat to democracy; the means by which they are being implemented represent what is perhaps an even greater threat. Again they must be counteracted by access to relevant information and the generation of an open debate by an informed and educated citizenry.

Some of the sociological accounts of the legitimation of discourse, as we saw in Chapter 3, take the view that control through discourse is an inevitable process, that this is what happens in any society and that we are all, as a result, the products of the discourse rather than its authors, that the discourse determines what we think rather than vice versa. However, as we also saw in Chapter 3, it is not necessary to assume or accept this kind of inevitability. Indeed, as we noted there, such a determinist view would render our whole discussion of democracy otiose, since it implies that we must accept whatever social system we find ourselves in and that we cannot do anything to change it. Furthermore, the clear evidence before us of the manipulation of discourse by those in power can leave us in no doubt that discourses are socially constructed. And as such they can be deconstructed or reconstructed.

For, as we saw, to recognize these features of discursive practices and, indeed, of rhetoric and metaphor too, is to achieve a position from which one can protect oneself from the manipulation of one's thinking which they are seeking to effect. It is to have gained 'greater freedom from ideological and linguistic traps' (Slaughter, 1989, p. 264). It is to have learnt to do our own thinking rather than have others do it for us. It is to have developed that 'reflexive perspective' which we have seen Freire (1972) regards as the only defence we have against those who would control the distribution of knowledge and the rest of society through that distribution. It is again to be empowered.

This is a process which we have also seen enables us to 'feel deeply involved in the process of cultural reconstruction and renewal' (Slaughter, 1989, p. 265). And it is that kind of involvement which we have seen to be of the essence of a democratic society. The education system in a democracy, like all other social institutions, belongs not to the politicians and their henchpersons but to every member of society. In a democratic context, even if social policy cannot be made by all of those affected by it, it should be open to the challenge and the debate of all concerned. And that requires again open access to information and the provision of adequately supported justifications for policy decisions.

To make policy without providing such access and to seek to implement it by stealth, by rhetoric and the manipulation of discourse is a practice which would be quite unacceptable and incompatible with democratic principles even if the policy itself were democratically sound. For the very practice puts democratic principles at risk, by seeking to change and control the lives of others without involving them in the process, even by the giving of justificatory evidence or reasons. There is no place in a democratic society for those who would deny others their democratic rights.

Current policies for education in the UK, then, stand convicted of being anti-democratic in terms of the procedures adopted for their implementation as well as of their content and nature. Empowerment rather than social control must be the keynote and the central purpose of educational planning and practice. And indeed, if there is a common denominator of those principles of education in a democratic setting which this book has sought to identify, then that is it.

One of the ways in which a democratically appropriate form of education can seek to achieve that aim is by ensuring that those principles are reflected in all aspects of its own practice. How that might be done and, more importantly, how and why it is often not done, have been the themes of the last two chapters.

A second way in which it must be tackled, however, is through a deliberate and positive attempt to prepare pupils for life in a democratic society. How that might be approached, and again how it can be bungled, will be the twin themes of Chapter 8.

8

EDUCATION FOR A
DEMOCRATIC SOCIETY

Education should serve as a means of training well-balanced citizens for a democracy.
(Bruner, 1960, p. 1)

The previous three chapters have considered some of the ways in which those democratic principles which were identified in Part 1 of this book, and especially those related to a twentieth-century perspective on human knowledge which we explored in Part 2, should be expected to permeate the practice of education in a democratic society. Those chapters have also attempted an evaluation of current trends and practices against the backcloth of those principles, and have identified the major threats to them, and thus to the maintenance and development of democracy itself.

The theme of those chapters, and indeed of the book as a whole, has been that, if we are serious about democracy we must recognize it as a moral rather than merely a political concept and thus as offering moral imperatives and placing upon us certain moral obligations. Those imperatives and obligations must govern all policies and practices in a democratic society so that, in the particular sphere of education, which is our central concern here, policies and practices must conform with those basic principles of democracy we have identified. A major element, then, in the preparation of young people for democratic forms of social living must be the experience of an education system which reflects those democratic principles.

Another aspect of this moral dimension of democracy, which we have also stressed, is that it is predicated on a view of human beings as capable of moral behaviour, of altruism, of making 'evaluations' (Wollheim, 1962), decisions reached in the light of the common interest rather than purely selfishly.

If this is so, it must follow that education in a democratic society must seek to develop these moral capabilities in all pupils. It is not enough, however, to expect them to imbibe these moral principles through some form of osmosis, or to develop these moral capabilities by some kind of natural process of maturation. Alongside our democratic practices, therefore, there must be a more positive attempt to induct them into the democratic moral system.

This chapter, then, will address the more positive and explicit issue of what the education system should be doing consciously to prepare the young for life in a democratic society. In particular, we will need to consider how they can be prepared for active participation in that society. We have already seen that one of the most serious threats to any democratic community is apathy on the part of its citizens, an unwillingness to become involved in public affairs, even at the level of informed comment on them, or a sense of inability to participate. For it is apathy which opens the way for those who do wish to become so involved to do so to their own advantage rather than to that of the community as a whole. In Chapter 1 we noted Pericles' comment that in ancient Athens 'we alone consider the person who takes no interest in public affairs not as impractical but as useless' and that 'we are able to make sound judgments on public policies even if we cannot originate them'. And that is the only position one can take if one is committed to those basic democratic values we have identified – human rights, equality, individual freedom and, perhaps above all in this context, the sovereignty of the people.

In a democratic society, then, education should be expected to take deliberate steps towards producing citizens who, even if they will not themselves be centrally engaged in policy-making, will appreciate the need to be aware of the actions of those who are and competent to form opinions and judgements about them, if for no other purpose than to be able to use their voting rights in a considered manner. How education might achieve this will be the subject of this chapter. And as we have done throughout, we will seek both to outline the ideal and to evaluate the realities of current policies and practices against that.

There are three main dimensions of this issue which we will need to explore. For, first, we must consider how pupils can most appropriately be initiated into a democratic form of morality. Second, we must consider what might be a suitable kind of institutional context to support that process of initiation. And, third, we will need to evaluate, against that backcloth, some of the current practices which are subsumed under the heading of education for citizenship or citizenship studies.

PERSONAL, SOCIAL AND MORAL EDUCATION

Moral education has always had a central role in theories of education. We have seen more than once that it was the main concern of Plato's theory, that the point and purpose of all the intellectual activity which he prescribed for his 'philospher-kings' was their development towards that stage of perfect moral understanding which constituted their entitlement to rule. And it is equally clear that the theories of education offered by all the other 'great educators', from Plato to Dewey, were similarly focused on the need for moral upbringing.

It is also clear that some form of moral upbringing was a central concern at the practical level in the private schools (or, in the UK, 'public' schools) which through most of these years provided the only forms of education available. The approaches to moral upbringing adopted may be considered to be somewhat ill conceived and perhaps even more badly translated into practice. Nevertheless, there can be no doubt that the moral dimension of education continued to loom large. Like Plato's theory, however, this provision was directed towards the production of a ruling class, towards the preparation of a small group of people, most usually men, to take all decisions on behalf of the uneducated mass of citizens.

With the advent of state-maintained education, less attention came to be given to the moral education of children, and universal education came to be viewed as having three functions – to offer opportunity for a limited degree of upward mobility for exceptionally talented pupils, to provide some kind of basic vocational/industrial training for the rest and to seek to reinforce concerns for law and order by offering them a form of training in obedience, a 'gentling of the masses'. This last function comes nearest to demonstrating a concern with moral upbringing but, in doing so, it takes us back to the Platonic system, in which a select few are educated to rule and the mass of those not so selected are trained to obey. We have seen that Plato's system has the exonerating feature of basing its selectivity on merit, on moral and intellectual quality. Modern versions have based it, in the main, on the privilege of birth and wealth.

Such a form of moral upbringing cannot be consonant with those principles of democracy we have identified. In particular, it cannot be reconciled with a political system in which political authority is, in some sense, invested in all citizens rather than in a privileged minority. A bipartite or tripartite ('tripartheid' I once came across as one of those examination paper howlers which has its own significance) system of moral education, then, is not a starter. It is a part of that 'minimalist' ideology (Lawton, 1989) which, it was suggested in Chapter 5, has no place in any society with pretensions to being described as democratic. Democracy, as has been reiterated frequently throughout this book, is a moral concept. And moral education in a democratic setting must reflect the essential elements of the democratic moral ideal.

There has been a good deal of debate about moral education in recent times, although significantly less since the advent of those instrumental, 'value-for-money' educational policies we have noted in earlier chapters. In the 1960s and 1970s, at a time when those egalitarian principles expressed in the Education Act 1944 and in such documents as the Crowther Report (CACE, 1959) continued to prevail, that debate focused on how a proper form of moral education might be provided for all pupils and, in particular, what might constitute a proper form of moral education for all.

The general thrust of the debate was away from the limited ambition of 'gentling the masses' and thus away from the notion that moral education is merely a matter of imbibing moral rules and obeying them in a largely uncritical manner, a process we would much more readily characterize as indoctrination rather than as education. Rather, moral education came to be seen as fundamentally concerned with the development of individual autonomy, the ability to think for oneself and reach one's own conclusions on moral issues.

We saw in our brief discussion of autonomy in Chapter 5 the support this view of moral education has received from the work of people such as Jean Piaget and Lawrence Kohlberg who have sought to trace the course of moral development in human beings and, in doing so, have seen the final stage of that development as the autonomous level of self-accepted moral principles (Kohlberg, 1966). What we must now note is that it is this kind of autonomous moral behaviour which is central to the moral system we call democracy. An authoritarian form of morality is unacceptable in a democratic context. For whose authority is the democratic citizen to be subservient to other than his or her own? In a democratic society, moral principles must be self-accepted rather than uncritically imbibed; they must be freely chosen rather than externally imposed; the democratic citizen must, in Kantian terms and in literal terms, give him or herself the laws he or she obeys. He or she must do this, however, in the light of an awareness of the collective 'good' of the community. Individualism must be tailored to communal responsibility.

That is the foundation of moral education in a democratic society. Its prime aim and purpose must be the production of autonomous, self-regulating and socially responsible citizens. This of course, like every other principle of democracy we have identified, is easier said than done. There are, however, a number of practical lessons which follow from it. And, first, there are those inevitable negative points, those things which a recognition of this basic principle of moral education must steer us away from.

For example, it must steer us away from all forms of authoritarianism. It is to misconceive moral education, and indeed to misconceive democracy, to advocate the inculcation of values, whether 'basic', 'traditional' or of any other kind. Etymology is an unreliable source of meanings, but it is often indicative of them. And it is worth noting that the etymological roots of the word 'inculcate' are the Latin words for 'tread' and 'heel'. Moral education in a democratic society cannot be conceived as a process of 'treading' values into future citizens, and especially not with one's heel.

This is one reason why religion and religious education are quite unsatisfactory vehicles for moral education (Downey and Kelly, 1978). Religious morality must be authoritarian in that it is based on religious fiat, on the law of God; and it requires of its adherents an acceptance of that fiat or law – 'laws which never shall be broken'. It must be some form of sacrilege to seek within a religious context to 'give oneself the law one obeys' or to seek to claim any kind of moral autonomy, other than the willing acceptance of a religious authority. Truly moral behaviour, however, can never be a matter of obedience – to any kind of law. It must entail a willing acceptance of that law, and an acceptance of it which derives from a recognition of its rightness rather than from an acknowledgement of, or even a respect for, the authority of its source.

To attempt to base morality, and thus moral education, on religion is to put at risk the development of forms of morality suitable to a democratic context. For it is to discourage that process of challenge, debate, dialogue and autonomous decision-making that are essential both to morality and to democracy.

Morality in a democratic society must be essentially humanist. Democratic values, as we have seen, are human values. They must reflect those values we have identified as central to any concept of democracy itself. They must involve respect for the human rights of one's fellows, a recognition of their right to equality of treatment, respect and opportunity, a tolerance of their right to appropriate forms of freedom – of thought, of speech, of action – and an acknowledgement of their right to full participation in decision-making.

Few of these values, incidentally, are to be discerned within most religious moral systems, and even fewer *between* religious moral systems, whose intolerance of each other is legendary and continues to block the attainment of reasoned solutions to social problems and even to prompt inhuman barbarities at an individual and public level throughout the world. A properly democratic form of moral education must seek not only to promote autonomous thinking on moral issues but it must also seek to promote those human values we have suggested are endemic to democratic forms of social living. Purists may argue here that there is an incoherence, a fundamental contradiction between these two goals, between the desire to promote individual autonomy and the intention to establish particular kinds of values, so that they may wish to raise the age-old debate about the justification of particular moral values.

The coherence and consistency of our case, however, comes, as we have indicated before, from the context in which it is being presented. If we have been right to claim that democracy is a moral concept, it must follow that to prepare future citizens for democracy involves introducing them to the moral principles which the concept of democracy encapsulates. Since, however, one of those principles is that of individual freedom, and especially freedom of opinion, it must further follow that the preparation of citizens for a democratic society must also involve assisting them to make full use of that freedom. If they accept democratic values they must do so freely and willingly. If, on the other hand, they exercise their freedom to adopt other values, as we know many people do, they must also be educated to recognize that it is democracy itself they are rejecting. For, as we have seen before, no one can consistently claim to be committed to democracy while at the same time rejecting any of the ideals or values we are claiming such a commitment entails. It must also be recognized, however, that, in rejecting democracy, they are also rejecting that very freedom they are seeking to exercise. For the so-called 'paradox of freedom' ceases to appear as a paradox once one acknowledges democracy as the only moral system within which true freedom can continue to flourish.

We do not need, therefore to be mealy-mouthed in our advocacy of human values within a democratic context. For we are merely drawing attention to the fact that any commitment to democracy entails a parallel commitment to those values. As has been pointed out on several occasions within this book, there is no compulsion to accept democracy or its values. There is, however, an intellectual and rational compulsion to recognize and accept the ineluctable inter-relationship between the two, and the consequent illogicality of seeking to accept one without the other. Moral education in a democratic society must seek to draw pupils' attention to this inter-relationship, but it must do so while stressing the centrality of autonomy and freedom of thought.

Further, in the process of seeking to achieve this it must not only reject all forms of authoritarianism but it must also assist pupils in the process of protecting themselves against other forces and agencies within society which would seek to do their thinking for them. This is a part of that function of education which we have noted on several occasions was Paulo Freire's (1972) sole justification for its provision, the function of arming the young against all those agencies which seek to ensure that they are 'dopes' whose destinies can be planned for them.

We have seen that there are many agencies in society which have a vested interest in discouraging autonomous thinking and reflection, not only in the young but also in everyone. Politicians, for example, want us to accept their policies without too much detailed analysis. And manufacturers want us to purchase their products without too much careful inspection or comparison with alternatives. This is the point and purpose of advertising, whether political or commercial. In neither case is it aimed at encouraging challenge, critique, debate or reflection. On the contrary, it is concerned to discourage that kind of approach and to promote a largely uncritical acceptance of its offerings. In a democratic society such uncritical acceptance must be quite unacceptable. And so in a democratic society moral education must seek positively to counteract it. And it must set about this by encouraging that critical, inquiring, challenging approach which we have suggested is essential to all forms of learning in a democratic society.

It must also, however, take a more positive stance than this. It must offer pupils opportunities to look critically at aspects of current society, and it must seek to help them to develop those critical faculties which they need if they are to learn to see beyond rhetoric, and to avoid the manipulation of their thinking by agencies in society which are concerned solely to promote their own sectional interests.

Moreover, to a large extent, this must be a process of self-reflection. For it must never be forgotten that moral education is not like, say, French, to which most pupils come completely anew. A great deal of moral learning has occurred before most children even enter formal group educational settings – from parents, from other adults, from peers, from children's literature and, above all, from the media (Downey and Kelly, 1978). It is this previous learning, then, that must form the basis of any positive attempts at moral education. And so in being encouraged to think about moral issues, pupils, from the earliest age, must be assisted to undertake this thinking in parallel with a process of self-reflection, of increasingly critical awareness of their own beliefs, however acquired, and indeed of their own behaviour. It will be clear that all areas of the school curriculum have a contribution to make to one or more aspects of this process of moral education, and equally that no teacher can avoid a share of the responsibility for it. As the Newsom Report (CACE, 1963, para. 160) said, 'teachers can only escape from their influence over the moral and spiritual development of their pupils by closing their schools'.

This reinforces the argument offered earlier for an approach to all forms of school learning that emphasizes challenge and critique and discourages uncritical acceptance. For as we have seen before, it is the *manner* in which knowledge is presented that is crucial. It also suggests that the social/moral dimension of every area of the curriculum or school subject should be stressed – in science and technology, for example, as well as in the humanities.

It also raises, however, a further point which is of great importance to any consideration of moral education in a democratic society. So far we have discussed moral education as if it were a purely cognitive matter, a question of learning how to cogitate about moral issues and reach intellectually honest conclusions about them. That dimension of morality and of moral education is of course very important. We saw earlier, however, that one of the major criticisms of rationalist epistemology, and especially of rationalist views of morals, was that they are incapable of accommodating anything other than the cognitive dimension. They cannot allow for the affective dimension of moral behaviour other than by rejecting it as an unfortunate barrier to what they see as a purely rational and cognitive process. We saw that this has been a major criticism of such theories, since they offer a form of morality which is largely 'inhuman' in so far as it cannot accommodate what we all recognize as being a significant feature of human life, its affective or emotional side. And there can be few people who would not be prepared to acknowledge the part that feeling plays in their moral lives, the extent to which their moral decisions are influenced by how they *feel* about things as well as, as much as and sometimes even more than, how they *think* about them. Any form of moral education which does not allow for this affective dimension must be recognized as inadequate. And if we have been right to argue that democratic values are human values, no form of moral education for a democratic society can ignore the affective or emotional dimension of the moral life of every human being.

In fact, it is important to recognize that there are several dimensions to moral decision-making and moral behaviour. An extremely detailed and helpful analysis was offered as long ago as 1967 by the Farmington Trust project, directed by John Wilson (Wilson, Williams and Sugarman, 1967), although, like many such things, it is part of an earlier form of discourse and it has been lost sight of as we have been taken ever further into the era of instrumentalism and 'value for money'.

This project identified several qualities which it claimed were necessary for moral decison-making and moral behaviour and which, consequently, it should be the function of moral education to promote. It suggested that the morally educated person must have learnt to respect others and acknowledge their rights; must have developed an empathetic capability to understand and be sensitive to the feelings of others; must have come to appreciate the need for relevant information in the reaching of moral decisions; must have developed whatever skills, particularly interpersonal skills, are needed to implement moral decisions made; must have acquired the ability to formulate his or her own general moral principles; must have become capable of translating those general principles into particular decisions; and must have acquired the self-discipline needed to translate those decisions into action.

It is not the intention here to debate the essentiality of these qualities at length, although it must be noted that there is nothing there that conflicts with what we are defining as a democratic form of moral education. Rather it refines our definition. What must be noted, however, is that, while perhaps no single area of the school curriculum, whether that is conceived in terms of subjects or 'areas of experience', can attend single handedly to the development of all of these qualities, every area has some part to play, either in the cognitive or the affective dimensions of moral development. The study of literature and drama, for example, provides an invaluable route to the development of empathy and sensitivity to the feelings and the perspectives of others. Aspects of physical education, perhaps especially outdoor pursuits, have much to contribute to the development of the self-discipline needed to translate decisions into action, what might be, perhaps glibly, described as 'character-building'. And so on.

We must finally note that, since no one area of the curriculum can meet all the needs of moral education, even if it sets out deliberately to do so, there is need for a form of provision which seeks to co-ordinate the disparate contributions of each. And a number of such forms have been devised and implemented, perhaps most notably Lawrence Stenhouse's Humanities Curriculum Project (HCP) (Schools Council, 1970), which set out to offer pupils opportunities to explore, freely and without teacher direction, controversial issues of social importance, and to form their own – informed – opinions on them. This project, although itself controversial in some respects, provides a very good model for the kind of provision that will genuinely support the development in pupils of those qualities we have identified as essential for proper participation in a democratic society. Again, however, we must note that it has been overtaken by educational policies that are directed towards other ends.

In spite of that, we must note further that the kind of National Curriculum which is now being operated in England and Wales makes it even more important that this kind of positive provision for moral education be made. For not only is it needed as a counter balance to the basic, instrumental, 'value-for-money' ideology of that curriculum but it is also particularly necessary in the context of a curriculum which is framed in terms of subjects rather than 'areas of experience', and where, beyond that, those subjects are conceived, as we have seen they are, in terms of 'useful' knowledge to be acquired rather than in terms of the contribution they make to the overall development of the individual. The National Curriculum is conceived and planned simply as a vehicle for the acquisition of knowledge and not as a support for personal development through that acquisition. And so it can no more support personal, social or moral development than it can promote any other kind of development.

It is for this reason that the National Curriculum Council (NCC, 1990a) has identified 'personal and social education' as a 'crosscurricular' issue and sought to advise schools on how they might tackle it as such. Unfortunately, there are some serious defects in this approach (apart from the omission of the word 'moral' from the new designation of this dimension of education).

First, in the context of a curriculum most of which is clearly specified and prescribed, anything which is not so specified and prescribed, and which thus does not contribute 'league-table' points, is inevitably regarded as of lesser importance and thus mariginalized, so that personal and social education becomes a kind of optional extra rather than being recognized as one of the most important tasks the schools should be addressing. It is significant that this dimension of education is given no mention in the revised version of the National Curriculum recommended in the 'Dearing Report' (SCAA, 1993). This problem is of particular concern where it has resulted from the imposition of this same National Curriculum on primary schools, and especially on early education, where an emphasis on the personal, social and moral development of children has traditionally, and for very good developmental reasons, been central. There is no logic in a government imposing policies that marginalize personal, social and moral education and then castigating parents and teachers for an apparent decline in behavioural standards among the young.

Second, as the change in terminology from 'moral' to 'personal and social' may denote, the approach to this area of the curriculum which is advocated leaves a good deal to be desired when evaluated against the criteria for moral education in a democratic society we have identified. There is more of a flavour of education for conformity about it than of education for autonomy.

Finally, we must note that there is an inevitable problem for those who would advise us on personal, social and moral education in the context of a national curriculum which, as we saw in Chapter 7, does not in itself evince the values it asserts it is desirable to promote. One cannot help children to develop empathy in a context that encourages competition. One cannot support decison-making capability when choice is limited and/or made on one's behalf by 'authority'. And one cannot promote individual autonomy where freedom, of pupil and teacher alike, is severely controlled.

Moral education, or personal, social and moral education, can only succeed when the institutional context supports and reinforces its central goals and purposes. We must practise what we preach. To do otherwise is hypocrisy, and is soon recognized as such by our pupils. And the net result of that is the diametric opposite of what we are suggesting is required.

THE INSTITUTIONAL CONTEXT OF MORAL EDUCATION

The importance of the context, the social and cultural environment, for the development of values has long been appreciated. It is this which is at the root of censorship in totalitarian societies, a practice that, like so many others, can be dated back to Plato. In Plato's 'ideal state', all forms of art were to be tightly controlled by his 'philosopher-kings' to ensure that the mass of citizens, from the very beginning, were exposed only to the 'right' moral values:

> First, then, it seems, we must supervise those who write stories, and select those stories they make which are proper and reject those which are not. And we will persuade nurses and mothers to tell the selected stories to their children. For they shape their minds much more with stories than they shape their bodies with their hands.
>
> *(The Republic, para. 377)*

There is no doubting the effectiveness with which subsequent totalitarian regimes have followed this advice to control the values and attitudes of their citizens.

Here, as elsewhere, however, it is not necessary to let the devil have all the best tunes. And it is important to recognize that the social and cultural environment is as significant in the development of a free and autonomous morality as it is in attempts to control and manipulate people's thinking, to do that thinking for them. It is for this reason that it has been claimed throughout this book that all aspects of any democratic society must display those democratic principles upon which it is built. And it is especially important that this should be the case in education, where the minds of the young will be 'shaped' – for good or evil, in the interests of democracy and its maintenance or to its ultimate destruction.

The importance of this was fully recognized by John Dewey, who claimed that, in a truly democratic society, schools must themselves be democratic and have their own 'embryonic community life'. And this has been reinforced by those studies of moral education, such as the Schools Council project, Lifeline (McPhail, Ungoed-Thomas and Chapman, 1972), which have seen moral education as a fruitless undertaking unless it is backed by the organization, practices and structures of the school or school system that is seeking to promote it.

As always there are two aspects of this to be considered: the negative and the positive. For if one accepts that much moral learning and development occurs through a process of imbibing values from the experience of what goes on around one, from what has been called the 'hidden curriculum', from that influence which teachers have over moral and spiritual development which, the Newsom Report (CACE, 1963) claims, can only be avoided by closing the schools, then this kind of process can be either supportive of the development of a democratic morality or inimical to it.

It will be inimical to it when it reflects values that are at odds with those fundamental principles of democracy we have identified. This means, in the first place, that, as we have seen, a curriculum which offers knowledge as dogma and discourages challenge to what is offered will have the effect of eroding democratic values, since it will reflect an implicit denial of the human right to freedom of opinion. It will promote passivity rather than active participation. It will thus work against any attempt which might be being made elsewhere in the system to promote democratic values of this kind; for the practice will not match the preaching:

> Too often we just assume that we can preach the virtues of a democratic

life to children and that through such exhortation they will become active, participating citizens. Surely this is wrong, when the rest of the student's experience is passive, with little to say about daily life. In fact, what students do learn is that unquestioning submission, rather than active participation, is what is valued in citizens.

(Wood, undated, p. i)

The converse of this is a curriculum which deliberately sets out to promote the ability of pupils to think for themselves and reach their own conclusions on every issue, to support their development towards individual autonomy, to offer them that empowerment we have discussed in earlier chapters. We have suggested that this is the only kind of curriculum compatible with the notion of democracy. To that we must now add that it is the only form of curriculum that will support, rather than inhibit, that parallel development of an appropriate form of democratic morality. The kind of curriculum we offer, then is a crucial determinant of the kind of moral development we will promote.

In a similar way, the approach adopted to discipline will strongly influence moral development. For an authoritarian approach to discipline, on the part of the school as a whole or individual teachers within it, will inhibit moral development and, worse, it will lead to the development of moral attitudes which are unsuited to democratic social living. To expect children to do as they are told simply because they have been told is to impart to them a view of moral behaviour as obedience to authority. And to expect good behaviour because of little more than a fear of punishment is to imply a 'social contract' view of social living and social morality in which anything goes if you can get away with it. Such a view of society we saw in Part 1 to be the very antithesis of democracy.

Conversely, where reasons are offered for injunctions on behaviour, where explanations are given for them, where the pupils' own views are listened to, the effect is to suggest that behaviour is a matter not of subservience to authority but of acceptance of the need for a rational order. One avoids certain kinds of behaviour not merely because they are forbidden but because one can see, or be led to see, that they are 'wrong' in the sense of being antisocial or undemocratic.

Patterns of authority thus become crucial. And it is most important for the development of a properly democratic form of morality that the teacher be seen, and obeyed, as *an* authority rather than as *in* authority; that the teacher's authority be based on *expertise* rather than on *position*.

Finally, we must note that school structures, and indeed the structure of the education system as a whole, also display particular sets of moral values, which become an element in the 'hidden curriculum' and play their parts in supporting or inhibiting moral development. Relationships between the headteacher, or others in senior positions, and classroom teachers, between the teachers themselves, and between teachers and pupils, will all reflect values and attitudes which will either support or inhibit the development of democratic forms of morality. Where these relationships evince a mutual respect and tolerance, their effects will be positive; where they are based on a strong form of stratification, they will promote a hierarchical view of society.

The ways in which the school system is organized and the internal forms of organization adopted by individual schools, perhaps particularly their arrangements for pastoral care, will also have their effect. The establishment of 'selective' schools says much about attitudes to schooling, for example, and as massive research has made clear, communicates 'wrong', i.e. undemocratic, messages to pupils. The parallel to this within schools is the adoption of systems of streaming by ability for the allocation of pupils to classes, the social effects of which have been documented with equal conviction.

This of course is one manifestation of the fundamental error of approaching the planning of education as if it were the same kind of competitive activity as commerce or industry. We have already noted this as a category error and one which prevents the education system from reflecting those democratic principles we have claimed every social institution in a democratic society must reflect. We must note here its further effects in inhibiting the moral development of those pupils who are exposed to such a system. For it is a nonsense to expect schools and teachers to be able to develop attitudes of co-operation and caring for others in their pupils when those pupils are being expected for most of their time to be competing with their fellows. If the main task of the pupil in school is to outdo every other pupil, to gain a better score on national tests in order to enable his or her school to gain a better placing in the 'league-table', it is unlikely that he or she will even be able to understand injunctions to be sensitive to others' feelings and needs or to work co-operatively with them.

An extreme example of the effects of this is to be seen in the recent revelation, which we noted in Chapter 7, that many headteachers of private schools in the UK have been excluding their weaker pupils from the official school entry to public examinations and persuading their parents to enter them privately, in order to ensure that their 'failures' did not adversely effect their 'league-table' placing. For pupils to find their own headteachers cheating in this way is far from conducive to their moral development. Whatever it might do to support their preparation for life in a competitive, capitalist society, its effect on their induction into democratic principles must be negative in the extreme. Perhaps nothing illustrates more clearly our claim that competitiveness has no place in democratic education.

The way in which the schooling system is organized, then, and in particular the arrangements selected by each school for its internal structure, will have a significant impact on the effectiveness with which pupils are prepared for life in a democratic society. As we saw Dewey asserting, if this preparation is to be successful, schools must have their own 'embryonic community life'.

Some have wished to take Dewey's claim further than this and have advocated a complete democratization of every school's management procedures, the purpose of which is to involve the pupils directly in all decision-making. Representation of students on all significant committees in university institutions has of course been accepted practice for some time, certainly since those disturbing student riots and demonstrations, most notably at Berkeley and at the Sorbonne, in the late 1960s. Similar arrangements for the involvement of pupils in schools have been advocated for some time, and indeed have been tried in a number of schools, especially in the USA. The most obvious and common feature of this development has been 'a commitment to the school as a community; a place where young people and the adults who work with them could experience what it means to be devoted to a sense of the common good' (Wood, 1991, p. 1), what Lawrence Kohlberg has called a 'just community'.

Most usually, the attempt to achieve this has been through the establishment of schools councils. These have taken various forms and have had varying powers. What they have all had in common, however, is the desire to involve pupils in the management of the community which is their school, both in order to ensure that that community should genuinely reflect the democratic values of the wider society and to support their pupils in coming to understand what those values are and why they are important. Such Schools Councils have usually taken an especially important role in the disciplinary arrangements within the school, sometimes having responsibility for 'passing judgement' on particular cases, and always being consulted on the general principles underpinning these arrangements. And, as a corollary of that, they have also played a major role in the development of pastoral care and support systems. In this way they have sought to encourage pupils to take increasing responsibility for their own affairs and to recognize the need to participate, to be active, to take action rather than to be acted upon. They have thus been seen not merely as a suppport to personal, social and moral education but also as an important element of education for citizenship.

This has been reinforced by the inevitable tendency for such attempts at building schools as communities to move outwards into considerations of how the school community fits into the wider community outside. For a growing understanding of that society, of how it impinges on one's own life and, most importantly, on how one can in a democratic society influence it oneself, is a crucial ingredient of democratic education. Moral education for democratic living takes us so far; it should help us to reach our own conclusions on, and make our own evaluations of, social policies. What is currently being called 'citizenship studies' or 'education for citizenship' should take us beyond that into all those issues which relate to what we might, can or should be doing about those policies.

How that might be done, and how far current practices succeed in doing it, then, are the matters we now turn to as the final area we need to explore in our attempt to identify the positive steps which society, through its education system, needs to take to ensure the production of people thoroughly prepared to take their place in a democratic community.

EDUCATION FOR CITIZENSHIP

Education for citizenship has become a major concern in most developed societies in recent years. In the UK the Speaker's Commission on Citizenship, led by the former Speaker of the House of Commons, Lord Weatherill, has been established and its work is underway, with education for citizenship as one of its central concerns. Education for citizenship has also been designated as one of the 'cross-curricular themes' of the 'whole curriculum' (NCC, 1990a), one of the several important dimensions of education omitted from the National Curriculum. In the Republic of Ireland, the National Council for Curriculum and Assessment is conducting a feasibility study on a new curriculum programme in this area and has published a discussion paper exploring the provision for civic, social and political education. And the Northern Ireland Curriculum Council has been involved in the development and implementation of a number of cross-curricular themes with similar dimensions. In many other countries too one can see a comparable increase in the focus of attention on this theme.

One explanation of this burgeoning interest is to be found in those extensive changes which have been occurring in the social fabric of western societies in recent years. For not only have rapid technological development and the advent of consumerism wrought changes in the material circumstances of our lives, and thus in our values, but there has also been, as we have seen, a massive intellectual shift, 'a major cultural reorientation, known by its protagonists as postmodernism, which is said to have wide-ranging implications for knowledge, morality, politics and individual identities' (Gilbert, 1992, p. 51). Some of those implications we have noted in earlier chapters, and it is not difficult to recognize the important questions they raise concerning the role of the citizen and his or her relationship to the community, about individual and social values and their inter-relationship. It is equally easy, therefore, as a consequence to understand the recent upsurge of interest in both citizenship itself and citizenship studies.

A second, and more disturbing, explanation is that citizenship is coming to be regarded as a possible source of cures for what are seen as the ills that are increasingly besetting modern society. Wilfred Carr (1991b, p. 373), for example, quotes from an article by Young in the *Guardian* in 1988:

> Something is rotten in the state of Britain, and all the parties know it . . . The buzz word emerging as the salve for this disease is something called 'citizenship' . . . Somewhere out there is an immense unsatisfied demand for it to mean something. But it needs to become much more than a word.

In order for it to become 'much more than a word', as is so often the case, the notion of citizenship needs to be clarified, and what it entails needs to be unpacked so that we may have a sound base for some form of practice, especially in relation to education for citizenship. There has, therefore, in recent years been considerable debate over what it means and over what kinds of educational practices it should lead to.

Within this debate, interpretations of citizenship have ranged as widely as those interpretations of the political implications of postmodernism which we considered in Chapter 4, and for the same reasons. At one extreme the view has been expressed that, since those changes in the fabric of society which we noted earlier, allied to those intellectual changes subsumed under the term postmodernism, have led to a fragmentation of culture and of society, and a corresponding loss of any serious idea of common interests, to seek for some unifying concept such as citizenship is to take on a lost cause (Wexler, 1990). As we have seen, however, to adopt such a view is to see democracy too as a lost cause. At the other extreme there have been those who have recognized the significance of these changes, and have acknowledged the tensions they are creating, but have accepted a concept of citizenship as providing a new unifying factor (Heater, 1990; Gilbert, 1992).

Furthermore, these more positive views of citizenship, in conformity with the more positive interpretation of postmodernism on which they are based, have, perhaps inevitably, adopted a world view. They have sought to transcend nationalism, to seek for unity in the notion of shared humanity and to define citizenship as international citizenship (Lynch, 1992). Or they have attempted to view citizenship as offering identity at every level – local, national and global. Heater's response, for example, as Gilbert (1992, p. 58) expresses it, 'is to continue to posit identity and virtue as the essence of citizenship, but to apply them at various geographical levels, from the local through the national and continental to the global, to acknowledge the tension of the nation state and its challenge from both local and cosmopolitan tendencies'.

Within the case which is being developed in this book, of course, there can be no question but that we must embrace the second of these perspectives. For to adopt the first is to surrender all hope for democracy. The current emphasis on an individualism that is divorced from any collective, democratic responsibility, on competitivism rather than co-operation, on market-forces rather than social policies as solutions to social problems, as we have noted elsewhere, is leading society away from democracy as well as away from any concept of citizenship. If we are to retain any hold on deocracy, then, we must adopt a positive view of the potentialities of citizenship. And we must translate that into a proper form of education for citizenship.

Furthermore, although there has been as much debate over the form which education for citizenship should take as over the meaning of citizenship itself, there can be no doubt concerning the meaning we must give it here. For within the context of our discussion of democracy and against the backcloth of those democratic principles we have identified, education for citizenship in a democratic society must be seen as an extension of that democratic form of moral education we discussed in the first section of this chapter. It must, as was suggested earlier, extend that democratic form of morality from theory into practice, from the making of informed moral decisions and evaluations into effective participation in the governance of society.

There are several implications of this basic stance that need to be identified. First, as we saw with moral education, many curriculum subjects have a contribution to make to education for democratic citizenship. History offers opportunities to plot the rise – and fall – of democratic systems, and to explore the characteristics of totalitarian states. English and drama can tell of, and seek to explain, that burgeoning of literature which was a salient feature of Athenian democracy, and the contrasting artistic poverty of totalitarianism. Drama can also assist in the development of skills such as those of public speaking, which may be seen as important to participation in democratic processes. Social studies can be planned as a critical examination of social policies and practices. Social geography can provide insights into other cultures and their practices. And the humanities generally are predicated on the view that the proper study of 'man' is 'man'.

All subjects have their contribution to make. However, as we saw when considering the National Curriculum for England and Wales in Chapter 7, if they are to make this kind of contribution to the education of citizens for a democracy they must be conceived and planned with that in view. When conceived merely as devices for the transmission of socially and economically useful knowledge, and particularly when they are planned in such a manner as to encourage a largely unquestioning acceptance of the value of that knowledge, they are unlikely to be able to pass beyond that narrow conception and open up these wider opportunities for individual and social development.

That is one reason why, although there are in any case good reasons for seeking to co-ordinate these disparate contributions, it has become particularly necessary to address the issue of education for citizenship in its own right in England and Wales. One must speculate again, however, in the light of our earlier discussion of the importance of a supportive context for such learning, whether the values implicit in the National Curriculum will not work against what education for democratic citizenship must seek to do.

For the second major implication of exploring the concept of citizenship in a democratic context is that such an exploration reveals that education for citizenship must seek to do at least three things. It must support the development of an understanding of the democratic processes and procedures and of the reasons why these are important. It must assist in the development of appropriate skills for participation in those processes and procedures, not least the ability to make informed choices. And, above all, it must promote the capacity to keep those processes and procedures, along with the practices through which they are implemented, under constant and critical review and to hold them up to continuous evaluation and challenge.

It is this last function that is central to the concept of citizenship in a democratic society. Education for democratic citizenship is not merely learning *about* social processes; it is, much more, a matter of learning to evaluate them and the practices and policies of those whose task it is to implement them on our behalf. More than education for citizenship, it must be education for *active* and *critical* citizenship.

It is this crucial ingredient that is, sadly, largely lacking in the recommendations of the National Curriculum Council for education for citizenship in England and Wales (NCC, 1990b). For too many of these recommendations begin with 'pupils need to know about . . .' and 'areas of study might include . . .'; and too few, in fact none, begin with 'pupils need to question . . .' or 'areas of *inquiry* might include'.

Indeed, the aims of education for citizenship which the document sets out (op.cit., p. 2) go no further than to

- establish the importance of positive, participative citizenship and provide the motivation to join in;
- help pupils to acquire and understand essential information on which to base the development of their skills, values and attitudes towards citizenship.

And its framework for education for citizenship is based on the following elements:

Objectives	knowledge, cross-curricular skills, attitudes, moral codes and values
Content	essential components
Activities	tasks, opportunities and experiences provided for pupils.

(ibid.)

There is nothing there which suggests that the most important aspect of education for democratic citizenship is challenge, evaluation and choice. All is content rather than process. And there is nothing to indicate a recognition that that content might have some implications for such things as the ways in which schools are governed and decisions taken.

This of course is not surprising when this set of recommendations is recognized as an extension of a narrowly conceived National Curriculum (explicit links with National Curriculum Attainment Targets are indicated throughout the document), which it could hardly be expected to contradict or challenge, even implicitly. Tissue rejection could be the only result of any attempt to graft active forms of learning through inquiry on to a curriculum whose fundamental principle is pupil passivity. As a blueprint for education for democratic citizenship, therefore, it is sadly inadequate, as we have seen the National Curriculum itself is.

One cannot avoid comparing and contrasting this, limited and limiting, view of education for citizenship with some of the more imaginative and open views expressed elsewhere. We read, for example, in the journal, *Encouraging Citizenship* (1990), published by the Speaker's Commission on Citizenship : 'The challenge to our society is to create conditions where all who wish can become actively involved, can understand and participate, can influence, persuade, campaign and whistleblow and, in the making of decisions, can work together for the mutual good'. And in a broadsheet on citizenship education, from the same source : 'Citizenship is also concerned with effective participation. This implies empowerment and access ... It is important to introduce concepts such as power, authority and legitimate protest into any discussion of political organisation.'

The full significance of this dimension of education for citizenship, the essential focus on challenge and empowerment, however, seems not always to be appreciated. In particular, it seems not to be recognized that there is a fundamental clash between this aim of education and the implicit aims of the National Curriculum. A project such as the 'Making Choices' project, directed by Karl Berger, (Saferworld 1993), sound as its basic philosophy seems to be in this respect, still insists on seeking to link what it is doing with National Curriculum Attainment Targets. And while this may be realistic in terms of persuading teachers that education for citizenship is a worthwhile area of study, it is doing so by selling it instrumentally, as a device for teaching aspects of the National Curriculum; and, more importantly, it is concealing that fundamental incompatibility of the National Curriculum's model of curriculum with the only model which can be conducive to supporting the kind of free thinking on the part of pupils which any view of democratic education must require.

For education for citizenship cannot at root be based on the transmission of knowledge. It is essentially a matter of developing in pupils a range of capabilities, especially the power of autonomous thinking. And that requires an approach to curriculum planning, a curriculum model, whose central feature is not knowledge to be acquired or facts to be stored or extrinsic objectives to be attained but the processes to be promoted and the procedural principles derived from those processes. And those principles must inform not only the initial planning but also, and more crucially, the individual adapations which must subsequently be made by teachers on the ground.

Such a curriculum cannot be integrated with a curriculum which, like the National Curriculum, is founded on preselected knowledge-content and predetermined behavioural objectives. They are oil and water (Kelly, 1989; 1990). In England and Wales, therefore, education for citizenship must be planned quite separately from, even in spite of, the curriculum pupils are being offered for most of their working week. And further, as was suggested above, it may even be the case that that curriculum will fundamentally act against what, in a democratic society, education for citizenship must seek to do.

For the aims of education for citizenship in a democratic society would seem to include – essentially and by definition – at least the following:

- To extend and deepen pupils' understanding of the concepts of democracy and citizenship and of their importance to humanity.
- To assist pupils to develop the skills necessary for full participation in democratic processes.
- To promote an understanding of the importance of participation.
- To encourage a properly thought-through and critical stance towards the activities of all agencies within society and a constant evaluation of the procedures in place for the implementation of democratic principles.

Of these aims it is the last which essentially distinguishes a properly democratic form of education for citizenship from education for passivity, compliance, obedience and thus a continued absence of substantial challenge to those who would wield power for their own ends and seek to undermine democratic principles and procedures in order to do so.

A further weakness in many of the projects one sees in the field of education for citizenship is a tendency to ethnocentricity, even a mild modern version of nationalism. 'The Choices for the 21st Century Education Project' in the USA, for example, is subtitled 'The Role of the United States in a Changing World'. And the parallel project in the UK, 'Making Choices', to which reference was made above, is similarly subtitled 'Choices for Britain'. Both of these projects do offer a global perspective, of the kind it was suggested earlier is implied by any notion we must have of democracy, especially in a postmodern age. The four *choices* they each offer include, in the USA project, 'co-operating globally' and, in the UK, 'global Britain', so that, through consideration of these choices, pupils will have the opportunity to consider citizenship as a global concept. In both cases, however, they are offered only as one possible future option for their own countries, so that a nationalistic stance would appear to be the starting point.

This concern is reinforced by the tendency in both projects to regard the status quo in each country as in general satisfactory, so that the democratic model of each is not offered up for challenge. Rather the question seems to be merely whether we should or should not be seeking to export it to other, less fortunate, countries. Both projects are thus, commendably, attempting to encourage pupils to debate, and to debate freely, issues, including international issues, which should be of concern to all citizens in any democratic society. It remains problematic, however, whether they are inviting pupils to go far enough, whether the debate is as free as it could, and should, be.

Finally, we should note that open and free debate, undirected discussion, is the method favoured by all the advocates of education for citizenship as the only appropriate method for achieving its aims. Students are to be invited to articulate their own opinions, and the teacher's role is one of value neutrality.

In the 'Making Choices' Project, for example, we are told

> Throughout the discussions, the primary role of the teacher is that of an
> impartial facilitator. Students may need to be reminded that . . . the issues
> they will be confronting are truly difficult ones on which the best experts
> disagree. In working with the Choices approach, students develop key
> decision-making, problem solving, communication and critical thinking
> skills. They also clarify their values, engage in co-operative learning, and
> learn to understand issues from multiple perspectives.

Such a statement is clearly well in line with what we are claiming education
for citizenship is about. And it also illustrates why we are asserting its
incompatibility with the National Curriculum for England and Wales. What
is perhaps most interesting about it, however, is the degree to which it
reflects the stated philosophy of the Schools Council's Humanities Curriculum
Project (HCP) of a quarter century ago. For there we read (Schools Council,
1970, p. 1):

> The work of the Project has been based upon five major prem-
> ises:
>
> 1. that controversial issues should be handled in the classroom with
> adolescents;
> 2. that the teacher accepts the need to submit his [or her] teaching in
> controversial areas to the criterion of neutrality at this stage of education,
> i.e. that he [or she] regards it as part of his [or her] responsibility not to
> promote his [or her] own view;
> 3. that the mode of enquiry in controversial areas should have discussion,
> rather then instruction, as its core;
> 4. that the discussion should protect divergence of view among partici-
> pants, rather than attempt to achieve consensus;
> 5. that the teacher as chairman [or chairwoman] of the discussion should
> have responsibility for quality and standards in learning.

The Humanities Curriculum Project was not of course focused on education
for citizenship as such, although it was centrally concerned with what we
are claiming is the essence of such education, namely the development
of autonomy of opinion. The point to be noted, however, is how close
we had come, 25 years ago, to the notion of free and open debate on
controversial issues. For here we have the best possible evidence of the ways
in which curriculum development has been held up by political policies since
that time.

Those policies, as we have seen, have not permitted curriculum development
to follow a natural course towards greater and better understanding of curricular
issues, but have dammed that course up in order to channel views, ideologies,
policies and practices in a particular, unnatural and politically predetermined
direction. And so, as a result of that rechannelling, we find ourselves
reinventing several wheels every 20 years or so. And the consequence
of this, again as we have seen in earlier chapters, is not only that the

development of education is inhibited; the march of democracy is also arrested. That of course, as we have also seen, is not only the effect, it is also the intention.

The last point to be made about education for citizenship in a democratic society is that, although free and open discussion and debate must play a major part, activity on the part of pupils must loom very large too. For as we noted in our discussion of moral education earlier in this chapter, the making of decisions, moral, social or political, is not merely a cognitive activity. Indeed, just as we questioned the wisdom and effectiveness of regarding moral education in that light, we must similarly question the validity of such a view of education for citizenship. This was one of the reasons why we explored the arguments for creating an environment in the school which will support what we are attempting to do in relation to personal, social and moral education. And the case we made there must apply with similar force to education for citizenship.

We must also note at this point that education for citizenship must not be seen as something which begins at adolescence, as some of the projects we have considered would seem to imply. And that is another strong reason for not viewing it entirely in terms of debate and discussion, although even very young children can show strikingly interesting levels of perception in such contexts.

One thing all pupils, of whatever age, can be encouraged to do is to take an active interest in events in the immediacy of their own environment – home, school and local community. And, furthermore, they can be assisted to play an active role in some of these. In this way they can be introduced to that concept of 'legitimate protest' which we saw earlier the Speaker's Commission on Citizenship, rightly, regards as essential. There are many local issues which directly affect children and their parents and which they can be encouraged to take action on, even if that action goes no further than letters written to local councils, councillors or Members of Parliament.

In ways such as this, children from a very early age can be helped to develop that sense of community which it was suggested earlier is an important part of learning to be a citizen, and from which by stages can be fostered an awareness of global citizenship. And there is the added advantage that they are being encouraged not merely to be active, although that, as we have seen, is important, but to be active on live issues rather than on imagined problems set as exercises. As George Wood (undated, p. i) says in his Preface to the occasional paper of the Institute of Democracy in Education, *Students Writing about Community Affairs*:

> We all believe that if students are to learn the skills and abilities it takes to be democratic citizens – and writing well is one of them – they should learn them through real experiences: through working on something they care about, that affects them in some way, and that they can do something about.

There are, then, many approaches to education for citizenship. What they must all have in common, however, is a genuine desire to encourage freedom of thought and opinion, to engender a sense of empowerment rather than of hopeless resignation, to invite challenge of *all* processes and procedures and to encourage active participation in real issues.

These are all matters of process rather than merely of knowledge. They thus require a curriculum which is planned in terms of processes rather than subjects or knowledge-content. And the base from which teachers must start to promote education for citizenship is not bodies of knowledge to be transmitted, nor targets to be attained, but principles or guidelines to inform day-to-day planning and decision-making.

This, then, is further evidence of the unsuitability for education for citizenship of the National Curriculum in England and Wales, and of other curricula elsewhere which are planned in terms only of objectives to be attained or knowledge to be acquired. And further, it reinforces the assertion made earlier in this book, that such curricula are unsuited to any form of education which lays claim to being democratic, or appropriate to educational provision in a democratic society. For, as we have seen, democratic education requires a reconceptualization of curriculum, and that reconceptualization must take us to a form of curriculum which emphasizes, and is based on, fundamental principles rather than on the imposition of preselected syllabus content.

What we have learnt in this chapter, then, about suitable and unsuitable forms of provision for education for citizenship has reinforced our earlier claims concerning the unsuitability of much that is currently being done, not only under this heading but in education generally. It has thus strengthened our claim that a genuine commitment to democracy demands an extensive overhaul of current policies and practices in many parts of the world.

AFTERWORD

This book began by suggesting that 'democracy' is a 'trouser' word, something you only notice or discuss when you are aware that it is not there or that it is about to fall. In other words, we began by indicating that the research was being undertaken because of a sense that democracy is currently at risk and, further, that what is happening to education systems throughout the world, but perhaps especially in the UK, is a particularly clear, and disturbing, illustration of this.

This view has been reinforced by the research itself, as earlier chapters will have revealed. Furthermore, throughout the period during which that research has been proceeding, there has been continuous evidence not only that democratic principles and practices continue to be eroded but also that, if anything, that process is accelerating. Indeed, it has hardly been possible to read a newspaper or journal, or to listen to and/or watch newscasts and current-affairs programmes on radio and television, without seeing further evidence of this erosion.

Nothing which has happened, then, while this book has been in preparation has done anything to allay the concerns which prompted the project in the first instance. Indeed there has been constant exacerbation of those concerns.

It remains the case that democracy is fragile, vulnerable and continuously open to the inroads of totalitarianism. There is a continuing need for it to be cherished and protected if it is to be maintained and developed. And if this is to be done, it can only be by a careful and thorough analysis of its essential principles and an eternal vigilance to ensure that those principles are translated into practice as effectively as is humanly possible in every area of social living.

It is clear that the defenders of democracy have been fighting a losing battle for some time. Or perhaps they have not been fighting at all, have not recognized the need.

Perhaps this book will alert people to that need, and will do so particularly in relation to the provision of a properly democratic form of education, before it is too late.

REFERENCES AND BIBLIOGRAPHY

Aldrich, R. (1988) 'The National Curriculum: an historical perspective,' in Lawton and Chitty (eds) (1988) *op. cit.*, pp. 34–48.

Apple, M.W. (1990) The Politics of Official Knowledge in the United States of America, *Journal of Curriculum Studies*, Vol. 22, no. 4, pp. 377–83.

Archambault, R.D. (ed.) (1965) *Philosophical Analysis and Education.* Routledge, London.

Atkin, J.M. (1979) 'Educational accountability in the United States,' in Stenhouse (ed.) (1979) *op. cit.*, pp. 15–21.

Ayer, A.J. (1936) *Language, Truth and Logic.* Gollancz, London.

Ball, S.J. (1990) *Politics and Policy Making in Education: Exploration in Policy Sociology.* Routledge, London.

Barber, B. (1984) *Strong Democracy.* University of California Press, Berkeley, Calif., Los Angeles, Calif. and London.

Barnett, R. (1988) 'Limits to academic freedom: imposed-upon or self-imposed,' in Tight (ed.) (1988) *op. cit.*, pp. 88–103.

Barrett, G. (1989) *Disaffection from School. The Early Years.* Falmer, London.

Bennis, W.G., Benne, K.D. and Chin, R. (eds) (1969) *The Planning of Change.* Holt, Rinehart & Winston, New York.

Berkley, J., Lackey, D. and Wood, G. (eds) (undated) *Students Writing About Community Affairs. Occasional Paper* 3. The Institute for Democracy in Education, Ohio University, Athens, OH.

Berlin, I (1969) *Four Essays on Liberty.* Basil Blackwell, Oxford.

Bernstein, B. (1967) 'Open schools, open society?,' *New Society*, 14 September.

Bernstein, B. (1972) 'On the classification and framing of educational knowledge,' in Young (ed.) (1972) *op. cit.*, pp. 47–69.

Blenkin, G.M., Edwards, G. and Kelly, A.V. (1992) *Change and the Curriculum.* Paul Chapman Publishing, London.

Blenkin, G.M. and Kelly, A.V. (1981) *The Primary Curriculum.* Paul Chapman Publishing, London (Second edition 1987).

Blenkin, G.M. and Kelly, A.V. (1993) 'Never mind the quality: feel the breadth and balance,' in Campbell (ed.) (1993) *op. cit.*, pp. 49–63.

Blenkin, G.M. and Kelly, A.V. (eds) (1994) *The National Curriculum and Early Learning.* Paul Chapman Publishing, London.

Bower, T. (1977) *The Perceptual World of the Child.* Fontana, London.

Boyne, R. and Rattansi, A. (eds) (1990) *Postmodernism and Society.* Macmillan, London.

Bruner, J.S. (1960) *The Process of Education.* Vintage Books, New York.

Bruner, J.S. (1981) 'The pragmatics of acquisition,' in Deutsche (ed.) (1981) *op. cit.*, pp. 39–55.

Bruner, J.S. and Haste, H. (eds) (1987) *Making Sense: The Child's Construction of the World*. Methuen, London and New York.

Burbules, N.C. and Rice, S. (1991) 'Dialogue across differences: continuing the conversation,' *Harvard Educational Review*, Vol. 61, no. 4, pp. 393–416.

Campbell, R.J. (ed.) (1993) *Breadth and Balance in the Primary Curriculum*. Falmer, London and Washington, DC.

Carr, W. (1991a) 'Education for democracy? A philosophical analysis of the National Curriculum,' *Journal of Philosophy of Education*, Vol. 25, no. 2, pp. 183–91.

Carr, W. (1991b) 'Education for citizenship,' *British Journal of Educational Studies*, Vol. XXXIX, no. 4, pp. 373–85.

Cherryholmes, C.H. (1987) 'A social project for curriculum: post-structural perspectives,' *Journal of Curriculum Studies*, Vol. 19, no. 4, pp. 295–316.

Childs, J.L. (1956) *American Pragmatism and Education*. Holt, New York.

Copleston, F.C. (1955) *Aquinas*. Penguin Books, Harmondsworth.

Crosland, A. (1961) 'Some thoughts on English education,' *Encounter*,

Dahrendorf, R. (1962) 'On the origin of social inequality,' in Laslett and Runciman (eds) (1962) *op. cit.*, pp. 88–109.

Daignault, J. (1992) 'Traces at work from different places,' in Pinar and Reynolds (eds) (1992) *op. cit.*, pp. 195–215.

Dearden, R.F. (1976) *Problems in Primary Education*. Routledge & Kegan Paul, London, Henley and Boston, Mass.

Dewey, J. (1916) *Democracy and Education*. Macmillan, New York.

Dewey, J. (1938) *Logic: The Theory of Enquiry*. Holt, New York.

Deutsche, W. (ed.) (1981) *The Childs Construction of Language*. Academic Press, London.

Doll, W.E. (1989) 'Foundations for a post-modern curriculum,' *Journal of Curriculum Studies*, Vol. 21, pp. 243–53.

Downey, M. and Kelly, A.V. (1978) *Moral Education: Theory and Practice*. Paul Chapman Publishing, London.

Eco, U. (1987) *Travels in Hyperreality (Essays Translated from the Italian by William Weaver)*. Pan, London.

Eisner, E. (1982) *Cognition and Curriculum: A Basis for Deciding What to Teach*. Longman, New York and London.

Etzioni, H. (1961) *A Comparative Analysis of Complex Organizations*. Free Press, New York.

Featherstone, M. (1988) 'In pursuit of the postmodern: an introduction,' in *Theory, Culture and Society*, Vol. 5, pp. 195–215. Sage, London, Newbury Park, Beverly Hills and New Delhi.

Feinberg, W. (1975) *Reason and Rhetoric: the intellectual foundations of twentieth-century liberal education policy*, Wiley, New York.

Feinberg, W. (1983) *Understanding Education*. Cambridge University Press.

Feinberg, W. (1993) 'Dewey and democracy at the dawn of the twenty-first century,' *Educational Theory*, Vol. 43, no. 2, pp. 195–216.

Foucault, M. (1979) *The History of Sexuality. Volume 1: An Introduction* (trans. Robert Hurley). Allen Lane, London.

Freire, P. (1972) *Pedagogy of the Oppressed*. Penguin Books, Harmondsworth.

Freire, P. (1976) *Education: The Practice of Freedom*. Writers & Readers Cooperative, London.

Gilbert, R. (1992) 'Citizenship, education and postmodernity,' *British Journal of Sociology of Education*, Vol. 13, no. 1, pp. 51–68.

Giroux, H. (1988a) *Schooling and the Struggle for Public Life*. University of Minnesota Press, Minneapolis, Minn.

Giroux, H. (ed.) (1988b) *Teachers as Intellectuals*. Bergin & Garvey, Granby, Mass.

Giroux, H. (1991) 'Democracy, and the Discourse of Cultural Difference: towards a politics of border pedagogy,' *British Journal of the Sociology of Education*, Vol. 12, no. 4, pp. 501–19.

Giroux, H. and Aronowitz, S. (1991) *Postmodern Education*. University of Minnesota Press, Minneapolis, Minn.

Goddard, D. (1985) 'Assessing teachers: a critical response to the government's proposals,' *The Journal of Evaluation in Education*, Vol. 8, pp. 35–8.

Goodson, I.F. (1981) 'Becoming an academic subject: patterns of explanation and evolution,' *British Journal of Sociology of Education*, Vol. 2, no. 2, pp. 163–80.

Goodson, I.F. (1983) *School Subjects and Curriculum Change*. Croom Helm, Beckenham.

Goodson, I.F. (1985a) 'Subjects for study,' in Goodson (ed.) (1985b) *op. cit.*, pp. 343–67.

Goodson, I.F. (ed.) (1985b) *Social Histories of the Secondary Curriculum: Subjects for study*. Falmer, London and Philadelphia, Pa.

Goodson, I.F. and Ball, S.J. (eds) (1984) *Defining the Curriculum: Histories and Ethnographies*. Falmer, London and Philadelphia, Pa.

Gordon, P. and Lawton, D. (1978) *Curriculum Change in the Nineteenth and Twentieth Centuries*. Hodder & Stoughton, London.

Gott, R. (1986) 'The crisis of contemporary culture,' *Guardian, 1 December*, p. 10.

Graham, W. (1989) 'From the President,' *Ontario Confederation of University Faculty Associations Bulletin*, Vol. 6, no. 15, pp. 2–3.

Gutmann, A. (1987) *Democratic Education*. Princeton University Press, Princeton, NJ.

Harris K. (1979) *Education and Knowledge: the structured misrepresentation of reality*. Routledge, London.

Heater, D. (1990) *Citizenship: The Civic Ideal in World History, Politics and Education*. Longman, London.

Held, D. (1987) *Models of Democracy*. Polity Press, Cambridge.

Hoggart, R. (1992) *An Imagined Life (Life and Times Volume III: 1959–91.)* Chatto & Windus, London.

Hollins, T.H.B. (ed.) (1964) *Aims in Education: the Philosophic Approach*. Manchester University Press.

Hooper, R. (ed.) (1971) *The Curriculum: Context, Design and Development*. Oliver & Boyd, Edinburgh.

Illich, I. (1971) *Deschooling Society*. Calder, London.

Inglis, F. (1989) 'Theory and tyranny: the strange death of democratic England,' *Cambridge Journal of Education*, Vol. 19, no. 2, pp. 123–30.

James, C.M. (1968) *Young Lives at Stake*. Collins, London.

Kanpol, B. (1992) 'Postmodernism in education revisited: similarities within differences and the democratic imaginary,' *Educational Theory*, Vol. 42, no. 2, pp. 217–26.

Kelly, A.V. (1974) *Teaching Mixed Ability Classes*. Paul Chapman Publishing, London.

Kelly, A.V. (ed.) (1975) *Case Studies in Mixed Ability Teaching*. Paul Chapman Publishing, London.

Kelly, A.V. (1977) *The Curriculum: Theory and Practice*. Harper & Row, London (second edition, 1982; third edition, published by Paul Chapman Publishing, London, 1989).

Kelly, A.V. (1978) *Mixed Ability Grouping*. Paul Chapman Publishing London.

Kelly, A.V. (1986) *Knowledge and Curriculum Planning*. Paul Chapman Publishing, London.

Kelly, A.V. (1987) 'The Assessment of Performance Unit and the school curriculum,' *Curriculum*, Vol. 8, no. 1, pp. 19–28.

Kelly, A.V. (1989) *The Curriculum: theory and practice (third edition)* Paul Chapman, London.

Kelly, A.V. (1990) *The National Curriculum: A Critical Review*. Paul Chapman Publishing, London.

Kelly, A.V. (1993) 'Education as a field of study in a university: challenge, critique, dialogue, debate,' *Journal of Education for Teaching: International Research and Pedagogy*, Vol. 19, no. 2, pp. 125–39.

Kelly, A.V. (1994) 'Beyond the rhetoric and the discourse,' in Blenkin and Kelly (eds.) (1994) *op. cit.*, pp. 1–23.

Kohlberg, L. (1966) 'Moral education in the schools: a developmental view,' *School Review*, Vol. 74, pp. 1–30.

Lancaster, L.W. (1959) *Masters of Political Thought. Vol. 3: Hegel to Dewey*. Harrap, London, Toronto, Wellington and Sydney.

Laslett, P. (ed.) (1956) *Philosophy Politics and Society* (First Series). Basil Blackwell, Oxford (reprinted in 1957 and 1963).

Laslett, P. and Runciman, W.G. (eds.) (1962) *Philosophy, Politics and Society* (Second Series). Basil Blackwell, Oxford (reprinted in 1964 and 1967).

Lawn, M. (1990) 'From responsibility to competency: a new context for curriculum studies in England and Wales,' *Journal of Curriculum Studies*, Vol. 22, no. 4, pp. 388–92.

Lawton, D. (1987) 'Fundamentally flawed,' *The Times Educational Supplement*, 18 September.

Lawton, D. (1989) *Education, Culture and the National Curriculum*. Hodder & Stoughton, London, Sydney, Auckland and Toronto.

Lawton, D. (1992) *Education and Politics in the 1990s: Conflict or Consensus*. Falmer, London and Washington, DC.

Lawton, D. and Chitty, C. (eds.) (1988) *The National Curriculum. Bedford Way Paper* 33. Institute of Education, London.

Levitas, R. (1986) *The Ideology of the New Right*. Polity Press, Cambridge.

Lewin, R. (ed.) (1975) *Child Alive: New Insights into the Development of Young Children*. Temple Smith, London.

Lucas, J.R. (1965) 'Against equality,' *Philosophy*, Vol. XL, no. 154, pp. 296–307.

Lynch, J. (1992) *Education for Citizenship in a Multicultural Society*. Cassell, London.

Lyotard, J.-F. (1984) *The Postmodern Condition: A Report on Knowledge*. University of Minnesota Press, Minneapolis, Minn.

Macdonald, M. (1956) 'Natural rights,' in Laslett (ed.) (1956) *op. cit.*, pp. 35–55.

MacPherson, C.B. (1973) *Democratic Theory: Essays in Retrieval*, Clarendon, Oxford.

MacPherson, C.B. (1974) *The Life and Times of Liberal Democracy*. Oxford University Press.

Madison, G. (1988) *The Hermeneutics of Postmodernity*. University of Indiana Press, Bloomington, Ind.

McLaren, P. (1988) 'Forward: critical theory and the meaning of hope,' in Giroux (ed.) (1988) *op. cit.*, pp. ix–xxi.

McMurtry, J. (1991) 'Education and the market model,' *Journal of Philosophy of Education*, Vol. 25, no. 2, pp. 209–17.

McPhail, P., Ungoed-Thomas, J.R. and Chapman, H. (1972) *Moral Education in the Secondary School*. Longman, London.

Minsky, L. and Noble, D. (1989) 'Corporate takeover on campus,' *The Nation*, p. 496.

Nathanson, P. (1951) *John Dewey. The Reconstruction of the Democratic Life*. Twentieth Century Library, New York.

Ortony, A. (ed.) (1979) *Metaphor and Thought*. Cambridge University Press.

Peters, R.S. (1965) 'Education as initiation,' in Archambault (ed.) (1965) *op. cit.*, pp. 87–111.

Peters, R. S. (1966) *Ethics and Education*. Allen & Unwin, London.

Peters, R.S. (ed.) (1969) *Perspectives on Plowden*. London, Routledge.

Peukertruth, H. (1993) 'Basic problems of a critical theory of education,' *Journal of Philosophy of Education*, Vol. 27, no. 2, pp. 159–70.

Phenix, P.H. (1958) *The Philosophy of Education*. Holt, Rinehart & Winston, New York.

Piaget, J. (1932) *The Moral Judgement of the Child*. Routledge & Kegan Paul, London.

Pinar, W.F. and Reynolds, W.M. (eds) (1992) *Understanding Curriculum as Phenomenological and Deconstructed Text*. Teachers College Press, Columbia University, New York and London.

Plamenatz, J. (1963) *Man and Society, Vols. I and II*. Longman, London (revised edition by M.E. Plamenatz and R. Wokler published in three volumes in 1992 by Longman, London and New York).

Popper, K. (1945) *The Open Society and its Enemies, Vols. 1 and 2*. Routledge & Kegan Paul, London.

Popper, K. (1957) *The Poverty of Historicism*. Routledge & Kegan Paul, London.

Powell, E. (1985) 'A modern barbarism,' *The Times Educational Supplement*, 4 January.

Ranson, S. (1993) 'Markets or democracy for education,' *British Journal of Educational Studies*, Vol. XXXI, no. 4, pp. 333–50.

Rosenthal, S. (1993) 'Democracy and education: a Deweyan approach,' *Educational Theory*, Vol. 43, no. 4, pp. 377–89.

Saferworld, (1993) *Choices for Britain*, Saferworld, Bristol.

Schools Council (1970) *The Humanities Project: An Introduction*. Heinemann Educational for the Schools Council, London.

Schools Curriculum Assessment Authority (SCAA) (1993) *The National Curriculum and its Assessment, Final Report*. SCAA, York.

Shapiro, M. (1981) Post-structuralist political pedagogy, *News for Teachers of Political Science*, no. 44.

Shipman, M. (1971) 'Curriculum for inequality?,' in Hooper (ed.) (1971) *op. cit.*, pp. 101–106.

Sholle, D. (1992) 'Authority on the left: critical pedagogy, postmodernism and vital strategies,' *Cultural Studies*, Vol. 6, no. 2, pp. 271–89.

Slaughter, R.A. (1989) 'Cultural reconstruction in the post-modern world,' *Journal of Curriculum Studies*, Vol. 21, no. 3, pp. 255–70.

Sockett, H. (1976) 'Teacher accountability,' *Proceedings of the Philosophy of Education Society*, July, pp. 34–57.

Soltis, J.F. (1993) 'Democracy and teaching,' *Journal of Philosophy of Education*, Vol. 27, no. 2, pp. 149–58.

Speaker's Commission on Citizenship (1990) *Encouraging Citizenship*. HMSO, London.

Stenhouse, L. (1975) *An Introduction to Curriculum Research and Development*. Heinemann, London.

Stenhouse, L. (ed.) (1979) *Educational Analysis, Vol. 1, no. 1*. Falmer, Lewes.

Stutt, T. (1990) 'Cutbacks in university funding,' *Canadian Association of University Teachers Bulletin*, Vol. 38, no. 4, pp. 1–4.

Sylva, K. (1992) 'Quality care for the under fives; is it worth it?', *Royal Society of Arts Journal*, Vol. CXL, no. 5433, pp. 683–90.

Tight, M. (1988a) 'Editorial introduction,' in Tight (ed.) (1988b) *op. cit.*, pp. 1–5.

Tight, M. (ed.) (1988b) *Academic Freedom and Responsibility*. Open University Press, Milton Keynes.

Turner, B. (ed.) (1990) *Theories of Modernity and Postmodernity*. Sage, London.

Warnock, M. (1977) *Schools of Thought*. Faber & Faber, London.

Wellington, J.J. (1981) 'Determining a core curriculum: the limitations of transcendental deductions,' *Journal of Curriculum Studies*, Vol. 13, no. 1, pp. 17–24.

West, E.G. (1965) 'Liberty and education: John Stuart Mill's dilemma,' *Philosophy*, Vol.XL, no. 152, pp. 129–42.

Westbrook, R. (1991) *John Dewey and American Democracy*. Cornell University Press, Ithaca, NY.

Wexler, P. (1990) 'Citizenship in the semiotic society,' in Turner (ed.) (1990) *op. cit.*, pp. 164–75.

White, J.P. (1968) 'Education in obedience,' *New Society*, 2 May.

White, J.P. (1971) 'The concept of curriculum evaluation,' *Journal of Curriculum Studies*, Vol. 3, no. 2, pp. 101–12.

White, J.P. (1973) *Towards a Compulsory Curriculum*. Routledge, London.

Williams, R. (1958) *Culture and Society 1780–1950*. Penguin Books in association with Chatto & Windus, Harmondsworth.

Williams, R. (1961) *The Long Revolution*. Chatto & Windus, London.

Wilson, J. (1964) 'Education and indoctrination,' in Hollins (ed.) (1964) *op. cit.*, pp. 24–46.

Wilson, J. Williams, N. and Sugarman, B. (1967) *Introduction to Moral Education*. Penguin Books, Harmondsworth.

Winter, R. (1991) 'Post-modern sociology, as a democratic educational practice? Some suggestions,' *British Journal of Sociology of Education*, Vol. 12, no.4, pp. 467–81.

Wittgenstein, L. (1975) *The Blue and Brown Books*. Basil Blackwell, Oxford.

Wollheim, R. (1962) 'A paradox in the theory of democracy,' in Laslett and Runciman (eds.) (1962) *op. cit.*, pp. 71–87.

Wood, G. (1991) 'Dialogue,' *Democracy and Education*, Vol. 5, no. 3, p. 1.

Wood, G. (undated) 'Preface,' in Berkley, Lackey and Wood (eds.) (undated) *op. cit.*, p. i.

Young, H. (1988) '"Citizen" the catch-all rallying cry,' *Guardian*, 1 September.

Young, M.F.D. (ed.) (1972) *Knowledge and Control*. Collier-Macmillan, London.

Government reports and other official publications referred to in the text

Board of Education (1931) *Primary Education* (The Hadow Report). HMSO, London.

Central Advisory Council for Education (1959) *15 to 18* (The Crowther Report). HMSO, London.

Central Advisory Council for Education (1963) *Half our Future* (The Newsom Report), HMSO, London.

Central Advisory Council for Education (1967) *Children and Their Primary Schools* (The Plowden Report). HMSO, London.

Committee on Higher Education (1963) *Higher Education.* (The Robbins Report). HMSO, London.

Department for Education (1993) *Higher Quality and Choice: The Charter for Higher Education*. DFE, London.

Department of Education and Science (1977) *Curriculum 11–16*. HMSO, London.

Department of Education and Science (1984) *Curriculum 11–16: Towards a Statement of Entitlement*. HMSO, London.

National Curriculum Council (1990a) *Curriculum Guidance 3: The Whole Curriculum*. NCC, York.

National Curriculum Council (1990b) *Curriculum Guidance 8: Education for Citizenship*. NCC, York.

School Curriculum and Assessment Authority (SCAA) (1993) *The National Curriculum and its Assessment*, Final Report: SCAA, York.

Classical works referred to in the text

Aristotle, *Politics*.
Burke, Edmund, *Reflections on the Revolution in France*.
Darwin, Charles, *Origin of Species*.
Hegel, Georg Wilhelm Friedrich, *Philosophy of Right*.
Hobbes, Thomas, *Leviathan*.
Hume, David, *Treatise of Human Nature*.
Hume, David, *An Enquiry Concerning Human Understanding*.
Hume, David, *An Enquiry Concerning the Principles of Morals*.
Hume, David, *Dialogues Concerning Natural Religion*.
Kant, Immanuel, *Groundwork of the Metaphysics of Morals*.
Locke, John, *Two Treatises of Government*.
Locke, John, *An Essay Concerning Human Understanding*.
Machiavelli, Niccolo, *The Prince*.
Mill, John Stuart, *On Liberty*.
Newman, J.H., *On the Scope and Nature of University Education*.
Orwell, George, *Animal Farm*.
Paine, Thomas, *The Rights of Man*.
Plato, *Gorgias*.
Plato, *The Republic*.
Rousseau, Jean-Jacques, *Émile*.
Rousseau, Jean-Jacques, *The Social Contract*.
Spinoza, Baruch, *Ethics*.
Thucydides, *The History of the Peloponnesian War*.

INDEX